GCSE AQA

Spanish

You've probably come across a few revision books in your time, but this is *nacho* average GCSE Spanish Revision Guide.

It covers the full AQA course, with examples and practice questions on all the vocab and grammar you'll need for the exams.

It also has lots of online revision in the CGP RevisionHub — there are quick quizzes, summary tests, audio, Q&A videos and more, all matched to your book! Yep, you'll be a Spanish pro before you've finished your second siesta of the day.

Unlock CGP RevisionHub

Just scan a QR code in the book to access the CGP RevisionHub.
Or go to **cgpbooks.co.uk/revise** and enter this code!

Revision Hub

3194 0249 0387 1054

By the way, this code only works for one person. If somebody else has used this book before you, they might have already claimed the code.

Revision Guide

with new CGP RevisionHub

Published by CGP

Editors:
Siân Butler
Daniel Chapero-Hall
Becca Clifford
Elliott Garraway
Brooke McCreight
Hannah Roscoe
Matt Topping

Contributors:
Jacqui Richards

With thanks to Helen Clements for the proofreading.
With thanks to Alice Dent for the copyright research.

Acknowledgements:
Audio produced by Voice Talent Online.

AQA material is reproduced by permission of AQA.
The worked solutions to questions and commentaries on questions and possible answers in this book have neither been provided by nor approved by AQA.

iPad is a trademark of Apple Inc., registered in the U.S. and other countries.

ISBN: 978 1 83774 123 6
Printed by Elanders Ltd, Newcastle upon Tyne.
Clipart from Corel®

Based on the classic CGP style created by Richard Parsons.

Contents

Contents

Contents

Section Fourteen — Adjectives and Adverbs

Section Fifteen — Verbs and Tenses

Pronunciation in Spanish

Exam Advice

How to Use this Book

This isn't a book. Or rather, this isn't *just* a book. It's full of online resources designed to help you get top marks. To learn how it all works, read these pages or scan the QR code for a walkthrough.

Video

This book follows the AQA specification

1) The content for AQA GCSE Spanish is divided into nine topics. Each topic falls under one of three themes:

People and lifestyle | Popular culture | Communication and the world around us

2) In this book, there is usually one section for each topic. However, some topics have been split into two sections to make things more manageable.
3) There are also three grammar sections that cover the grammar you need to know.
4) The resources on the CGP RevisionHub are split up in the same way as the book.

There's also a 'General Stuff' topic in the book and online with content that's useful across the course.

The CGP RevisionHub is full of resources

- You can use the online resources on the CGP RevisionHub alongside this book as you're revising.
- There's audio, quick quizzes and summary tests, as well as printable vocab lists and transcripts.

There are resources for Foundation tier and Higher tier on the CGP RevisionHub. The Hub is automatically set to Higher, but you can switch to Foundation to only see Foundation content.

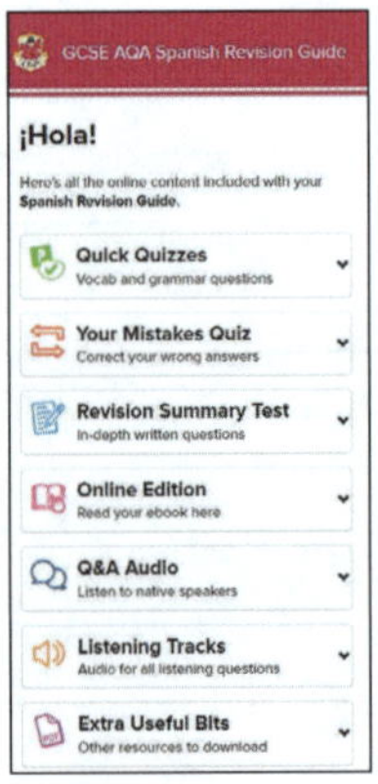

Revision Hub

Scan this QR code to access the CGP RevisionHub, or if you're on a computer, go to www.cgpbooks.co.uk/Bueno.

Get ready for the exams

1) In your exams, you can sit Foundation-tier or Higher-tier papers.
2) In each tier, there are four papers: Listening, Speaking, Reading and Writing. You have to choose the same tier for all four papers.

For more about the exams, see p.150-151.

- In Foundation tier, there's less vocabulary and less grammar to learn and the questions are slightly easier. In this tier, you can earn up to Grade 5.
- In Higher tier, you can achieve Grades 4-9, but you'll need to learn more vocab and more complex grammar.

3) Throughout this book, there's practice for all the key skills you'll need in the exams.
4) Most of this book is helpful for both tiers, but some vocab and questions have been marked with a bracket if they only apply to one tier.
5) If you aren't sure which tier to take, trying out the questions should help you and your teacher make a decision.

Higher

el canal	*channel*
la telenovela	*soap opera, TV serial*
el documental	*documentary*

H

privado/a	*private*
internacional	*international*

Learn the set vocabulary

- The AQA specification contains a list of words you could be tested on in your Listening and Reading papers, depending on your tier.
- This vocab will also help you in your Speaking and Writing papers. In these two papers, you can use non-specification vocab, too.
- The key vocab is on the main pages of each section. At the end of each section, there's a list of all the vocab relevant to the topic. Every word on the specification is on at least one of these lists.
- There are printable versions of these lists on the CGP RevisionHub.

Identity and Relationships with Others — Vocabulary

Practise your listening skills

1) In this book, you'll find questions and example answers:

Q&A Audio	Question	Simple Answer	Extended Answer
	¿Te gustaría ser una persona famosa? *Would you like to be a famous person?*	Sí, porque mi sueño es ser un músico conocido. *Yes, because my dream is to be a well-known musician.*	No me interesa nada ser una estrella. No me gustaría ni la atención ni la presión. *I'm not interested at all in being a star. I would like neither the attention nor the pressure.*

Scan the QR code to hear the sentences out loud and to practise your pronunciation.

2) There are also QR codes that take you to Listening Tracks. Each track comes with questions that test you on what you've heard.

Test your knowledge

Quick Quizzes

- The QR codes at the top of the page take you to a quick quiz.
- These quizzes test you on the vocab (or the grammar in Sections 13-15) on that page.
- They're a great way to keep your knowledge fresh.
- You can easily revisit questions that you answer incorrectly by doing the 'Your Mistakes' quiz.

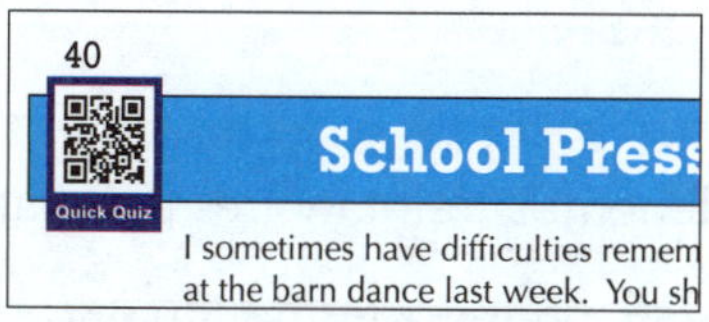
40
Quick Quiz
School Press
I sometimes have difficulties remem
at the barn dance last week. You sh

Revision Summary Tests

- For more of a challenge, try a revision summary test. These are found at the end of each section.
- These tests cover the most important information in a topic and are a good way to see how much you can remember.
- You can do these tests on paper or you can complete them online. Online, you can find sample answers, assess your progress, and look at previous topics to see the areas you need to work on.

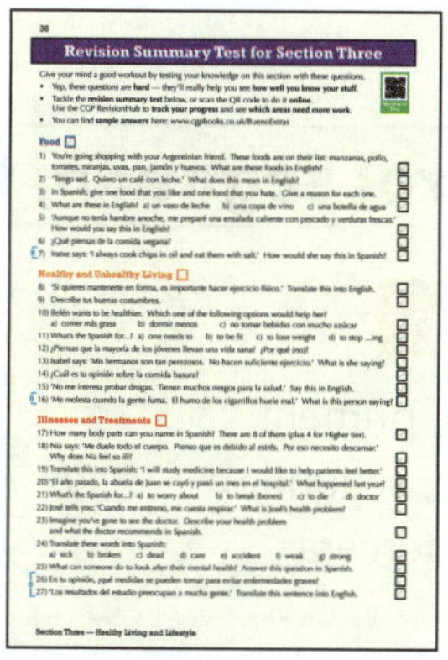
Revision Summary Test for Section Three

Fun fact — rearrange the letters of 'RevisionHub' and you get...

...'SnoivierUbh', which makes no sense. But do you know what *does* make sense? Using the RevisionHub alongside this book — it'll help you to get the most out of your revision and impress all those examiners.

Quick Quiz

Numbers and Times

Your GCSE Spanish Revision is ready to launch in 3...2...1...

Remember there's also lots of online content here: www.cgpbooks.co.uk/Bueno

Uno, dos, tres — *One, two, three*

Vocabulary

cero	*0*	veinte, veinti-	*20*
uno	*1*	veintiuno	*21*
dos	*2*	veintidós	*22*
tres	*3*	veintitrés	*23*
cuatro	*4*	treinta	*30*
cinco	*5*	treinta y uno	*31*
seis	*6*	cuarenta	*40*
siete	*7*	cincuenta	*50*
ocho	*8*	sesenta	*60*
nueve	*9*	setenta	*70*
diez	*10*	ochenta	*80*
once	*11*	noventa	*90*
doce	*12*	cien(to)	*100*
trece	*13*	ciento uno	*101*
catorce	*14*	doscientos	*200*
quince	*15*	quinientos	*500*
dieciséis	*16*	setecientos	*700*
diecisiete	*17*	novecientos	*900*
dieciocho	*18*	mil	*1000*
diecinueve	*19*	un millón	*1 000 000*

All twenty-something numbers are rolled into one — like 'veintiuno' (twenty-one). After 30, numbers are joined by 'y' (and), but written separately — like 'treinta y uno' (thirty-one).

Grammar — using 'one' with masculine nouns

When you put 'one' in front of a masculine word, uno becomes 'un'.

veintiún alumnos — ***21 pupils***
treinta y un alumnos — ***31 pupils***

Before a feminine word, the 'o' changes to 'a':

veintiuna naranjas — ***21 oranges***

See p.103 for more on masculine and feminine nouns.

'Cien' becomes 'ciento' when used in front of another number (except 'mil').

mil ochocientos veintiséis	*1826*
mil novecientos ochenta y cuatro	*1984*
dos mil once	*2011*

Tenemos treinta y tres bolígrafos. — *We have 33 pens.*

Hay ciento veintiún alumnos. — *There are 121 students.*

Nací en dos mil diez. — *I was born in 2010.*

Quiero cinco manzanas, por favor. — *I want five apples, please.*

Each of our 33 pens can hold up to 6 students.

Primero, segundo, tercero — *First, second, third*

Vocabulary

primero, primera	*1st*
segundo, segunda	*2nd*
tercero, tercera	*3rd*

Grammar — 'primero', 'tercero' + masculine nouns

You can drop the 'o' at the end of 'primero' or 'tercero' when they appear in front of a masculine word.

el primer baile — ***the first dance***
el tercer cantante — ***the third singer***

Vivo en la primera planta del edificio. — *I live on the first floor of the building.*

Mi hermano terminó en el tercer lugar. — *My brother finished in third place.*

¿Qué hora es? — *What time is it?*

Vocabulary

Es la...	*It's...*
Son las...	*It's...*
el cuarto	*quarter (used in time expressions)*
medio/a	*half*
el segundo	*second*
el minuto	*minute*
la hora	*hour, time (specific)*

Grammar — at / it's X o'clock

To say 'at X o'clock', you need 'a':

a la una — ***at one o'clock***
a las ocho — ***at eight o'clock***

'La' changes to 'las' for anything other than 'one o'clock'.

To say 'it's X o'clock', use 'es' or 'son':

es la una — ***it's one o'clock***
son las ocho — ***it's eight o'clock***

'Es' changes to 'son' for anything other than 'one o'clock'.

Es la una y media.	*It's half past one.*
Es la una menos veinte.	*It's twenty to one.*
Son las ocho y cinco.	*It's five past eight.*
Son las cinco y cuarto.	*It's quarter past five.*

five to — menos cinco

quarter to — menos cuarto

Instead of saying 'to' when telling the time in Spanish, you use 'menos' ('less' or 'minus'). So 'Son las cinco menos diez' literally means 'It's five o'clock minus ten'.

The 24-hour clock

The 24-hour clock is also used in many Spanish-speaking countries, so make sure you can tell the time both ways.

(Son) las veintiuna horas treinta minutos.	***(It's) 21.30.***
(Son) las tres horas catorce minutos.	***(It's) 03.14.***
(Son) las diecinueve horas cincuenta y cinco minutos.	***(It's) 19.55.***

The only time Max cares about is nap time.

Practice Questions

Q1 Read the text and answer the questions in English.

READING

Laia tiene veintidós años. Su hermana solo tiene diecisiete años, pero su abuelo tiene ochenta y ocho años. Laia vive muy cerca — en la segunda calle a la derecha.

e.g. *How old is Laia?* She is 22.

a) How old is Laia's sister? *[1 mark]*

b) How old is Laia's grandad? *[1 mark]*

c) On which street does Laia live? *[1 mark]*

Higher

Q2 Ignacio is talking about his routine. What does he normally do?
Write A if only statement A is correct. Write B if only statement B is correct.
Write A + B if both statements A and B are correct.

LISTENING

Listening Track 01

a) Ignacio normally wakes up...
A. at half past seven. **B.** at nine o'clock. *[1 mark]*

b) At quarter to ten, Ignacio...
A. reads his book. **B.** gets out of bed. *[1 mark]*

c) Ignacio prefers to...
A. have a wash before breakfast. **B.** eat breakfast at half past ten. *[1 mark]*

1st the worst, 2nd the best, 3rd the one with the Spanish test...

They might feel like a basic topic, but numbers are quite important. You can do some pretty incredible things with them too: tell the time, give your birthday, ask for enormous quantities of cheese at the supermarket...

Quick Quiz

Times and Dates

I'm partial to prunes myself — dates get stuck in my teeth. Anyway, it's times and dates um... time.

Los momentos del día — *Times of the day*

Vocabulary

la mañana	*morning*	mañana	*tomorrow*
la tarde	*afternoon, evening*	ayer	*yesterday*
la noche	*night, evening*	anoche	*last night*
por la mañana	*in the morning*	pasado/a	*past, last*
por la tarde	*in the afternoon / evening*	siguiente	*following, next*
por la noche	*at night, in the evening*	a veces	*sometimes*
esta noche	*tonight*	antes	*before, beforehand*
hoy	*today*	después	*after, afterwards*

You need to add 'de' after 'antes' or 'después' if you want to say before or after something. E.g. say 'después de la fiesta', not just 'después la fiesta'.

Iré a España mañana por la mañana.	*I will go to Spain tomorrow morning.*
Esta mañana fui al castillo.	*This morning I went to the castle.*
Perdió su mochila la semana pasada.	*He lost his rucksack last week.*
Juego al fútbol por la mañana.	*I play football in the morning.*

next week — la semana que viene

the following week — la semana siguiente

in the afternoon — por la tarde

Q&A Audio

Question

¿Qué haces el fin de semana?

What do you do at the weekend?

Simple Answer

Me gusta salir con mis amigos el fin de semana.

I like to go out with my friends at the weekend.

Extended Answer

A veces me gusta salir con mis amigos el fin de semana, pero prefiero descansar o leer si estoy cansada.

Sometimes I like to go out with my friends at the weekend, but I prefer to relax or read if I am tired.

Los días de la semana — *The days of the week*

Days of the week are always masculine and lower case.

Vocabulary

la fecha	*date (in calendar), day*	lunes	*Monday*	viernes	*Friday*
el día	*day*	martes	*Tuesday*	sábado	*Saturday*
la semana	*week*	miércoles	*Wednesday*	domingo	*Sunday*
el fin de semana	*(at the) weekend*	jueves	*Thursday*		

Voy al centro comercial los sábados para ir de compras con mis amigos.	*I go to the shopping centre on Saturdays to go shopping with my friends.*
Intento salir todos los días. Paseo al perro después del colegio.	*I try to go out every day. I walk the dog after school.*
Fui a la biblioteca ayer porque tengo un examen de inglés el miércoles.	*I went to the library yesterday because I have an English exam on Wednesday.*
Suelo descansar los domingos.	*I tend to relax on Sundays.*

You don't translate 'at' here — you just say 'the weekend'.

at the weekend — el fin de semana

on Friday afternoons — los viernes por la tarde

Los meses del año — *The months of the year*

Just like the days of the week, the months of the year are all masculine and shouldn't have capital letters.

Vocabulary

enero	*January*	abril	*April*	julio	*July*	octubre	*October*
febrero	*February*	mayo	*May*	agosto	*August*	noviembre	*November*
marzo	*March*	junio	*June*	septiembre	*September*	diciembre	*December*

Voy a la playa todos los años en agosto.	*I go to the beach every year in August.*
En enero, iremos de vacaciones.	*In January, we will go on holiday.*
Mi hermano menor nació en abril.	*My younger brother was born in April.*

¿Qué fecha es? — *What's the date?*

In English, you say 'the third of May' or 'the twentieth of December'. In Spanish, you can say either 'el primero de' or 'el uno de' for the first of the month, but for all the other dates, you say 'the three of May' or 'the twenty of December'...

el tres de mayo	*(on) the third of May*
el veinte de diciembre	*(on) the twentieth of December*
Es el uno de / el primero de febrero.	*It's the first of February.*
Es el dos de octubre de dos mil veinticuatro.	*It's the second of October 2024.*

You don't translate 'on' at the start of dates in Spanish, so both 'the third of May' and 'on the third of May' are written 'el tres de mayo'.

Practice Questions

Q1 *Read aloud the following text in Spanish.* *[5 marks]*

SPEAKING

Mi cumpleaños es lunes el quince de agosto. Quiero tener una fiesta grande con mis amigos. Siempre me gusta pasar tiempo con ellos. Mañana a las seis, tengo que llamar a mi restaurante favorito. Quiero reservar una mesa que está al lado de la cocina.

Answer the following questions in Spanish.

a) ¿Cuándo es tu cumpleaños?
b) Describe tu fiesta perfecta.
c) ¿Qué te gusta hacer con tus amigos?
d) ¿Qué vas a hacer mañana? *[10 marks]*

Top Tips for Higher Students
✓ Try to use complex structures like the subjunctive.
✓ Give at least two details in each answer.

Q2 *Listen to what Carlos, Anabel and Julia have to say, and then answer the questions in English.*

e.g. *How often does Carlos go to the gym?* Every day.
a) When was Anabel's birthday meal? *[1 mark]*
b) Where did Anabel go last week? *[1 mark]*
c) When is Julia going to the theatre? *[1 mark]*

Listening Track 02

LISTENING

Time to *fecha* your calendar and revise your days and months...

It might be tempting to put capital letters everywhere you'd expect to see them in English, but it's best avoided. Lots of Spanish words don't actually need them — even the word 'Spanish' (write 'español', not 'Español').

Quick Quiz

Questions

I'm afraid it's a bit late to question your GCSE options now... but if you wanted to do this *en español*, these pages will give you a few pointers. They're going to prove pretty handy in your speaking exam...

Question marks and tone of voice

To turn a statement into a question, put an upside down question mark at the beginning and a normal one at the end.

When speaking, raise your voice at the end of the sentence to show you're asking a question.

Literally: 'Your dress is blue?'

¿Tu vestido es azul? — *Is your dress blue?*

¿Tienes un coche? — *Do you have a car?*

Literally: 'You have a car?'

¿Qué... — *What...?*

If your question starts with 'What...', you normally need to start it with '¿Qué...' in Spanish.

¿Qué comes por la mañana? — *What do you eat in the morning?*

¿Qué quieres hacer el fin de semana? — *What do you want to do at the weekend?*

Go back to p.6-7 for more time phrases.

¿Cuál... — *Which one..? What...?*

1. '¿Cuál...' normally means 'Which...' or 'Which one...':

¿Cuál quieres? — *Which (one) do you want?*

2. However, sometimes you might need to use '¿Cuál...' even if you'd use 'What...' in English. This is usually when you use the verb 'ser' and you're asking for a piece of information, rather than a definition.

¿Cuál es tu problema? — *What is your problem?*

¿Cuál es tu dirección? — *What is your address?*

¿Cuándo? ¿Por qué? ¿Dónde? — *When? Why? Where?*

There are lots of other words you can use to begin a question — get them all learnt.

Vocabulary

¿Cuándo?	*When?*	¿Dónde?	*Where?*	¿Cuánto/a?	*How much?*	¿Quién(es)?	*Who?*
¿Por qué?	*Why?*	¿Cómo?	*How?*	¿Cuántos/as?	*How many?*	¿Cuál(es)?	*Which?*

Remember that question words need accents.

¿Cuántos/as tienes?	*How many do you have?*
¿Por qué haces eso?	*Why are you doing that?*
¿De dónde eres?	*Where are you from?*
¿Cuál prefieres?	*Which do you prefer?*

Noodles definitely has questions this time...

Question words like this are known as interrogatives. See p.109.

Tengo una pregunta — *I have a question*

Here are some of the most common ways you can use the question words.

¿Cuándo es tu cumpleaños?	*When is your birthday?*
¿Cuántos años tienes?	*How old are you?*
¿Cuánto cuesta(n)?	*How much does it (do they) cost?*

You shouldn't use '¿Cómo...?' to ask how old someone is in Spanish. You have to ask 'How many years do you have?' instead.

Q&A Audio

Question

¿Cuánto cuesta ir al cine?

How much does it cost to go to the cinema?

Simple Answer

Cuesta diecisiete euros.

It costs seventeen euros.

Extended Answer

Cuesta diecisiete euros, cincuenta céntimos. Es muy caro, por eso prefiero ver las películas en casa.

It costs seventeen euros, fifty cents. It's very expensive, so I prefer to watch films at home.

Grammar (Higher only) — prepositions in questions

If you need to include a preposition (see p.110) in your question, it should come before the question word. Prepositions should never go at the end of a question in Spanish.

¿Con quién hablas? — ***Who are you talking to? (literally 'With whom are you talking?')***

¿Para qué te entrenas? — ***What are you training for? (literally 'For what are you training?')***

Practice Questions

Q1 *Read Carla and Olaya's role-play. Then, use the instructions on the role-play card to prepare your own role-play. You should address your friend as 'tú'. Aim to speak for about one and a half minutes.*

Top Tips for Higher Students
✓ Try to use multiple tenses in your role-play.
✓ Back up all of your opinions.

SPEAKING

Olaya: *¿Cuántas veces haces deporte a la semana?*

Carla: *Juego al fútbol dos veces a la semana. Y tú, ¿qué deportes haces?*

Olaya: *Me gusta nadar y voy a la piscina cada semana. ¿Qué piensas de la televisión?*

Carla: *Me gusta la tele porque me ayuda a descansar.*

Olaya: *Ahora, háblame de los libros que te gustan.*

Carla: *Me gusta leer libros románticos. Me hacen feliz.*

Olaya: *¿Hay alguna actividad que te gustaría probar?*

Carla: *Me gustaría aprender a tocar la guitarra.*

You are talking to your Spanish friend.

1. *Say how often you play sports.*
2. *? Ask what sports they do.*
3. *Say what you think about TV.*
4. *Say what sort of books you like.*
5. *Say an activity you would like to try in your free time.*

When you see '?', you need to ask a question.

[10 marks]

Higher

Q2 *Translate these sentences into Spanish.*

a) *Which laptop should I buy?*
b) *Who were you dancing with?*
c) *How many TV channels are there?*
d) *What are you talking about?*

[8 marks]

Why does that hamster have a better film set up than me?

Look at him — a sofa all to himself, free reign of the remote and even some popcorn. Who do I need to speak to about getting that? Whatever you want to question, make sure you know which words you need to use.

Quick Quiz

Being Polite

Can you learn all of the lovely vocab on these pages? Pretty please with a cherry on top?

Tú y usted — *Informal and formal 'you'*

In Spanish, there are four different ways of saying 'you' depending on how formal you want to be.

Grammar — 'tú' and 'usted'

Tú	Vosotros/as	Usted	Ustedes
Informal singular 'you'. For one person who's your friend, a family member or of a similar age.	Informal plural 'you'. For a group of two or more people that you know. Only use 'vosotras' if everyone you're talking to is female.	Formal singular 'you'. For one person that is older than you or someone you don't know.	Formal plural 'you'. For a group of two or more people that you don't know.

Ewe better learn these...

So, there are four different ways to ask a question like 'Where are you from?':

Tú	Vosotros/as	Usted	Ustedes
¿De dónde eres?	¿De dónde sois?	¿De dónde es?	¿De dónde son?

You need to use the 'he/she/it' part of the verb for 'usted' (see p.127-147). For 'ustedes', use the 'they' part of the verb.

Hola y adiós — *Hello and goodbye*

You can also say '¿Cómo estás?' (informal) or '¿Cómo está?' (formal) to ask how someone is.

Vocabulary

hola	*hello, hi*	¿Qué tal?	*How are you? (informal)*	mal	*badly*
buenos días	*good morning*	bien	*well*	adiós	*goodbye*

Q&A Audio

Question

¿Qué tal?
How are you?

Simple Answer

Bien, gracias.
Well, thanks.

Extended Answer

Me siento fatal. Tengo dolor de cabeza.
I feel terrible. I've got a headache.

See p.32 for more illnesses.

Le presento a... — *May I introduce...?*

You need to know two things in order to introduce someone: the verb 'presentar' and an indirect object pronoun — usually 'te' (informal) or 'le' (formal).

'Este/Esta es...' ('This is...') is another way to introduce someone.

Shula:	Hola Señora Valls. ¿Cómo está?	*Hello Señora Valls. How are you?*
Señora Valls:	Muy bien, gracias.	*Very well, thank you.*
Shula:	Le presento a mi novio, Arturo.	*May I introduce my boyfriend Arturo?*
Señora Valls:	Encantada.	*Pleased to meet you.*
Arturo:	Encantado.	*Pleased to meet you.*
Señora Valls:	Lo siento, tengo que irme. ¡Hasta luego!	*I'm sorry, I have to go. See you soon!*
Shula & Arturo:	¡Adiós!	*Goodbye!*

Shula is using the 'usted' form because Señora Valls is older than her.

Señora Valls says 'Encantada' because she is female.

Arturo says 'Encantado' because he is male.

See you on Monday! — ¡Hasta el lunes!
See you tomorrow! — ¡Hasta mañana!

Por favor y gracias — *Please and thank you*

Vocabulary

por favor	*please*	claro	*of course*
gracias	*thanks, thank you*	lo siento	*I'm sorry, I apologise*
vale	*OK*	¡Perdón!	*Sorry!*

'Perdone' is the formal version of 'Perdón' — it's used to get someone's attention, e.g. when asking someone the way. 'Con permiso' is used if you want to get past someone.

¿Me puedes ayudar, por favor?	*Can you help me, please?*
Sí, claro.	*Yes, of course.*
¡Perfecto! ¡Muchas gracias!	*Perfect! Thank you very much!*
¡No te preocupes!	*No worries!*

You're welcome! — ¡De nada!

Quisiera... — *I would like...*

1) Don't just say 'I want to...' — make sure you ask what you would like to do politely using 'quisiera' and an infinitive.
2) You can also ask for a specific object if you put a noun after 'quisiera'.
3) Or you can phrase what you would like to do as a question using 'puedo' and an infinitive.

Quisiera hablar.	*I would like to talk.*
Quisiera un café.	*I would like a coffee.*
¿Puedo sentarme?	*May I sit down?*

go to the toilet — ir al baño

eat here — comer aquí

Practice Question

Q1 Andrés is introducing his two friends Mateo and Sakura to each other.

Andrés: ¡Buenos días, Mateo! ¿Qué tal?
Mateo: Muy bien, gracias, ¿y tú?
Andrés: Sí, bien. Esta es mi amiga, Sakura.
Mateo: ¡Hola Sakura! Encantado.
Sakura: Encantada.
Mateo: ¿Cómo estás, Sakura?
Sakura: No muy bien. Estoy enferma.
*Mateo: Ay, ¡qué lástima!**
Sakura: Sí, es una pena.
Andrés: Pues, hasta luego, Mateo.*
Mateo: ¡Adiós!

Ay, ¡qué lástima — Oh, what a shame!
Pues — Well

WRITING

Top Tips for Higher Students
✓ Ask additional questions to develop your conversation.
✓ Use varied adjectives to talk about how you feel.

Now have a go yourself:
Write a conversation between you and your friend Diego. Write approximately 50 words in Spanish.
You should:

- *say how you both feel.*
- *introduce another friend to Diego.*
- *say what you and Diego are going to do.*

[10 marks]

Mind your manners — and yours and yours and yours...

If you're unsure which 'you' to use, it's better to start with 'usted(es)' as it's politer. If whoever you're speaking to thinks 'usted' is too formal, they might say that you can 'tutear', which just means you can use the 'tú' form.

Quick Quiz

Opinions

Having opinions is great, but spicing them up with exotic adjectives makes them even better.

Las opiniones — *Opinions*

Vocabulary

gustar	*to like, please, be pleasing (to)*	interesar	*to interest*	pensar	*to think*
		acordar	*to agree on*	parecer	*to seem*
encantar	*to love, delight, be delightful to*	de acuerdo	*in agreement*	sentir	*to feel, sense*
		odiar	*to hate*	imaginar (H)	*to imagine*
encontrar	*to find*	creer	*to believe, think*	indicar (H)	*to point (out)*

Grammar — 'gustar' and 'encantar'

Use 'me gusta' and 'me encanta' when you want to say you like or love a singular thing.
If you want to say you like or love a plural thing, add an 'n' to the end.

Me gustan las uvas. ***I like grapes.*** **Me encantan las películas.** ***I love films.***

To say you like doing an activity, use an infinitive (see p.127) after the correct form of 'gustar' or 'encantar'.

Me gusta bailar. ***I like dancing.*** **Me encanta dormir.** ***I love sleeping.***

(No) me gustan las verduras.	*I (don't) like vegetables.*
Los idiomas (no) me interesan.	*Languages (don't) interest me.*
Encuentro la paella deliciosa.	*I find paella delicious.*
Me encantan los perros.	*I love dogs.*
¿Qué piensas de mi amigo? Pienso que es muy simpático.	*What do you think of my friend? I think he's very friendly.*
Estoy de acuerdo contigo. Me parece un chico amable.	*I am in agreement with you. He seems to me like a kind boy.*

You need an indirect object pronoun with verbs like 'gustar' because you're literally saying 'it pleases me'. See p.107 for more information.

What's your opinion of...? — ¿Cuál es tu opinión de...?

I am not in agreement — No estoy de acuerdo

shy — tímido

Prefiero... — *I prefer...*

If you dislike something, try to say what you prefer:

Me gusta el té, pero prefiero el café.	*I like tea, but I prefer coffee.*
No me gusta pintar — prefiero correr.	*I don't like painting — I prefer running.*

Grammar — 'preferir' is a stem-changing verb

'Preferir' (*to prefer*) is a stem-changing verb (see p.128). The second 'e' changes to 'ie' in the present tense:

prefiero	***I prefer***
prefieres	***you prefer***
prefiere	***he/she/it prefers***
prefieren	***they prefer***

The stem doesn't change for the 'we' form ('preferimos'), nor does it change for the 'you inf., pl.' form ('preferís').

Porque — *Because*

To start justifying your opinion, you need 'porque' (because).

Look out, though — 'porque' and '¿por qué?' sound very similar, but they're written differently and mean different things.

¿Por qué te gusta cocinar?	*Why do you like cooking?*
Me gusta cocinar porque...	*I like cooking because...*

(No) me gusta porque es... — *I (don't) like it because it's...*

Vocabulary

bueno/a	*good*	perfecto/a	*perfect*	aburrido/a	*boring*
estupendo/a	*wonderful, marvellous*	agradable	*pleasant, nice*	horrible	*horrible*
		increíble	*incredible*	malo/a	*bad*
excelente	*excellent*	bonito/a	*pretty, nice, beautiful*	maravilloso/a (Higher)	*wonderful, marvellous*
genial	*great*	interesante	*interesting*		
guay	*cool*	divertido/a	*fun, enjoyable*	precioso/a (Higher)	*beautiful*
emocionante	*exciting*	raro/a	*strange*	decepcionante (Higher)	*disappointing*

Grammar — nouns and adjectives agree

The ending of the adjective must agree with the noun (p.117).

El libro es bueno. ***The book is good.*** 'el libro' is masculine so 'bueno' must end in 'o'.

La película es buena. ***The film is good.*** 'la película' is feminine so the adjective ends in 'a'.

Q&A Audio

Question

¿Cuál es tu opinión de esta revista?

What is your opinion of this magazine?

Simple Answer

Me gusta mucho esta revista.

I really like this magazine.

Extended Answer

Me gusta mucho esta revista porque es muy interesante.

I really like this magazine because it's very interesting.

If an adjective doesn't end in an 'o', it usually stays the same for both masculine and feminine nouns.

Practice Questions

Q1 Dike and Elena are discussing the cinema. Read the dialogue and answer the questions in English.

READING

Dike: *¿Te gusta ir al cine, Elena?*

Elena: *Sí, ir al cine es muy divertido. Me gustan las películas de acción. ¿Y tú qué piensas?*

Dike: *No me gusta ir al cine. Prefiero ver las películas en casa. Me encantan las comedias pero odio las películas románticas porque me parecen aburridas. ¿Qué piensas, Elena?*

Elena: *Sí, estoy de acuerdo. A veces son tontas.*

e.g. *Why does Elena like going to the cinema?* Because it's fun.

a) Does Dike prefer going to the cinema or watching films at home? *[1 mark]*

b) What is Dike's opinion of romantic films? *[1 mark]*

c) What does Elena think of romantic films? *[1 mark]*

Higher

Q2 Carolina and Antonio are talking about what they do at the weekend. What are their opinions? Write P for a positive one, N for a negative one, or P+N for a positive and negative one.

Listening Track 03

LISTENING

e.g. *Carolina — swimming* P

a) i) Carolina — reading *[1 mark]*

ii) Carolina — listening to music *[1 mark]*

b) i) Antonio — listening to music *[1 mark]*

ii) Antonio — going out with friends *[1 mark]*

I think sharing your opinions is positively splendiferous...

It is a real word — I checked. Though I wonder how you say it in Spanish... Anyway, whenever you do share your opinion, you should try to explain why you like or dislike something — you'll pick up more marks for it.

General Stuff — Vocabulary

Phew that was a lot, but don't worry — I've popped all the words you need across the next four pages. How kind of me...

Numbers

el número	*number*
cero	*zero*
uno	*one*
dos	*two*
tres	*three*
cuatro	*four*
cinco	*five*
seis	*six*
siete	*seven*
ocho	*eight*
nueve	*nine*
diez	*ten*
once	*eleven*
doce	*twelve*
trece	*thirteen*
catorce	*fourteen*
quince	*fifteen*
dieciséis	*sixteen*
diecisiete	*seventeen*
dieciocho	*eighteen*
diecinueve	*nineteen*
veinte, veinti-	*twenty*
veintiuno	*twenty-one*
veintidós	*twenty-two*
veintitrés	*twenty-three*
treinta	*thirty*
treinta y uno	*thirty-one*
cuarenta	*forty*
cincuenta	*fifty*
sesenta	*sixty*
setenta	*seventy*
ochenta	*eighty*
noventa	*ninety*
cien(to)	*one hundred (and...)*
ciento uno	*one hundred and one*
doscientos	*two hundred (and...)*
quinientos	*five hundred (and...)*
setecientos	*seven hundred (and...)*
novecientos	*nine hundred (and...)*
mil	*thousand*
un millón	*one million*
dos millones	*two million*
primer	*first (pre-noun, m only)*
primero/a	*first*
segundo/a	*second (pre- and post-noun)*
tercer	*third (pre-noun, m only)*
tercero/a	*third*
varios/as	*several, various*
la mayoría	*majority*
la mitad	*half, middle*
el resto	*rest, remainder*

Higher

total	*total, entire*
entero/a	*entire, whole*
junto/a	*together*
máximo/a	*maximum*
mínimo/a	*minimum*
numeroso/a	*numerous, large, big*

Time

el tiempo	*time (general)*
Es la...	*It's...*
Son las...	*It's...*
el cuarto	*quarter (used in time expressions)*
medio/a	*half*
el segundo	*second*
el minuto	*minute*
la hora	*hour, time (specific)*
ahora	*now, these days*
de momento	*at the moment*
luego	*then, later*
el principio	*beginning, start*
el fin	*end*
el final	*end, ending*
el momento	*moment*
el rato	*moment, while, time*
el pasado	*past*
la vez	*time (specific occurrence)*
la mañana	*morning*
la tarde	*afternoon, evening*
la noche	*night, evening*
por la mañana	*in the morning*
por la tarde	*in the afternoon / evening*
por la noche	*at night, in the evening*
esta noche	*tonight*
hoy	*today, nowadays*
mañana	*tomorrow*
ayer	*yesterday*
anoche	*last night*
reciente	*recent*
tarde	*late*
pasado/a	*past, last*
último/a	*last, past*
siguiente	*following, next*
a veces	*sometimes*
antes	*before, beforehand*
después	*after, afterwards*
finalmente	*finally, at last*

H

el comienzo	*start, beginning*
la frecuencia	*frequency*
ocurrir	*to happen, occur*

For more information about words related to telling the time, head to p.5. For other time words, see p.6.

Dates

la fecha	*date (in calendar), day*
el día	*day*
la semana	*week*
el fin de semana	*(at the) weekend*
el puente	*long weekend*
lunes	*Monday*
martes	*Tuesday*
miércoles	*Wednesday*
jueves	*Thursday*
viernes	*Friday*
sábado	*Saturday*
domingo	*Sunday*
el mes	*month*
el año	*year*
la estación	*season (of the year)*
la primavera	*spring*
el verano	*summer*
el otoño	*autumn*
el invierno	*winter*

enero	*January*
febrero	*February*
marzo	*March*
abril	*April*
mayo	*May*
junio	*June*
julio	*July*
agosto	*August*
septiembre	*September*
octubre	*October*
noviembre	*November*
diciembre	*December*
H anterior	*previous, preceding*
H la época	*time, age, period*

If you want to say 'on Mondays', you shouldn't use 'en'. Instead, just add 'los' before 'lunes' or any other day of the week. E.g. 'I swim on Mondays' would be 'Nado los lunes'.

Questions

¿Qué?	*What?*
¿Cuál(es)?	*Which?*
¿Cuándo?	*When?*
¿Por qué?	*Why?*
¿Dónde?	*Where?*
¿Cómo?	*How?*
¿Cuánto/a?	*How much?*
¿Cuántos/as?	*How many?*
¿Quién(es)?	*Who?*
sí	*yes*
no	*no*
la pregunta	*question*
responder	*to reply, respond, answer*

When writing questions in Spanish, don't forget to add an upside down question mark at the start of your question. If you're asking a question out loud, remember to raise your voice at the end of the sentence.

For more on interrogative pronouns, see p.109.

Quick, they're looking! Let's pretend I've said something really witty and inspiring.

Being Polite

hola	*hello, hi*
buenos días	*good morning*
¿Qué tal?	*How are you? (informal), How is...? (someone or something)*
bien	*well*
mal	*badly*
adiós	*goodbye*
presentar	*to introduce, present*
por favor	*please, excuse me*
el favor	*favour*
gracias	*thanks, thank you*
vale	*OK*
de acuerdo	*OK*
claro	*of course, clearly*

lo siento	*I'm sorry, I apologise*
¡Perdón!	*Sorry!*
quisiera	*(I) would like (to), would love (formal)*
¡Vamos!	*Come on!, Let's go!*
¿Cómo es?	*What is it like?*
el señor	*Mr., man, Sir, gentleman*
la señora	*Mrs., lady*
H introducir	*to introduce, bring in*
H el permiso	*permission*

General Stuff — Vocabulary

Opinions

la opinión	*opinion, view*
gustar	*to like, please, be pleasing (to)*
me/te/le gustaría	*(I, you, he, she, it, you (sing. form) would like (informal)*
encantar	*to love, delight, be delightful to*
encontrar	*to find*
interesar	*to interest*
acordar	*to agree on, remind*
de acuerdo	*in agreement*
la razón	*reason*
la decisión	*decision*
la idea	*idea*
el lado	*side*
el ejemplo	*example*
el detalle	*detail*
odiar	*to hate*
creer	*to believe, think*
pensar	*to think*
la verdad	*truth*
la mentira	*lie*
parecer	*to seem*
sentir	*to feel, sense*
preferir	*to prefer*
aparte (de)	*besides, apart (from)*
completamente	*completely*
bueno/a	*good*
estupendo/a	*wonderful, marvellous*
excelente	*excellent*
genial	*great*
guay	*cool*
emocionante	*exciting*
perfecto/a	*perfect*
ideal	*ideal*
agradable	*pleasant, nice*
increíble	*incredible*
bonito/a	*pretty, nice, beautiful*
interesante	*interesting*
divertido/a	*fun, enjoyable*
cierto/a	*certain, sure, true*
correcto/a	*correct, suitable*
exacto/a	*exact, true*
raro/a	*strange, rare*
aburrido/a	*bored, boring*
horrible	*horrible*
malo/a	*bad*
falso/a	*false*
general	*general*
semejante	*similar*
típico/a	*typical*
común	*common*
diferente	*different*
imposible	*impossible*
posible	*possible*

Higher

el punto	*point, full stop, dot*
imaginar	*to imagine*
significar	*to mean*
sugerir	*to suggest*
proponer	*to propose, suggest*
considerar	*to consider*
mencionar	*to mention*
referir	*to refer*
incluir	*to include*
indicar	*to point (out), indicate*
destacar	*to emphasise, stand out, highlight*
insistir	*to insist*
vale la pena	*it's worth it*
estupendo/a	*great, brilliant*
maravilloso/a	*wonderful, marvellous*
precioso/a	*beautiful, precious*
preferible	*preferable*
evidente	*evident, obvious*
verdadero/a	*true, real*
decepcionante	*disappointing*
distinto/a	*distinct, different*
la posibilidad	*possibility*
la duda	*doubt*

Useful Nouns

la caja	*box*
las ganas	*desire*
el miedo	*fear*
la pena	*sadness, shame, pity, trouble*
el recuerdo	*memory*
(un) montón	*(a) lot of, heap, pile*
la variedad	*variety*
el plan	*plan*
la intención	*intention*
la letra	*letter*
la cosa	*thing*
la situación	*situation*
el tipo	*type, kind*
la clase	*kind, type*
el sentido	*sense, meaning*

Higher

la línea	*course*
la calidad	*quality*
la creación	*creation*
la sensación	*feeling, sensation*
la emoción	*emotion, excitement*
la impresión	*impression*
la expresión	*expression*
la manera	*way, manner*
la forma	*form, shape, way*
la parte	*part*
el objeto	*object, thing*
el caso	*case, occasion*
el deseo	*desire, wish*
el fondo	*bottom, back, end (of area), back, background*

When you learn a new noun, make sure you learn its article too. That way, you'll know how to make any adjectives agree with it.

Useful Adjectives & Adverbs

corto/a	*brief*
lento/a	*slow*
libre	*free, vacant*
vacío/a	*empty, vacant*
lleno/a	*full*
medio/a	*half, middle, average*
real	*real*
listo/a	*ready (after estar)*
seguro/a	*sure*
como	*like*
encima	*on top*
rápidamente	*quickly*

Higher

dispuesto/a	*ready, willing, prepared*
ocupado/a	*busy, taken, occupied*
oscuro/a	*dark, obscure*
vivo/a	*bright*
pesado/a	*heavy, boring*
ligero/a	*light (in weight)*
suave	*soft, gentle, mild*
inútil	*useless*
despacio	*slow*

Remember — Spanish adjectives need to agree in gender and number with the noun they describe. However, adverbs don't need to agree.

Colours

el color	*colour*
amarillo/a	*yellow*
azul	*blue*
blanco/a	*white*
gris	*grey*
marrón	*brown*
negro/a	*black*
rojo/a	*red*
verde	*green*

Mercè believed in a 'more is more' approach.

Useful Verbs

abrir	*to open, unwrap*
abrirse	*to open up*
acercarse	*to come closer*
acordarse	*to remember*
afectar	*to affect*
afectarse	*to be moved*
bajar	*to lower*
cambiar	*to change*
convertirse	*to become, transform*
crear	*to create*
decidir	*to decide*
dejar	*to let, leave*
depender	*to depend*
diseñar	*to design*
empujar	*to push*
entrar	*to enter, go in*
escoger	*to choose*
esperar	*to wait (for), hope (for), expect*
hablar	*to speak, talk*
intentar	*to try, attempt (to)*
mirar	*to look, watch*
mostrar	*to show*
necesitar	*to need*
oír	*to hear*
ponerse	*to get, become (+ adjective)*
quedar	*to arrange to meet, remain, be left*
quitar	*to remove, take away*
recordar	*to remember, recall, remind*
repetir	*to repeat*
volver a	*to do again*
romper	*to break (object)*
separar	*to separate*

Higher

acompañar	*to go with, accompany*
agradecer	*to be grateful for*
añadir	*to add*
alcanzar	*to reach, catch up with*
aparecer	*to turn up, appear*
apreciar	*to appreciate*
arreglar	*to repair, fix, tidy*
arreglarse	*to get ready*
asegurar	*to assure*
asegurarse (de que)	*to ensure (that), make sure (that)*
atreverse	*to dare*
¡Basta!	*(that's) enough!*
consistir (en)	*to consist (of)*
contar	*to tell, count*
controlar	*to control*
cubrir	*to cover*
dedicar	*to devote, dedicate*
despedirse (de)	*to say goodbye (to)*
escapar	*to escape*
esconder	*to hide*
exigir	*to demand*
formar	*to form, set up*
identificar	*to identify*
impedir	*to prevent*
meter	*to put, place*
mezclar	*to mix*
mover	*to move*
notar	*to notice*
obtener	*to obtain, get*
¡Ojalá!	*I hope so!, I wish!*
tratar de	*to try to*

Revision Summary Test for Section One

That's the first section (nearly) done and dusted. Time to test yourself on what you can remember.

- These questions are **hard**, but they'll really help you see **how well you know your stuff**.
- Tackle the **revision summary test** below, or scan the QR code to do it **online**. You can **track your progress** online and see **which areas need more work**.
- There are **sample answers** for the test here: www.cgpbooks.co.uk/BuenoExtras

Summary Test

Numbers and Times

1) Count out loud from 0 to 20 in Spanish.
2) How do you say these numbers in Spanish? a) 25 b) 37 c) 60 d) 104 e) 2003
3) 'Hay mil setecientas cuarenta y nueve razónes.' What does this mean in English?
4) Say the following phrases in Spanish: a) the first example b) the second day c) the third detail
5) Describe your daily routine using at least three different times.
6) H 'The maximum number of points you could obtain is five hundred.' Translate this into Spanish.

Times and Dates

7) Say all 7 days of the week and all 12 months of the year in Spanish.
8) ¿Cuándo es tu cumpleaños?
9) Say these words and phrases in English: a) hoy b) el fin de semana c) anoche d) ayer
10) Your Chilean friend says: 'Decidiré mañana por la mañana.' What does this mean in English?
11) Describe what you like to do on long weekends.
12) H Paloma says: 'El futuro es el comienzo de una época de posibilidad. Es un deseo mío crear millones de recuerdos bonitos llenos de emoción.' What is she saying?

Questions

13) What is the difference between '¿Qué...?' and '¿Cuál...?'?
14) '¿Cuánto cuesta el reloj blanco? El precio no está en la caja.' What is this person asking?
15) Write a question for each of the following question words:
    a) ¿Quién...? b) ¿Cuántos/as...? c) ¿Dónde...? d) ¿Cómo...? e) ¿Por qué...?

Being Polite

16) What are the differences between 'tú', 'vosotros/as', 'usted' and 'ustedes'?
17) How do you say these in English?
    a) hola b) ¿Qué tal? c) bien d) mal e) adiós f) por favor g) gracias h) lo siento
18) Imagine you're introducing a friend to your headteacher. Write out 2 sentences for each person.
19) How would you ask someone politely to repeat their idea in Spanish?

Opinions

20) How would you say that you love to design objects that don't seem real in Spanish?
21) Pepe says: 'Me gusta jugar al baloncesto porque es emocionante.' What's he saying?
22) 'I find this situation strange and boring.' How would you say this in Spanish?
23) Gonzalo asks: '¿Estás de acuerdo con mi opinión?' What does he want to know?
24) a) Explain why you dislike your least favourite school subject in Spanish.
    b) Say a subject that you like using the word 'prefiero'. Give a reason why you like it.
25) H Give a review of a book that you have recently read or a film that you have recently watched.

About Yourself

Quick Quiz

I know you're probably not supposed to admit this, but I do love talking about myself. And why wouldn't I when I can limbo skate better than the pros...

Head to the CGP RevisionHub for all your online content: www.cgpbooks.co.uk/Bueno

Preséntate — *Introduce yourself*

Vocabulary

el nombre	*name*	nacer	*to be born*	gay	*gay*
el apellido	*surname*	inglés(a)	*English*	hetero(sexual)	*straight*
llamarse	*to be called*	español(a)	*Spanish*	la religión	*religion*
la edad	*age*	europeo/a	*European*	religioso/a	*religious*
el año	*year*	transgénero	*transgender*	H la nacionalidad	*nationality*
el cumpleaños	*birthday*	bi(sexual)	*bi(sexual)*	H el género	*gender*

¡Hola! Me llamo Riku y tengo quince años. — *Hello! I'm called Riku and I'm 15 years old.*

Mi cumpleaños es el dos de abril. Nací en dos mil doce. — *My birthday is the 2nd of April. I was born in 2012.*

Vivo en España, pero soy francesa. — *I live in Spain, but I am French.*

Mi familia es religiosa. — *My family is religious.*

Varios aspectos forman mi identidad, como la edad y el género. — *Various aspects form my identity, like age and gender.*

I'm... — Soy...
My name is... — Mi nombre es...

Check p.7 for a reminder of how to say dates.

Scottish — escocés / escocesa
Irish — irlandés / irlandesa
Welsh — galés / galesa

See p.26 for more nationalities and religions.

Grammar — saying your age

In Spanish, you '<u>have</u>' an age, so you need '<u>tener</u>' to say <u>how old you are</u>. 'Tener' is a <u>stem-changing</u> verb — see p.128.

<u>Tengo</u> 16 años. ***<u>I'm</u> 16 years old.***

Grammar — nationalities

Nationalities are <u>adjectives</u>. Some have an <u>accent</u> in the <u>masculine singular</u> form, but drop the accent and add '<u>a</u>' in the <u>feminine</u> form.

inglés (m., sing.) — **inglesa** (f., sing.)
ingleses (m., pl.) — **inglesas** (f., pl.)

The accent is dropped in the plural forms too.

Practice Question

Q1 *Read the following text out loud.* *[5 marks]*

SPEAKING

¡Hola! Me llamo Estefanía y soy de Venezuela. Vivo en el norte del país, cerca de la ciudad de Caracas. Mi cumpleaños es el veinticuatro de julio. Nací en el año dos mil diez.

Now answer the questions about yourself below in Spanish.

a) *¿Cómo te llamas?*
b) *¿Dónde vives?*
c) *¿Cuántos años tienes?*
d) *¿Cuándo es tu cumpleaños?* *[10 marks]*

Top Tip for Higher Students
✓ Try to give more than one detail for your answers, e.g. say the year you were born in.

The only llamas I'm interested in have four legs and a fluffy tail...

When you're introducing yourself to someone new in Spanish, you could say the same stuff as you would in English, like your name, age, and where you're from. Or you could make up a cool alter ego instead...

Quick Quiz

My Family and Friends

OK, it's not *all* about you — you'll have to be able to talk about your family and friends too. Examiners are a nosy bunch, so prepare yourself for a friendly interrogation...

Mi familia — *My family*

Vocabulary

el miembro	*member*	los hijos	*children*	el perro	*dog*
los padres	*parents*	el hijo	*son, child (m)*	el gato	*cat*
el padre	*father*	la hija	*daughter, child (f)*	el caballo	*horse*
la madre	*mother*	el hermano	*brother*	el pájaro	*bird*
el padrastro	*stepfather*	la hermana	*sister*	el papá (Higher)	*dad*
la madrastra	*stepmother*	el tío	*uncle*	la mamá (Higher)	*mum*
los abuelos	*grandparents*	la tía	*aunt*	el familiar (Higher)	*relative*
el abuelo	*grandfather*	el primo	*cousin (m)*	familiar (Higher)	*of the family*
la abuela	*grandmother*	la prima	*cousin (f)*	la mascota (Higher)	*pet*

Háblame de tu familia — *Tell me about your family*

Grammar — saying 'my' and 'your'

Possessive adjectives like 'my' and 'your' have to agree with the noun they come before (see p.119). Remember — 'su(s)' could also mean 'your' if you're being formal.

mi padre — *my father*	tu hermana — *your sister*	su tía — *his / her / their aunt*
mis padres — *my parents*	tus hermanas — *your sisters*	sus tías — *his / her / their aunts*

I wonder who the favourite is...

Tengo una hermana mayor. Se llama Ramona.	*I have an older sister. She is called Ramona.*
Hay cinco personas en mi familia: mi madre, mi padrastro, mis dos hermanos menores y yo. Mis hermanos se llaman Waisea y Gabriel.	*There are five people in my family: my mother, my stepfather, my two younger brothers and me. My brothers are called Waisea and Gabriel.*
Soy hijo único, pero me gustaría tener hermanos.	*I'm an only child (m), but I'd like to have siblings.*
Para mí, mi perro Joey es parte de la familia también.	*For me, my dog Joey is part of the family too.*

a younger sister — una hermana menor
a bird — un pájaro

older brothers — hermanos mayores

an only child (f) — hija única
the oldest — el/la mayor
the youngest — el/la menor

I like not having siblings — me gusta no tener hermanos

Q&A Audio

Question

¿Cómo es tu familia?
What's your family like?

Simple Answer

Soy hijo único, pero tengo muchos primos.
I'm an only child, but I have a lot of cousins.

Extended Answer

Soy hijo único, pero mi padre tiene cinco hermanos, entonces en realidad, tengo muchos familiares. Mis primos viven cerca de aquí y siempre lo pasamos bien juntos.
I'm an only child, but my father has five siblings, so really, I have lots of relatives. My cousins live near here and we always have a good time together.

Mis amigos — *My friends*

Vocabulary

la amistad	*friendship*	conocer	*to know (person, place), meet (for the first time)*
el amigo	*friend (m)*	pasar	*to spend (time)*
la amiga	*friend (f)*		
mejor	*better, best*		

Grammar — prenominal adjectives

'Bueno' becomes 'buen' before masculine nouns. 'Buen' is a prenominal adjective (see p.118).

Eres un buen amigo. *You're a good friend.*

The other forms don't need to change.

Eres una buena amiga. *You're a good friend.*
Sois buenos amigos. *You're good friends.*

Tengo muchas amigas pero no tengo una mejor amiga. — *I have lots of friends but I don't have a best friend.*

Mis amigos y yo somos muy similares. — *My friends and I are very similar.*

La amistad es muy importante. Soy feliz porque tengo buenos amigos. — *Friendship is very important. I am happy because I have good friends.*

Para mí, es bastante fácil hacer amigos. Pero a veces puede ser difícil. — *For me, it's quite easy to make friends. But sometimes it can be difficult.*

Mi buen amigo Benicio es argentino. Me gusta cuando pasamos tiempo juntos porque le conozco muy bien. — *My good friend Benicio is Argentinian. I like it when we spend time together because I know him really well.*

to meet new people — conocer a nueva gente

Mexican — mexicano
Chilean — chileno
Colombian — colombiano

'Conozco' (I know) is the only irregular bit of the verb 'conocer' in the present tense.

Practice Questions

Q1 *Describe your family and friends.*
You should write about 50 words in Spanish. Mention:
- *who's in your family*
- *whether you have a best friend*
- *whether you have any pets.* *[10 marks]*

WRITING

Top Tip for Higher Students
✓ Use possessive pronouns to talk about your family, e.g. 'Tu amigo es mayor que el mío.'

Higher

Q2 *Qori has written about her family.*
Read her comments and then answer the questions below in English.

READING

> Vivo con mi mamá, mi hermana mayor y mis dos hermanas menores. Paso mucho tiempo con ellas porque disfrutamos de las mismas actividades . Los fines de semana, visito a mi padre, su mujer italiana y mi hermanastro*, que se llama Marco. Tenemos la misma edad y el mismo cumpleaños. Sí, ¡nació el mismo día que yo! Me gustaría pasar más tiempo allí con ellos porque es muy divertido.

*hermanastro — stepbrother

a) How many sisters does Qori have? *[1 mark]*
b) Why does Qori spend lots of time with them? *[1 mark]*
c) Who does Qori visit on the weekend? *[1 mark]*
d) What coincidence does Qori mention? *[1 mark]*

Pineapple on pizza — that's what true friendship looks like...

You can tut all you like, but it won't change my mind. No matter who makes up your family or friendship groups, you need to be able to talk about them in your exams. You'd better give these pages another read...

Quick Quiz

Describing People

Adjectives are a key ingredient of Spanish success, so it's always worth having some to hand...

¿Cómo eres? — *What are you like?*

You'll need the verbs 'tener' (to have) and 'ser' (to be) for this page. They're irregular, so check p.129-130 to see how they work.

Vocabulary

guapo/a	*good-looking*	las gafas	*glasses*	moreno/a	*brown (hair), dark (skin)*
feo/a	*ugly*	el ojo	*eye*	el tatuaje	*tattoo*
alto/a	*tall*	marrón	*brown*	el adulto	*adult*
bajo/a	*short*	verde	*green*	el anciano	*elderly person*
gordo/a	*fat*	azul	*blue*	la altura	*height*
delgado/a	*thin, slim*	gris	*grey*	la cara	*face*
pequeño/a	*little, small, young*	el pelo	*hair*	oscuro/a	*dark*
joven	*young*	corto/a	*short (hair)*	precioso/a	*beautiful, precious*
viejo/a	*old, elderly*	largo/a	*long*	infantil	*of children, children's*
describir	*to describe*	rubio/a	*blond, fair (hair)*		
parecerse a	*to look like*	negro/a	*black*		

'Marrón' loses its accent in the plural form.

Higher: el adulto, el anciano, la altura, la cara, oscuro/a, precioso/a, infantil

Tengo... — *I have...*

Q&A Audio

Question

¿Cómo eres?

What are you like?

Simple Answer

Soy alta. Tengo los ojos azules y tengo el pelo moreno.

I'm tall. I have blue eyes and I have brown hair.

Extended Answer

Soy de altura media — no soy ni alta ni baja. Tengo los ojos azules y llevo gafas. Tengo una cara pequeña y tengo el pelo corto.

I am average height — I'm neither tall nor short. I have blue eyes and I wear glasses. I have a small face and I have short hair.

Soy muy bajo como mis padres. Sin embargo, mi hermano es mucho más alto que yo. Tengo el pelo rubio y tengo los ojos verdes.

I'm very short like my parents. However, my brother is much taller than me. I have blond hair and I have green eyes.

Grammar — adjectives agree

Adjectives must agree with the noun they describe.

'Los ojos' are masculine plural, so adjectives like 'blue' must be in the masculine plural form — 'azules'.

'El pelo' is masculine singular, so adjectives like 'short' need to be in the masculine singular form — 'corto' — even if you're a girl.

Tiene el pelo rubio y largo. Es altísima. Lleva gafas y tiene los ojos azules.

She has long, blond hair. She's really tall. She wears glasses and she has blue eyes.

really short — bajísima

No soy ni gorda ni delgada. Tengo los ojos marrones y el pelo negro.

I'm neither fat nor slim. I have brown eyes and black hair.

dark skin — la piel morena

dark hair — el pelo oscuro

Creo que te pareces a tu padre, pero él es más bajo y tiene el pelo gris.

I think that you look like your father, but he is shorter and has grey hair.

he's red-haired — es pelirrojo

Mis abuelos son viejos pero mi abuelo todavía se considera joven.

My grandparents are old but my grandfather still considers himself young.

Es un chico guapísimo con los ojos verdes. Tiene una sonrisa preciosa.

He's a very good-looking boy with green eyes. He has a beautiful smile.

face — cara

Mi carácter — *My personality*

Vocabulary

simpático/a	*nice, friendly*	trabajador(a)	*hardworking*	fiel	*faithful, loyal*
alegre	*cheerful*	perezoso/a	*lazy*	sensible	*sensitive*
gracioso/a	*funny*	serio/a	*serious*	tolerante	*tolerant*
animado/a	*lively*	tranquilo/a	*calm, relaxed*	ambicioso/a	*ambitious*
tonto/a	*silly*	nervioso/a	*nervous, uptight*	orgulloso/a	*proud*
optimista	*optimistic*	contento/a	*happy, content*	vago/a	*lazy*

Higher (fiel – vago/a)

Grammar — making adjectives agree

Adjectives must agree with the nouns they describe — see p.117.

Some adjectives don't follow the normal rules:

1) '-or' endings, e.g. '**trabajador**' — add an 'a' on the end for the feminine form and then 'es' and 'as' for the masculine and feminine plurals.
2) '-ísta/-ista' endings, e.g. '**optimista**' — stay the same in the singular and add an 's' for both the masculine and feminine plurals.

Grammar — 'ser' vs 'estar'

Both 'ser' and 'estar' mean 'to be'.

To describe someone's personality use 'ser', but to describe how they feel at a given moment, use 'estar' — see p.130.

Está tranquilo. ***He is feeling calm.***

Es tranquilo. ***He is calm. (a calm person)***

Mi mejor amigo es sensible. Es optimista también. Sin embargo, hoy está triste. — *My best friend is sensitive. He is optimistic too. However, today he is feeling sad.*

He has a good sense of humour — Tiene un buen sentido del humor

Mis padres son estrictos pero divertidos al mismo tiempo. Mi madre es muy deportiva pero mi padre es más artístico. — *My parents are strict but fun at the same time. My mother is very sporty but my father is more artistic.*

Mis profesoras son listas y simpáticas. — *My teachers are intelligent and friendly.*

understanding — comprensivas

Practice Questions

Q1 *Ana and Pablo are describing these four people. Write the correct order in which they are mentioned.* LISTENING

Listening Track 04

A

B

C

D

[4 marks]

Q2 *You're writing an introduction about you and your best friend for your new blog. Write about 90 words in Spanish. You must write something about each bullet point. Mention:* WRITING

- *your appearance and personality*
- *your best friend's appearance and personality*
- *why they are your best friend.*

Top Tip for Higher Students
✓ Use additional tenses, e.g. to talk about when you first met your friend.

[15 marks]

I reckon I'm funny, intelligent and humble...

Oh, this space isn't for me to keep describing myself? Shame. Remember — if you want to call your sister silly, you'll need the feminine form of the adjective. Also, try to avoid describing everyone in the same way.

Quick Quiz

Relationships and Partnerships

Here's your chance to say who you get on best with — or vent about someone who winds you up...

Las relaciones — *Relationships*

You need the personal 'a' with verbs like 'aguantar'. Have a look at p.112 for more information.

Vocabulary

aguantar	*to put up with, stand*	escuchar	*to listen (to)*
discutir	*to argue, discuss*	respetar	*to respect*
molestar	*to bother, annoy*	ayudar	*to help*
pelearse	*to fight*	apoyar	*to support*
llevarse	*to get on, relate*	comprender (Higher)	*to understand*
entenderse	*to get on*	confiar (Higher)	*to trust, confide*
entender	*to understand*	animar (Higher)	*to cheer up*

Willow could always lean on her friends for support.

Grammar — reflexive verbs

'Pelearse', 'entenderse', 'llevarse' and 'enamorarse' are reflexive verbs. Take off the 'se' and add the correct ending to the stem like a normal verb (see p.127). Then choose the right pronoun (see p.137) and put it in front of the verb.

¿Te entiendes con ella?	***Do you get on with her?***
Nos peleamos mucho.	***We fight a lot.***
Me llevo bien con mi hermana.	***I get on well with my sister.***

Grammar (Higher only) — 'confiar'

'Confiar' is an irregular verb. In the present tense, the 'i' has an accent on it in every form except the 'we' and 'you inf., plural' forms.

Confío en él. ***I trust him.***

To say you trust someone, you need to use 'en'.

¿Te llevas bien con ellos? — *Do you get on well with them?*

Mis padres tienen una buena relación pero yo no me llevo bien con ellos. — *My parents have a good relationship but I don't get on with them.*

I don't get on very well with them — no me relaciono muy bien con ellos

Me llevo mejor con mi hermana porque me ayuda mucho. La encuentro muy graciosa. — *I get on better with my sister because she helps me a lot. I find her very funny.*

I don't like to argue with my sister — No me gusta discutir con mi hermana

Mi hermano y yo nos peleamos mucho porque me molesta. — *My brother and I fight a lot because he annoys me.*

I can't stand my brother — No aguanto a mi hermano

Un buen amigo siempre te escucha y te apoya. — *A good friend always listens to you and supports you.*

helps you and cheers you up — te ayuda y te anima

El amor — *Love*

Vocabulary

el novio	*boyfriend, groom*	el matrimonio	*marriage*	divorciarse	*to get divorced*
la novia	*girlfriend, bride*	casado/a	*married*	soltero/a	*single, unmarried*
la pareja	*couple, partner*	casarse	*to get married*	el estado civil (Higher)	*marital status*
la boda	*wedding*	besar	*to kiss*	prometerse (Higher)	*to get engaged*
el marido	*husband*	cuidar	*to take care of*	enamorarse (de) (Higher)	*to fall in love (with)*
la mujer	*wife*	separarse	*to separate*	abrazar (Higher)	*to hug*

¿Qué piensas del matrimonio? — *What do you think about marriage?*

Las bodas son muy románticas. Me gustaría enamorarme y casarme porque parece emocionante.

Weddings are very romantic. I would like to fall in love and get married because it seems exciting.

Debo decir que preferiría no casarme, porque una boda puede costar mucho dinero.

I must say that I would prefer not to get married, because a wedding can cost a lot of money.

I never want to get married — no quiero casarme nunca

I'd prefer to buy myself a house — preferiría comprarme una casa

En mi opinión, no es necesario casarse antes de tener hijos, pero todavía me gustaría hacerlo.

In my opinion, it's not necessary to get married before having children, but I'd still like to do it.

marriage can give you security — el matrimonio te puede dar seguridad

En el futuro... — *In the future...*

Q&A Audio

Question

¿Te gustaría casarte y tener hijos en el futuro?

Would you like to get married and have children in the future?

Simple Answer

No sé si quiero casarme, pero me gustaría tener hijos.

I don't know if I want to get married, but I'd like to have children.

Extended Answer

Quiero casarme porque me importa mucho. Me gustaría tener hijos cuando tenga treinta años, pero no sé cuántos hijos quiero tener.

I want to get married because it's very important to me. I'd like to have children when I'm 30, but I don't know how many children I want to have.

Grammar (Higher only) — When I'm X years old...

To say 'when I'm 30' (or to say 'when' with a future event), use the subjunctive. See p.142.

Cuando tenga 60 años...
When I'm 60 years old...

Practice Questions

Q1 *Read Chea's message about her boyfriend and choose the correct options below.*

READING

Conocí a mi novio en una fiesta de cumpleaños cuando tenía quince años. Me llevo muy bien con él porque los dos tenemos el mismo sentido del humor. Aunque discutimos muy poco, no quiero casarme con él ahora porque somos muy jóvenes. Quizás en unos años ¡si me aguanta y yo le aguanto!

a) *Where did Chea meet her boyfriend?*

A. A party
B. A cafe
C. At school
D. Online *[1 mark]*

b) *When does she want to get married?*

A. In 15 years
B. She's not sure
C. Never
D. Now *[1 mark]*

Higher

Q2 *Miguel is talking about his relationships. Choose the correct statement from each list below to complete the sentences in English.*

LISTENING

Listening Track 05

a) Miguel used to fight with...

A. his mum.
B. his dad.
C. his brother. *[1 mark]*

b) Miguel's boyfriend says that Miguel...

A. is happy.
B. is lazy.
C. isn't very tolerant. *[1 mark]*

Luckily, I get on really well with Spanish revision...

I know it feels a bit weird to talk to a stranger about your relationships, but have a think about who you do or don't get on with (and why) so you'll be ready for whatever the examiner might throw your way.

Identity and Relationships with Others — Vocabulary

Use the next two pages to strike up a friendship with all the vocab from this section.

About Yourself

el nombre	*name*
el apellido	*surname*
presentar	*to introduce, present*
llamar	*to call, name*
llamarse	*to be called*
la edad	*age*
el año	*year*
tener ... años	*to be ... years old*
el cumpleaños	*birthday*
nacer	*to be born*
la identidad	*identity*
británico/a	*British*
inglés(a)	*English*

español(a)	*Spanish*
francés(a)	*French*
alemán(a)	*German*
italiano/a	*Italian*
europeo/a	*European*
mexicano/a	*Mexican*
cubano/a	*Cuban*
chileno/a	*Chilean*
colombiano/a	*Colombian*
argentino/a	*Argentinian*
chino/a	*Chinese*
el sexo	*sex*
transgénero	*transgender*

bi(sexual)	*bi(sexual)*
gay	*gay*
hetero(sexual)	*straight, heterosexual*
la religión	*religion*
religioso/a	*religious*
católico/a	*Catholic*
cristiano/a	*Christian*
musulmán(a)	*Muslim*
judío/a	*Jewish*

Higher

el nacimiento	*birth, origin*
la nacionalidad	*nationality*
latino/a	*Latin, Latin American*
el género	*gender*

My Family and Friends

la familia	*family*
el miembro	*member*
los padres	*parents*
el padre	*father*
la madre	*mother*
el padrastro	*stepfather*
la madrastra	*stepmother*
los abuelos	*grandparents*
el abuelo	*grandfather*
la abuela	*grandmother*
los hijos	*children*
el hijo	*son, child (m)*
la hija	*daughter, child (f)*
el hermano	*brother*
la hermana	*sister*
menor	*younger*

mayor	*older*
el tío	*uncle*
la tía	*aunt*
el primo	*cousin (m)*
la prima	*cousin (f)*
el niño	*child (m), little boy*
la niña	*child (f), young girl*
el bebé	*baby*
el perro	*dog*
el gato	*cat*
el caballo	*horse*
el pájaro	*bird*
la amistad	*friendship*
el amigo	*friend (m)*
la amiga	*friend (f)*
mejor	*better, best*

viejo/a	*old, long-standing (pre-noun)*
conocer	*to know (person, place), to meet (for the first time)*
pasar	*to spend (time)*

Higher

el papá	*dad*
la mamá	*mum*
familiar	*of/relating to the family*
el familiar	*relative, family member*
el/la menor	*the youngest*
el/la mayor	*the oldest*
la generación	*generation*
la mascota	*pet*
la cola	*tail*

Describing People — Appearances

guapo/a	*good-looking*
hermoso/a	*handsome*
feo/a	*ugly*
alto/a	*tall*
bajo/a	*short*
gordo/a	*fat*
delgado/a	*thin, slim*
pequeño/a	*little, small, young*
joven	*young*
viejo/a	*old, elderly (post-noun)*
describir	*to describe*
parecerse a	*to look like*
sonreír	*to smile*
la sonrisa	*smile*
llevar	*to wear*

las gafas	*glasses*
el ojo	*eye*
marrón	*brown*
verde	*green*
azul	*blue*
gris	*grey*
rojo/a	*red*
el pelo	*hair*
corto/a	*short (hair)*
largo/a	*long*
rubio/a	*blond, fair (hair)*
negro/a	*black*
moreno/a	*brown (hair), dark (skin)*
pintarse	*to put on makeup*

el tatuaje	*tattoo*
la persona	*person*
el chico	*boy*
la chica	*girl*
la mujer	*woman*
el hombre	*man*
la gente	*people*

Higher

precioso/a	*beautiful, precious*
oscuro/a	*dark*
infantil	*of children, children's*
la cara	*face*
la altura	*height*
el adulto	*adult*
el anciano	*elderly person*

Describing People — Personalities and Emotions

el carácter	*personality, character*
la personalidad	*personality*
simpático/a	*nice, friendly*
alegre	*cheerful, happy, lively*
contento/a	*happy, content, pleased*
feliz	*happy, glad, content*
gracioso/a	*funny*
el humor	*humour, mood*
animado/a	*lively*
tonto/a	*silly*
(ser) listo/a	*(to be) clever, intelligent*
trabajador(a)	*hardworking*
perezoso/a	*lazy*
deportivo/a	*sporty*
artístico/a	*artistic*
duro/a	*resilient*
optimista	*optimistic*
serio/a	*serious*
independiente	*independent*
tranquilo/a	*calm, relaxed*

nervioso/a	*nervous, uptight*
triste	*sad, unhappy, upset*
enojado/a	*angry*

Higher

comprensivo/a	*understanding*
fiel	*faithful, loyal*
sensible	*sensitive*
tolerante	*tolerant*
estricto/a	*strict*
loco/a	*crazy, insane*
ambicioso/a	*ambitious*
orgulloso/a	*proud*
vago/a	*lazy*

'listo/a' changes its meaning depending on whether you use it with 'ser' or 'estar'. Use 'ser' if you want to say that someone is clever, e.g. 'Es un hombre listo.' Use 'estar' if you want to say that someone is ready, e.g. 'La mujer está lista.'

Relationships and Partnerships

la relación	*relationship*
aguantar	*to put up with, stand*
discutir	*to argue, discuss*
molestar	*to bother, annoy, upset, disturb*
pelearse	*to fight (physically)*
llevarse	*to get on, relate*
entenderse	*to get on*
entender	*to understand*
escuchar	*to listen (to)*
respetar	*to respect*
ayudar	*to help*
apoyar	*to support*
el sentimiento	*feeling, sentiment*
el amor	*love*
la pareja	*couple, partner*
el/la compañero/a	*companion*
el novio	*boyfriend, groom*
la novia	*girlfriend, bride*
la boda	*wedding*
el marido	*husband*
la mujer	*wife*
el matrimonio	*marriage*
civil	*civil*
casado/a	*married*
casarse	*to get married*
besar	*to kiss*
cuidar	*to take care of*
separarse	*to separate (of a couple)*
divorciarse	*to get divorced*
soltero/a	*single, unmarried*

Higher

relacionarse con	*to relate to, get on with*
comprender	*to understand*
confiar	*to trust, confide*
el secreto	*secret*
perdonar	*to forgive, excuse*
animar	*to encourage, cheer up*
alegrar	*to make happy, cheer up*
la cita	*(romantic) date*
romántico/a	*romantic*
enamorarse (de)	*to fall in love (with)*
el cariño	*affection, love*
el estado civil	*marital status*
la independencia	*independence*
prometer	*to promise*
prometerse	*to get engaged*
llorar	*to cry*
abrazar	*to hug*
reírse	*to laugh*

Malai loved her personal space. Berto also loved Malai's personal space...

Revision Summary Test for Section Two

Improve your relationship with family and friendship vocab by giving this test a go.

- These questions are **really tricky**, but they'll help you see **how well you know your stuff**.
- Tackle the **revision summary test** below, or scan the QR code to do it **online**. You can **keep track of your progress** online and see **which areas need more work**.
- There are **sample answers** here: www.cgpbooks.co.uk/BuenoExtras

Summary Test

About Yourself

1) Preséntate en español. Da tu nombre, apellido, edad y cumpleaños.
2) How many words related to religion, gender and sexuality can you list in Spanish? There are 11 in this section (plus 1 for Higher tier).
3) 'Nací en Sudamérica y esto es una parte importante de mi identidad.' Translate this into English.
4) List the 13 Spanish words from this section (plus 2 for Higher tier) that describe where you're from.
5) [H] Pablo says: 'Te presento a mi amigo. Se llama Carlos y su lugar de nacimiento es Barcelona.' Translate his sentences into English.

My Family and Friends

6) How many words related to family members can you name in Spanish? There are at least 19 you need to know (plus 3 for Higher tier).
7) In Spanish, write about why you like your friends. Give at least two details.
8) 'I met my best friend for the first time when I was a baby. She is a special person in my life and her friendship is really important to me.' Translate this sentence into Spanish.
9) Would you like to have any pets? Why (or why not)? Answer in Spanish.
10) [H] 'De los niños en mi familia, Diego es el menor y Leya es la mayor. Esa niña es de una generación completamente diferente a la mía.' Translate these sentences into English.

Describing People

11) How would you say the following words in Spanish?
    a) tall b) short c) fat d) thin e) old f) young g) ugly h) good-looking i) small
12) 'Tiene el pelo largo y rubio, los ojos azules y lleva gafas rojas.' Translate this description into English.
13) ¿Cómo te describirías físicamente y cómo describirías tu carácter?
14) 'La chica que está allí con el pelo negro y los ojos marrones se parece a la mujer de la película que vimos ayer.' Translate this sentence into English.
15) How many adjectives can you think of to describe someone's personality or emotions in Spanish? There are 20 you need to know in this section (plus 9 for Higher tier).
16) [H] 'La anciana tenía una sonrisa preciosa y el pelo oscuro y corto. También tenía tatuajes y se pintaba la cara de un estilo tradicional.' Translate these sentences into English.

Relationships and Partnerships

17) What is your relationship like with your family and friends? Answer in Spanish.
18) How would you say the following words in Spanish?
    a) girlfriend b) husband c) wife d) married e) single f) to separate g) to divorce
19) 'My parents don't understand my feelings. It annoys me a lot.' Translate this into Spanish.
20) Write down the English for the following verbs: a) besar b) ayudar c) pelearse d) cuidar
21) 'No aguanto a mi hermano mayor. El hombre no me respeta y discutimos.' Translate this into English.
22) [Higher] In Spanish, write about the qualities you think are most important in a relationship or marriage.
23) [Higher] 'Me enamoré con mi novio en la primera cita. Es muy romántico y creo que nos prometeremos en el futuro.' Translate these sentences into English.

Food

Quick Quiz

It's time to devour some tasty food vocab. My stomach is already rumbling...

Don't forget you can access your online content here: www.cgpbooks.co.uk/Bueno

La comida — *Food*

Vocabulary

la fruta	*fruit*	el jamón	*ham*
la manzana	*apple*	el pollo	*chicken*
la naranja	*orange*	el pescado	*fish*
la uva	*grape*	la paella	*paella (dish usually of rice and seafood)*
la verdura	*vegetable*		
la ensalada	*salad*	el caramelo	*sweet*
el tomate	*tomato*	vegetariano/a	*vegetarian*
las patatas fritas	*chips, fries*	vegano/a	*vegan*
la hamburguesa	*burger*	la bebida	*drink*
la comida rápida	*fast food*	el agua (f)	*water*
la comida basura	*junk food*	la leche	*milk*
el bocadillo	*sandwich*	el café	*coffee*
el huevo	*egg*	el alimento (Higher)	*food, nourishment*
el pan	*bread*	el arroz (Higher)	*rice*
la carne	*meat*	el aceite (Higher)	*oil*

I said paella — not pie, Ella...

¿Qué comes? — *What do you eat?*

Suelo comer una ensalada de frutas para el desayuno. — *I usually eat a fruit salad for breakfast.*

'Soler' (*to usually do something*) is a stem-changing verb ('o' to 'ue'). See p.128.

Mi padre es vegano. Por eso nunca prepara comida con productos animales. — *My dad is vegan. Therefore, he never prepares food with animal products.*

cheese — queso
cream — nata

Para la comida, me gusta comer un bocadillo de pollo. — *For lunch, I like to eat a chicken sandwich.*

'el almuerzo' is another way to say lunch.

Grammar — meal times

These are the nouns for Spanish meals:

el desayuno	***breakfast***
la comida	***lunch*** ('comida' also means 'food' or 'meal'.)
la cena	***dinner, evening meal***

These nouns can be made into verbs:

desayunar	***to have breakfast***
comer (This also means 'to eat'.)	***to have lunch***
cenar	***to have dinner, tea (evening meal)***

Practice Question

Q1 *Three friends are talking about food. Answer the questions in English.*

e.g. *What did Joaquín eat a lot of when he was younger?* sweets

a) Joaquín avoids foods that are high in two things. Name one. *[1 mark]*

b) What does Alejandra say she needs to eat more of? *[1 mark]*

c) What does Raquel find difficult as a vegetarian? *[1 mark]*

LISTENING — Listening Track 06

Why did the tomato blush? Because it saw the salad dressing...

It doesn't get much better than food, so savour every morsel of this page. If you're struggling to remember how to say certain foods, give them a label in the kitchen and repeat the Spanish word every time you see it.

Quick Quiz

Healthy and Unhealthy Living

Now for two pages about healthy living, complete with reflexive verbs. Pass the biscuits, then.

Una vida sana — *A healthy life*

'la dieta' means your general diet, e.g. what you eat or drink normally. 'el régimen' means a specific diet, e.g. for weight loss or medical conditions.

Vocabulary

la vida	*life*	la dieta	*diet (general)*
la salud	*health*	equilibrado/a	*balanced*
sano/a	*healthy, wholesome*	la costumbre	*habit*
suficiente	*sufficient, enough*	el sueño	*sleep*
la importancia	*importance*	dormir	*to sleep*
activo/a	*active*	dormirse	*to fall asleep*
físico/a	*physical*	descansar	*to rest, relax*
el ejercicio	*exercise*	diario/a (Higher)	*daily*
estar en forma	*to be fit*	relajante (Higher)	*relaxing*
entrenarse	*to train, go training*	promover (Higher)	*to promote*

Q&A Audio

Question

¿Crees que es importante estar en forma?

Do you believe it's important to be fit?

Simple Answer

Sí, pienso que es importante entrenarse y comer bien.

Yes, I think it's important to train and to eat well.

Grammar — reflexive verbs

'entrenarse' is a reflexive verb (see p.137).

Me entreno todos los días.

I train every day.

Extended Answer

Diría que es importante entrenarse, pero no tengo tiempo para hacerlo todos los días. Voy al gimnasio dos veces a la semana y siempre elijo comida sana.

I would say that it's important to train, but I don't have time to do it every day. I go to the gym twice a week and I always choose healthy food.

Derek trains three times a week.

Las buenas costumbres — *Good habits*

Es importante intentar comer una dieta equilibrada todos los días.
It's important to try to eat a balanced diet every day.
(*to avoid junk food* — evitar la comida basura)

Hago ejercicio los fines de semana porque no tengo mucho tiempo libre durante la semana.
I do exercise at weekends because I don't have much free time during the week.
(*I prefer to rest after school* — prefiero descansar después del colegio)

Vale la pena tener buenas costumbres como beber dos litros de agua todos los días.
It's worth having good habits like drinking two litres of water every day.
(*getting enough sleep* — dormir lo suficiente)

Es importante cuidar la salud mental también.
It's important to take care of your mental health too.

En mi opinión, la mente y el cuerpo son igualmente importantes. Por eso siempre dedico tiempo a hacer actividades relajantes.
In my opinion, the mind and the body are equally important. Therefore, I always devote time to doing relaxing activities.
(*daily life causes a lot of stress* — la vida diaria causa mucho estrés)

Las malas costumbres — *Bad habits*

Vocabulary

perezoso/a	*lazy*
el peso	*weight*
perder	*to lose*
el riesgo	*risk*
la droga	*drug*
fumar	*to smoke*

Higher

la cantidad	*quantity, amount*
el consumo	*consumption*
el sobrepeso	*obesity, excess weight*
el cigarrillo	*cigarette*
el humo	*smoke, fumes*
el alcohol	*alcohol*

Soy una persona muy perezosa. Me encanta echarme en el sofá y ver la televisión durante horas.	*I'm a very lazy person. I love to lie down on the sofa and watch TV for hours.*
Los cigarrillos tienen muchos riesgos. El humo afecta la salud y puede causar enfermedades graves.	*Cigarettes have lots of risks. The smoke affects your health and it can cause serious illnesses.*
No quiero probar las drogas porque son peligrosas.	*I don't want to try drugs because they are dangerous.*
Una vez, bebí alcohol con mis amigos. No me gustó.	*Once, I drank alcohol with my friends. I didn't like it.*

to smoke because it smells horrible — fumar porque huele horrible
'Oler' *(to smell)* is an irregular verb.

Grammar — to stop ...ing

To say '<u>to stop ...ing</u>', use '<u>dejar de</u>' followed by the <u>infinitive</u>.

Quiero <u>dejar de fumar</u>.
I want <u>to stop smoking</u>.

Practice Questions

Q1 Write an article for a magazine about healthy living. You should write about 90 words in Spanish. Mention:

WRITING

- *whether you exercise or not*
- *if you have a balanced diet*
- *two things you could do to lead a healthier life* *[15 marks]*

Top Tips for Higher Students
✓ Give plenty of details about what makes your diet balanced.
✓ Use impersonal phrases like 'vale la pena' to say what is worth doing.

Higher

Q2 Read Karima's thoughts on alcohol and drugs. Answer the questions in English.

READING

Para mí, beber alcohol es tan peligroso como tomar drogas. Los jóvenes piensan que no importa si toman unas copas con los amigos, pero no prestan atención a las consecuencias. A veces, no saben ni dónde están ni cuánto han bebido. El año pasado, mi amigo bebió demasiado y tuvo que ir al hospital. Era muy irresponsable.

a) What is Karima's opinion on drinking alcohol? *[1 mark]*

b) What two consequences of drinking alcohol does Karima mention? *[2 marks]*

c) What happened to Karima's friend? *[1 mark]*

Balance is key — you won't get very far if you keep falling over...

I must be a magician because all the biscuits have disappeared... This topic isn't just about physical health, so practise talking about mental health as well. And make sure you cover both healthy and unhealthy living.

Quick Quiz

Illnesses and Treatments

You can boost your defences against examstressitis with a daily dose of vocab practice.

Las enfermedades — *Illnesses*

Vocabulary

sentirse	*to feel (+ adjective)*	el cuerpo	*body*	el dolor	*pain, ache*
enfermo/a	*ill, sick*	la cabeza	*head*	la herida	*wound, injury*
cansado/a	*tired, tiring*	el ojo	*eye*	el cáncer	*cancer*
preocuparse por	*to worry about*	la lengua	*tongue*	la sangre	*blood*
respirar	*to breathe*	el diente	*tooth*	la pierna	*leg*
romperse	*to break (bones)*	la mano	*hand*	el brazo	*arm*
roto/a	*broken*	el pie	*foot*	la boca	*mouth*
doler	*to hurt, be painful*	la piel	*skin*	el cerebro	*brain*
caerse	*to fall over*	el corazón	*heart*	la mente	*mind*

(Higher: el dolor – la mente)

Me siento... — *I feel...*

Q&A Audio

Question

¿Cómo te sientes?
How do you feel?

Simple Answer

Me duele la mano.
My hand hurts.

Extended Answer

Me duelen el pie y la pierna.
Tengo dolor de cabeza también.
My foot and leg hurt. I have a headache too.

Grammar — 'doler' — to hurt

'Doler' works in a similar way to 'gustar' — to say what's hurting you, you need to use an indirect object pronoun (see p.107) before the verb.
You also need to add an 'n' in the plural.

Me duele la pierna.	***My leg hurts.*** (Literally, 'the leg hurts me'.)
Me duelen los pies.	***My feet hurt.***
Le duelen el brazo y la mano.	***His / her arm and hand hurt.***

You also need to remember that 'doler' is a stem-changing verb. See p.128.

The verb 'romper' means 'to break', but you need the reflexive verb (see p.137) 'romperse' to talk about broken bones.

Ayer me caí mientras corría y me rompí el brazo.
Yesterday I fell over while I was running and I broke my arm.

I broke my wrist — me rompí la muñeca
I twisted my ankle — me torcí el tobillo

In Spanish, you need to use the definite article ('the') instead of 'my' when you talk about body parts that you've hurt.

El año pasado, un familiar mío sufría una enfermedad grave. Me preocupé mucho por él.
Last year, a relative of mine was suffering from a serious illness. I worried a lot about him.

Lucho contra el sobrepeso. Estoy tratando de perder peso, pero es más difícil de lo que pensaba.
I struggle with excess weight. I'm trying to lose weight, but it's more difficult than I thought.

Siempre me siento enferma. Es muy duro porque me impide hacer actividades físicas.
I always feel ill. It's very hard because it stops me doing physical activities.

I get tired quickly — me canso rápidamente

Mucha gente se preocupa por su peso y su apariencia.
Lots of people worry about their weight and their appearance.

have recurring health problems — tienen problemas de salud recurrentes

Necesito ir al médico — *I need to go to the doctor*

Vocabulary

el cuidado	*care, carefulness*	el/la médico/a	*doctor*	mental	*mental*
el accidente	*accident*	el/la paciente	*patient*	la cita	*appointment*
el hospital	*hospital*	la medicina	*medicine*	superar	*to overcome*

(Higher: mental, la cita, superar)

Cuando era niño, tenía que tomar medicina para poder respirar mejor. Ahora ya no la necesito. — *When I was a child, I had to take medicine to be able to breathe better. Now I no longer need it.*

Tengo una cita con el médico porque me duele una herida en la mano. — *I have an appointment with the doctor because a wound on my hand hurts.*

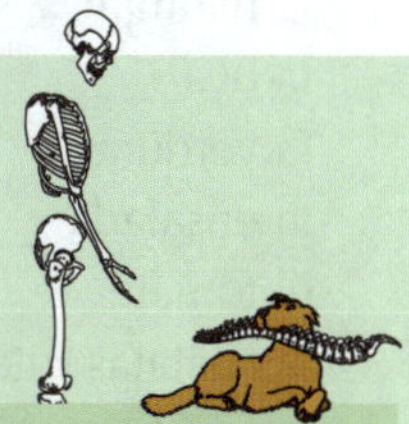

a pain in my back — un dolor en la espalda

Superar las enfermedades mentales puede ser muy difícil. Es importante hablar con alguien si tienes problemas. — *Overcoming mental illnesses can be very difficult. It's important to speak to someone if you have problems.*

Alguna gente se siente nerviosa antes de visitar al médico. — *Some people feel nervous before visiting the doctor.*

Los médicos pueden ofrecer a los pacientes tanto apoyo como sea posible. — *Doctors can offer patients as much support as possible.*

appropriate treatments — tratamientos apropiados

lots of useful advice — muchos consejos útiles

Practice Questions

Q1 *Read this passage about an accident.*

SPEAKING

> El mes pasado, mi hermano tuvo un accidente en el parque. Se cayó del equipo de patio y le dolía mucho la cabeza. Mi madre quería llevarle al hospital para preguntar a los médicos si había algún problema. Sin embargo, mi hermano tenía miedo de ir al hospital entonces quería quedarse en casa.

Top Tip for Higher Students
✓ Use relative pronouns to add more detailed clauses to your sentences, e.g. 'Me rompí el brazo, lo que me dolió mucho.'

Now it's your turn. Talk about an accident you or a family member had in the past and what was done about it. Aim to talk for about two minutes. *[10 marks]*

Higher

Q2 *Listen to the conversation between Aitor and the doctor, then answer the questions below.*

LISTENING

Listening Track 07

a) What caused Aitor to start feeling unwell? *[1 mark]*

b) What does the doctor ask Aitor? *[1 mark]*

c) Why is Aitor having trouble falling asleep? *[1 mark]*

d) Write down two pieces of advice that the doctor gives Aitor. *[2 marks]*

My friend gets heartburn when they eat birthday cake...

I told them to try taking the candles off first. Revision is the best medicine for GCSE Spanish woes, so don't skip over the vocab for this topic. Doing all the right prep will help you feel fighting fit for your exams.

Healthy Living and Lifestyle — Vocabulary

It's time for a recap of all the vocab from this section before you hop, skip and jump to the next topic.

Food

la fruta	*fruit*
la manzana	*apple*
la naranja	*orange*
la uva	*grape*
la verdura	*vegetable*
la ensalada	*salad*
el tomate	*tomato*
las patatas fritas	*chips, fries*
la hamburguesa	*burger*
la comida rápida	*fast food*
la comida basura	*junk food*
el bocadillo	*sandwich*
el huevo	*egg*
el pan	*bread*
la carne	*meat*
el jamón	*ham*
el pollo	*chicken*
el pescado	*fish*
la paella	*paella (dish usually of rice and seafood)*
el caramelo	*sweet*
vegetariano/a	*vegetarian*
vegano/a	*vegan*
la bebida	*drink*
el agua (f)	*water*
la leche	*milk*
el café	*coffee*
el vino	*wine*
el desayuno	*breakfast*
la comida	*food, meal, lunch*
la cena	*dinner, evening meal*
cenar	*to have dinner, tea (evening meal)*
preparar	*to prepare*
comer	*to eat*
beber	*to drink*
probar	*to try, taste*
gustar	*to please, be pleasing to*
odiar	*to hate*
el hambre (f)	*hunger*
la sed	*thirst*
dulce	*sweet*
rico/a	*tasty*
fresco/a	*fresh*
caliente	*hot (temperature), warm*
la sal	*salt*
la grasa	*fat, grease*
el azúcar	*sugar*
la botella	*bottle*
la copa	*cup, glass*
el vaso	*(drinking) glass*

Higher

el alimento	*food, nourishment*
el arroz	*rice*
el aceite	*oil*
cocinar	*to cook*
saludable	*healthy*
asqueroso/a	*disgusting, revolting*

Healthy Living

la vida	*life*
la salud	*health*
sano/a	*healthy, wholesome*
suficiente	*sufficient, enough*
la importancia	*importance*
se necesita	*you need (to) (general), one needs (to)*
evitar	*to avoid, prevent*
activo/a	*active*
físico/a	*physical*
el ejercicio	*exercise*
estar en forma	*to be fit*
mantenerse	*to keep, maintain*
entrenarse	*to train, go training*
entrenar	*to train*
la dieta	*diet (general)*
equilibrado/a	*balanced*
el paso	*step*
la costumbre	*habit*
el sueño	*sleep*
dormir	*to sleep*
dormirse	*to fall asleep*
descansar	*to rest, relax*

Higher

diario/a	*daily*
relajante	*relaxing*
acostarse	*to go to bed*
pasear	*to take for a walk, go for a walk*
promover	*to promote*

'Entrenar' means 'to train someone else', whereas 'entrenarse' means 'to train yourself'.

Unhealthy Living

demasiado(s)/a(s)	*too much (many) + noun, too much, too + adjective*
perezoso/a	*lazy*
el peso	*weight*
el régimen	*diet (for weight loss or medical conditions)*
perder	*to lose*
el riesgo	*risk*
la droga	*drug*
fumar	*to smoke*
dejar de (+ infinitive)	*to stop (+ ing)*
probar	*to try*

Higher

la cantidad	*quantity, amount*
el consumo	*consumption*
el sobrepeso	*obesity, excess weight*
el cigarrillo	*cigarette*
el humo	*smoke, fumes*
huele (a)	*it smells (of)*
el alcohol	*alcohol*
la consecuencia	*consequence*

Illnesses and Treatments

la enfermedad	*illness, disease*
grave	*serious*
sentirse	*to feel (+ adjective)*
sentir	*to feel, sense*
enfermo/a	*ill, sick*
cansado/a	*tired, tiring*
preocupar	*to (be a) worry*
preocuparse por	*to worry about*
el estrés	*stress*
respirar	*to breathe*
romperse	*to break (bones)*
roto/a	*broken*
doler	*to hurt, be painful*
morir	*to die*
muerto/a	*dead*
caer	*to fall*
caerse	*to fall over*
el cuerpo	*body*
la cabeza	*head (body part)*
el ojo	*eye*
la vista	*sight*
la lengua	*tongue*
el diente	*tooth*
la mano	*hand*
el pie	*foot*
débil	*weak*
fuerte	*strong*
la piel	*skin*
el corazón	*heart*
el cuidado	*care, carefulness*
el accidente	*accident*
el hospital	*hospital*
el/la médico/a	*doctor*
ayudar	*to help*
apoyar	*to support*
el apoyo	*support*

Use 'sentirse' when you want to talk about how you feel physically or mentally, e.g. 'Me siento mal'. Use 'sentir' when you want to talk about general feelings, emotions or sensations, e.g. 'Siento frío'.

el/la paciente	*patient*
la medicina	*medicine*
tomar	*to take, have, drink*
el resultado	*result*

Higher

luchar	*to fight, struggle*
sufrir	*to suffer*
el dolor	*pain, ache*
la herida	*wound, injury*
el cáncer	*cancer*
vivo/a	*alive*
la muerte	*death*
la sangre	*blood*
la pierna	*leg*
el brazo	*arm*
la boca	*mouth*
el cerebro	*brain*
la mente	*mind*
mental	*mental*
la cita	*appointment*
echarse	*to lie down*
la tasa	*rate*
la medida	*measure*
tratar	*to treat*
superar	*to get over, overcome*
resultar	*to be, to turn out (+ adjective)*

Revision Summary Test for Section Three

Give your mind a good workout by testing your knowledge on this section with these questions.

- Yep, these questions are **hard** — they'll really help you see **how well you know your stuff**.
- Tackle the **revision summary test** below, or scan the QR code to do it **online**.
  Use the CGP RevisionHub to **track your progress** and see **which areas need more work**.
- You can find **sample answers** here: www.cgpbooks.co.uk/BuenoExtras

Summary Test

Food

1) You're going shopping with your Argentinian friend. These foods are on their list: manzanas, pollo, tomates, naranjas, uvas, pan, jamón y huevos. What are these foods in English?
2) 'Tengo sed. Quiero un café con leche.' What does this mean in English?
3) In Spanish, give one food that you like and one food that you hate. Give a reason for each one.
4) What are these in English? a) un vaso de leche b) una copa de vino c) una botella de agua
5) 'Aunque no tenía hambre anoche, me preparé una ensalada caliente con pescado y verduras frescas.' How would you say this in English?
6) ¿Qué piensas de la comida vegana?
7) (H) Iratxe says: 'I always cook chips in oil and eat them with salt.' How would she say this in Spanish?

Healthy and Unhealthy Living

8) 'Si quieres mantenerte en forma, es importante hacer ejercicio físico.' Translate this into English.
9) Describe tus buenas costumbres.
10) Belén wants to be healthier. Which one of the following options would help her?
    a) comer más grasa b) dormir menos c) no tomar bebidas con mucho azúcar
11) What's the Spanish for...? a) one needs to b) to be fit c) to lose weight d) to stop ...ing
12) ¿Piensas que la mayoría de los jóvenes llevan una vida sana? ¿Por qué (no)?
13) Isabel says: 'Mis hermanos son tan perezosos. No hacen suficiente ejercicio.' What is she saying?
14) ¿Cuál es tu opinión sobre la comida basura?
15) 'No me interesa probar drogas. Tienen muchos riesgos para la salud.' Say this in English.
16) (H) 'Me molesta cuando la gente fuma. El humo de los cigarrillos huele mal.' What is this person saying?

Illnesses and Treatments

17) How many body parts can you name in Spanish? There are 8 of them (plus 4 for Higher tier).
18) Nia says: 'Me duele todo el cuerpo. Pienso que es debido al estrés. Por eso necesito descansar.' Why does Nia feel so ill?
19) Translate this into Spanish: 'I will study medicine because I would like to help patients feel better.'
20) 'El año pasado, la abuela de Juan se cayó y pasó un mes en el hospital.' What happened last year?
21) What's the Spanish for...? a) to worry about b) to break (bones) c) to die d) doctor
22) José tells you: 'Cuando me entreno, me cuesta respirar.' What is José's health problem?
23) Imagine you've gone to see the doctor. Describe your health problem and what the doctor recommends in Spanish.
24) Translate these words into Spanish:
    a) sick b) broken c) dead d) care e) accident f) weak g) strong
25) What can someone do to look after their mental health? Answer this question in Spanish.
26) (H) En tu opinión, ¿qué medidas se pueden tomar para evitar enfermedades graves?
27) (H) 'Los resultados del estudio preocupan a mucha gente.' Translate this sentence into English.

School Subjects

Quick Quiz

On the subject of school, it's time for — yep, you guessed it, school subjects.
It's important to learn them and be able to say what you think about them.

Remember there's also lots of online content here: www.cgpbooks.co.uk/Bueno

Las asignaturas — *School subjects*

Vocabulary

el inglés	*English*	las matemáticas	*maths*	la cocina	*food technology*
el español	*Spanish*	las ciencias	*science(s)*	la educación física	*physical education (PE)*
el francés	*French*	la geografía	*geography*		
el italiano	*Italian*	la historia	*history*	el dibujo	*art*
el alemán	*German*	la religión	*religion (RE)*	el teatro	*drama*
el chino	*Chinese*	la informática	*ICT*	la música	*music*

Mi asignatura favorita es... — *My favourite subject is...*

Q&A Audio

Question

¿Cuál es tu asignatura favorita?
What's your favourite subject?

Simple Answer

Mi asignatura favorita es la música. Me encanta tocar la guitarra.
My favourite subject is music. I love to play the guitar.

Extended Answer

El español es mi asignatura favorita ya que es muy interesante. Será útil también porque espero ir a España el verano que viene.
Spanish is my favourite subject as it's very interesting. It will be useful too because I hope to go to Spain next summer.

To be fair, I never said I was any good...

Me gusta la historia. Es interesante aprender sobre el pasado.	*I like history. It's interesting to learn about the past.*
Gonzalo odia las ciencias pero los idiomas son más fáciles para él.	*Gonzalo hates science but languages are easier for him.*
Nos encantan las matemáticas aunque para otros son una asignatura dura.	*We love maths even though for others it's a hard subject.*

still relevant — todavía relevante

biology — la biología
chemistry — la química
physics — la física

difficult — difícil
complicated — complicado/a

Practice Question

Q1 You are writing a blog post about your school subjects. You should write about 50-90 words in Spanish.

Write about:

- *which subject(s) you dislike*
- *which subject(s) you find hard or easy*
- *what your favourite subject is.* *[15 marks]*

WRITING

Top Tip for Higher Students
✓ Use the superlatives 'el/la mejor' or 'el/la peor' to say which subjects are the best or worst.

This is the part where I subject you to a pun...

Remember — each school subject has its own gender. Lots are masculine and singular, but some are feminine and/or plural, e.g. 'las ciencias'. Speaking of science, I need to go and check I definitely turned the gas off...

Quick Quiz

School Life

If you have some time to spare in your busy timetable, I'd recommend going over these pages. You'll get to gush about all the things you love about school — or moan about what's rubbish...

Mi horario — *My timetable*

Vocabulary

el día	*day*	comenzar	*to start, begin*
la lista	*list, register*	empezar	*to start, begin*
la clase	*class, lesson*	terminar	*to finish, end*
el recreo	*break*	durar	*to last*

Grammar — telling the time

If you're saying what time something is at, remember to put 'a' first.

La hora de comer es a la una.
Lunchtime is at one o'clock.

For more about time, see p.5.

Mi colegio empieza a las nueve y el profesor pasa la lista a las nueve y cinco. — *My school starts at nine o'clock and the teacher reads the register at five past nine.*

Tengo cinco clases al día y cada clase dura cuarenta minutos. — *I have five lessons a day and each lesson lasts forty minutes.*

A las tres y media vuelvo a casa. — *At half past three I return home.*

at twenty to nine — a las nueve menos veinte

we go to the assembly room — vamos al salón de actos

the school day finishes — el día escolar termina

Q&A Audio

Question

¿Qué haces durante el recreo?
What do you do during break?

Simple Answer

Durante el recreo, juego al fútbol con mis amigas.
During break, I play football with my friends.

Extended Answer

Prefiero leer durante el recreo porque mis amigos van al club de tenis, que a mí no me gusta.
I prefer to read during my break because my friends go to the tennis club, which I don't like.

En clase — *In class*

Vocabulary

la pantalla	*screen*
la puerta	*door*
la mesa	*table*
la silla	*chair*
olvidar (+ noun)	*to forget*
llevar	*to take, carry, wear*
el libro	*book*

el papel	*paper*
la regla	*ruler*
el bolígrafo	*pen*
la mochila	*school bag*
el aula (f) [Higher]	*classroom*
prestar [Higher]	*to lend*
el diario [Higher]	*diary, journal*

Grammar — el aula

'Aula' is feminine, but it uses 'el' when it's singular. Any adjectives must be in the feminine form.

El aula está llena.
The classroom is full.

¿Me puedes prestar un bolígrafo para la prueba de geografía? — *Can you lend me a pen for the geography test?*

Ayer, puse un estuche y varios libros en mi mochila. — *Yesterday, I put a pencil case and several books in my school bag.*

Me he olvidado de traer mi regla. — *I have forgotten to bring my ruler.*

a pencil — un lápiz

an exercise book — un cuaderno

'Olvidar' is usually followed by a noun, whereas 'olvidarse de' is usually followed by a verb.

¿Cómo es tu colegio? — *What's your school like?*

Vocabulary

el instituto	*secondary school*	el uniforme	*uniform*	el gimnasio	*gym*
la escuela	*(primary) school*	la instalación	*facility*	los servicios	*toilets*
público/a	*public*	el patio	*playground*	la biblioteca	*library*
religioso/a	*religious*	el campo	*pitch, field (sport)*	H privado/a	*private*
moderno/a	*modern*	la piscina	*swimming pool*	H internacional	*international*

Hay quinientos alumnos en mi instituto y llevamos uniforme. — *There are 500 students at my school and we wear a uniform.*

we don't have to wear a uniform — no tenemos que llevar uniforme

Soy alumna aquí desde hace tres años. Me gusta este colegio y me llevo bien con los profesores. — *I've been a student here for three years. I like this school and I get on well with the teachers.*

the teachers are very nice — los profesores son muy simpáticos

La escuela de mi hermano tiene un campo de deportes grande donde pueden jugar al hockey. — *My brother's school has a big sports field where they can play hockey.*

a small gym where they can keep fit — un gimnasio pequeño donde pueden mantenerse en forma

En mi colegio, las aulas no tienen suficientes sillas. — *In my school, the classrooms don't have enough chairs.*

the computers don't work well — los ordenadores no funcionan bien

Practice Questions

Q1 *Juan and Marta are talking about their timetables. Choose the correct option from the times below to complete the sentences in English.*

LISTENING — Listening Track 08

a) On Mondays, Juan and Marta have English at...
A. 8:30 **B.** 9:45 **C.** 9:20 *[1 mark]*

b) Then they go to their history class at...
A. 10:15 **B.** 10:30 **C.** 11:15 *[1 mark]*

c) Juan prefers Wednesdays, when they have music at...
A. 11:45 **B.** 12:15 **C.** 13:30 *[1 mark]*

Higher

Q2 *Read this message from Daraja about her school and answer the questions below in English.*

READING

¡Hola! Soy Daraja. Voy a un colegio privado y hay ochocientos alumnos. En general, me encantan las instalaciones. Lo mejor es la biblioteca — hay muchos libros y estoy segura de que podrías encontrar todo lo que necesitas. Además, tenemos una piscina enorme y un campo deportivo. Lo malo es el gimnasio porque está muy sucio.

a) How many people go to Daraja's school? *[1 mark]*
b) Why does she think the library is the best facility? *[1 mark]*
c) How does Daraja describe the pool? *[1 mark]*
d) Why does Daraja dislike the gym? *[1 mark]*

What did one chair say to the other? *Silla* later...

Just like the school day itself, revision can be a slog. Splitting up your revision into manageable chunks will definitely help. As will scheduling a break to put your feet up and grab a snack — I'll take an apple, thanks...

Quick Quiz

School Pressures and Difficulties

I sometimes have difficulties remembering my left from my right, which caused real problems at the barn dance last week. You should see my poor partner's feet. Right, back to school...

Las reglas — *The rules*

Vocabulary

necesario/a	*necessary, required*	pedir	*to ask for*
hay que	*you must (general)*	permitir	*to allow, permit*
tener que	*to have to, must*	prohibir	*to prohibit, forbid*
deber	*to have to, must*	H obligatorio/a	*compulsory*
poder	*to be able to, can*	H el permiso	*permission*

Ernie wasn't very impressed with the new uniform rules...

No deberías gritar la respuesta en clase. — *You should not shout the answer in class.*
(*arrive late* — llegar tarde)

Hay que levantar la mano antes de contestar. — *You must raise your hand before answering.*
(*write in blue or black ink* — escribir en tinta azul o negra)

Es obligatorio llevar camisa blanca y zapatos negros. — *It's compulsory to wear a white shirt and black shoes.*
(*to wear a tie* — llevar corbata)

Está prohibido usar el móvil en clase. — *It's forbidden to use your mobile phone in class.*
(*to run in the corridors* — correr en los pasillos; *to eat chewing gum* — comer chicle)

Las presiones del colegio — *School pressures*

Vocabulary

aprender	*to learn*	el examen	*exam*	Higher: lograr	*to achieve, manage to (+ verb)*
estudiar	*to study*	aprobar	*to pass*	Higher: conseguir	*to get, obtain*
repasar	*to revise*	la nota	*grade*	Higher: suspender	*to fail*
el estrés	*stress*	los deberes	*homework*	Higher: equivocarse	*to be wrong, make a mistake*

Los exámenes causan mucho estrés cuando necesitas aprobar. — *Exams cause lots of stress when you need to pass.*
(*you don't have enough support* — no tienes suficiente apoyo)

Sienten presión de sus padres para conseguir buenas notas. — *They feel pressure from their parents to get good grades.*

El acoso es un problema grave en mi colegio. Creo que más gente debería pensar en el efecto que pueden tener sus palabras. — *Bullying is a serious problem in my school. I think more people should think about the effect their words can have.*
(*exists in many forms* — existe en muchas formas)

Tengo miedo de equivocarme en los exámenes y suspenderlos. — *I'm afraid of making mistakes in the exams and failing them.*
(*not being able to study the Baccalaureate* — no poder estudiar el Bachillerato)

La presión de grupo es difícil. Me gustaría hacer felices a mis amigos, pero no quiero romper las reglas. — *Peer pressure is difficult. I would like to make my friends happy, but I don't want to break the rules.*

Evitar problemas — *Preventing problems*

Tengo suerte porque mis amigos me apoyan mucho.	*I'm lucky because my friends support me a lot.*	*my parents help me to study* — mis padres me ayudan a estudiar
Para reducir el estrés, intenta repasar poco a poco.	*To reduce stress, try to revise little by little.*	*to do sport or something fun* — hacer deporte o algo divertido
Es importante respetar a todos tus compañeros.	*It's important to respect all your classmates.*	*other students* — otros alumnos
Necesito confiar en mi profesora para contarle mis problemas.	*I need to trust in my teacher in order to tell her my problems.*	*not suffer in silence* — no sufrir en silencio

Q&A Audio

Question

¿Cómo puedes reducir el estrés del colegio?

How can you reduce stress from school?

Simple Answer

Para reducir el estrés, es importante hablar con alguien.

To reduce stress, it's important to talk with someone.

Extended Answer

En mi opinión, charlar con mis amigos es la mejor manera de reducir el estrés. Me ayudan mucho a pensar en soluciones prácticas.

In my opinion, chatting with my friends is the best way to reduce stress. They help me a lot to think of practical solutions.

Milo found his mallet was the practical solution to most everyday problems.

Practice Questions

Q1 *Look at the two photos below. Talk in Spanish about what is in the photos. You should talk for about a minute and say something about each photo.*

SPEAKING

Top Tip for Higher Students
✓ Use tricky conjunctions like 'sino' to link your ideas together.

[5 marks]

Higher

Q2 *Listen to Omar talking about causes of stress at school. There are two correct statements in each list below. Choose the correct options from each list.*

LISTENING

Listening Track 09

a) Omar...

A. has to do homework on Mondays.
B. gets more homework than others.
C. says exams stress him the most.
D. leaves it late to do his homework.

[2 marks]

b) His...

A. parents tell him to relax.
B. friends aren't as stressed.
C. parents support him a lot.
D. friends compete with him.

[2 marks]

Problems at school are no laughing matter...

They say a problem shared is a problem halved. So if you're struggling with something or feeling stressed, you should definitely speak to someone. Just had to get that off my chest... I'll go back to being hilarious now.

Education — Vocabulary

Learn all the vocab on this page and I'm sure you'll be top of the class in no time at all...

School Subjects

la asignatura	*school subject*
la educación	*education*
el inglés	*English*
el español	*Spanish*
el francés	*French*
el italiano	*Italian*
el alemán	*German*
el chino	*Chinese*
el idioma	*language*
la lengua	*language*
las matemáticas	*maths*
las ciencias	*science(s)*
la geografía	*geography*
la historia	*history*
la religión	*religion*
la informática	*ICT*
la cocina	*food technology*

la educación física	*physical education (PE)*
el dibujo	*art*
el teatro	*drama*
la música	*music*
favorito/a	*favourite*
práctico/a	*practical, useful*
útil	*useful*
fácil	*easy*
sencillo/a	*simple, easy*
duro/a	*hard*
difícil	*difficult, hard*
educativo/a	*educational*

Higher

la selección	*choice, selection*
el castellano	*(Castilian) Spanish*
el lenguaje	*language, speech*
la literatura	*literature*
complicado/a	*difficult, complicated*

School Life

el horario	*timetable, schedule*
el día	*day*
la lista	*list, (school) register*
la clase	*class, lesson, classroom*
el recreo	*break (at school)*
el club	*club*
comenzar	*to start, begin*
empezar	*to start, begin*
temprano/a	*early*
terminar	*to finish, end*
durar	*to last*
el/la director(a)	*headteacher*
el/la secretario/a	*secretary*
el/la profesor(a)	*teacher*
el/la estudiante	*student*
el/la alumno/a	*student, pupil*
el/la compañero/a	*classmate, group member*
la tecnología	*technology*
la pantalla	*screen*
la puerta	*door*
la mesa	*table*
la silla	*chair, seat*
olvidar (+ noun)	*to forget (something)*
olvidarse de (+ verb)	*to forget (to do something)*
llevar	*to take, carry, wear*
el libro	*book*
el papel	*paper*
la regla	*ruler*
el bolígrafo	*pen*
la mochila	*school bag, rucksack*

el colegio	*(secondary) school*
el instituto	*secondary school*
la escuela	*(primary) school*
público/a	*public*
religioso/a	*religious*
moderno/a	*modern*
el uniforme	*uniform*
la camisa	*shirt*
el pantalón	*trousers*
la falda	*skirt*
el zapato	*shoe*
la instalación	*facility*
el patio	*yard, playground*
el campo	*pitch, field (sport)*
la piscina	*swimming pool*
el gimnasio	*gym*
los servicios	*toilets*
la biblioteca	*library*
el equipo	*equipment*

Higher

el aula (f)	*classroom*
prestar	*to lend, pay (attention)*
el diario	*diary, journal*
privado/a	*private*
internacional	*international*
charlar	*to chat*
firmar	*to sign*
desde hace + present tense	*to have been + -ing + for + time*

School Pressures and Difficulties

la regla	*rule*
necesario/a	*necessary, required*
hay que	*you must (general), one must*
tener que	*to have to, must*
deber	*to have to, must*
poder	*to be able to, can*
pedir	*to ask for*
mandar	*to order*
permitir	*to allow, permit*
permitirse	*to afford*
prohibir	*to prohibit, forbid*
gritar	*to shout*
callarse	*to be quiet, quieten down*
levantar	*to raise*
preguntar	*to ask (a question)*
contestar	*to answer, reply, respond*
explicar	*to explain*
saber	*to know (how to)*
conocer	*to know (person, place)*
responsable	*responsible*
independiente	*independent*
escribir	*to write*
enseñar	*to teach, show*
aprender	*to learn*
estudiar	*to study*
el estudio	*study, learning*
repasar	*to revise, review*
preparar	*to prepare*
mejorar	*to improve, make better*
la presión	*pressure*
el estrés	*stress*
el examen	*exam*
la prueba	*test*
aprobar	*to pass (test)*
sacar	*to get, obtain*
la nota	*grade, note, mark*
el resultado	*result*
el error	*error, mistake*
la falta	*mistake*
costar	*to be hard*
el éxito	*success*
la suerte	*luck, fortune*
los deberes	*homework*
la tarea	*task, homework*
el proyecto	*project*
el trabajo	*work, effort*
trabajar	*to work*
trabajador(a)	*hardworking*
cansado/a	*tired, tiring*
el esfuerzo	*effort*
la confianza	*confidence, trust*

la palabra	*word*
la frase	*phrase, sentence*
el consejo	*(piece of) advice*
el apoyo	*support*
apoyar	*to support*
respetar	*to respect*
la discusión	*discussion, argument*
el acoso	*bullying*
la violencia	*violence*
el comportamiento	*behaviour*
causar	*to cause*
continuar	*to continue*

Higher

obligatorio/a	*compulsory*
el permiso	*permission*
lograr	*to achieve, manage to (+ verb)*
conseguir	*to get, obtain*
suspender	*to fail*
equivocarse	*to be wrong, make a mistake*
sentarse	*to sit (down)*
la respuesta	*answer, reply*
el nivel	*level*
pegar	*to hit, stick (on)*
castigar	*to punish*
estricto/a	*strict*
capaz	*capable, able*
consciente	*conscious, aware*
reflejar	*to reflect*
entregar	*to deliver, hand in*
confiar	*to trust, confide*
expresar	*to express*
ordenar	*to tidy, organise*
el orden	*order*
la enseñanza	*education, teaching*
la inteligencia	*intelligence*
la imaginación	*imagination*
el conocimiento	*knowledge*
el silencio	*silence*
la responsabilidad	*responsibility*
la independencia	*independence*

Elfa loved revising for food technology — it was a piece of cake...

Revision Summary Test for Section Four

I haven't heard the bell ring yet, so it looks like you've still got time to try your hand at this test.

- These questions are **hard**, but they'll really help you see **how well you know your stuff**.
- Tackle the **revision summary test** below, or scan the QR code to do it **online**. You can **track your progress** online and see **which areas need more work**.
- There are **sample answers** for the test here: www.cgpbooks.co.uk/BuenoExtras

Summary Test

School Subjects

1) List the school subjects covered in this section. There are 17 (plus 2 for Higher tier).
2) '¿Cuál es tu asignatura favorita y por qué?' Translate this question, then answer it in Spanish.
3) In Spanish, give two words that mean 'language' (plus another one for Higher tier).
4) How would you say the words below in Spanish?
   a) education b) practical c) useful d) simple e) hard f) educational g) difficult
5) (H) 'No logro encontrar la respuesta en la selección de libros complicados.' Translate this into English.

School Life

6) How would you say the words and phrases below in English?
   a) una escuela moderna b) un instituto religioso c) olvidarse de d) el horario
7) There are two different Spanish verbs meaning 'to start' or 'to begin'. Write down both of them.
8) Cruz says: 'Durante el recreo, me gusta ir al club de teatro. ¿Qué te gusta hacer?' Translate what they said into English, then answer their question in Spanish.
9) How do you say the words below in Spanish?
   a) headteacher b) secretary c) to forget (something) d) equipment e) technology f) register
10) Alex asks: '¿Qué uniforme llevas?' What is Alex's question? Answer it in Spanish.
11) Translate the words below into English:
    a) la pantalla b) la mesa c) la silla d) la puerta e) terminar f) temprano/a g) público/a
12) '¿Qué llevas en tu mochila?' Translate this question into English, then answer it in Spanish.

Higher

13) Raúl says: 'I have been going to an international school for two years and the facilities are great.' Translate his sentence into Spanish, then write two sentences about your own school's facilities.
14) 'La profesora ordena el aula mientras los alumnos escriben en silencio.' Translate this into English.

School Pressures and Difficulties

15) How do you say the words below in English?
    a) gritar b) callarse c) la frase d) preguntar e) pedir f) conocer g) la palabra h) la falta
16) Give a school rule starting with each phrase: a) Es necesario b) Hay que c) Tengo que d) Debo
17) 'Me cuesta mucho hacer los deberes y hago muchos errores.' Translate this sentence into English.
18) How do you say the words below in Spanish?
    a) to allow b) result c) explain d) to work e) hardworking f) to know (how to) g) to forbid
19) Antonio says: 'Estoy cansado de preparar tareas y proyectos para el colegio.' What is he saying?
20) Write at least two sentences in Spanish about bad behaviour at your school and how to improve it.
21) In your opinion, what do you need to do to succeed in exams? Answer in Spanish.
22) In Spanish, suggest two different things that might help with school pressures.

H

23) 'No puedo permitirme suspender la prueba. Confía en mí.' Translate these sentences into English.
24) What are two things that you would change about your school? Answer in Spanish.

Quick Quiz

Education Post-16

It's time to spare a thought for your future self and all the things they could get up to.

Remember there's also lots of online content here: www.cgpbooks.co.uk/Bueno

¿Qué harás? — *What will you do?*

Vocabulary

estudiar	*to study*	aprobar	*to pass (test)*	la formación	*training, education*
el Bachillerato	*Baccalaureate (equivalent to A levels)*	la prueba	*test*	el título	*title, (university) degree*
		el examen	*exam*	el derecho	*law (subject of study)*
		la nota	*grade, mark*	la traducción	*translation*
la universidad	*university*	la profesión	*profession*	conseguir	*to get, obtain*
la medicina	*medicine*	entrenarse	*to train*	suspender	*to fail*

Higher: la formación, el título, el derecho, la traducción, conseguir, suspender

See p.37 for more subjects.

Quiero hacer el Bachillerato porque espero conseguir un título en derecho en la universidad.

I want to do the Baccalaureate (A levels) because I hope to get a degree in law at university.

Todo depende de mis exámenes. Si los apruebo, continuaré estudiando. Si los suspendo, haré un curso de formación profesional.

It all depends on my exams. If I pass them, I will continue studying. If I fail them, I will do a professional training course.

to train as a plumber — entrenarme como fontanero

to work with my hands — trabajar con las manos

I will take a gap year — me tomaré un año sabático

Q&A Audio

Question

¿Cuáles son tus planes para el futuro?

What are your plans for the future?

Simple Answer

Quiero empezar a trabajar.

I want to start working.

Extended Answer

Me gustaría dejar de estudiar tan pronto como sea posible. Preferiría trabajar en una profesión para ganar experiencia laboral.

I would like to stop studying as soon as possible. I would prefer to work in a profession to gain work experience.

Grammar — conditional

To say that something could, should or would happen, use the conditional (p.135).

Me gustaría estudiar música.

I would like to study music.

'Quisiera' can also be used to say 'I would like' (p.136).

Practice Question

Q1 *Look at the two photos below. Talk in Spanish about what is in the photos. You should talk for about a minute and say something about each photo.*

SPEAKING

Top Tip for Higher Students
✓ Use the passive voice accurately, e.g. 'los estudiantes son enseñados por un experto.'

[5 marks]

I think I'll study circus skills — I'm good at clowning around...

I also have an endless supply of terrible jokes, but we'll save those for later in the book. Seriously though, you'll really impress the examiner if you can confidently talk about what you want to do after your GCSEs.

Quick Quiz

Career Choices and Ambitions

My job is to make sure you know your way around careers vocab in Spanish, so let's get to it...

Los empleos — *Jobs*

Vocabulary

trabajar	*to work*	el/la escritor(a)	*writer*	el/la soldado/a	*soldier*
el trabajo	*job*	el/la periodista	*journalist*	el/la empresario/a	*business person, entrepreneur*
la carrera	*career*	el/la pintor(a)	*painter*	el/la obrero/a	*worker, labourer*
el/la médico/a	*doctor*	el/la peluquero/a	*hairdresser*	la construcción	*construction (industry)*
el/la enfermero/a	*nurse*	el/la policía	*police officer*		
el/la cuidador(a)	*carer*	la policía	*police (organisation)*		
el/la abogado/a	*lawyer*	el ejército	*army*		
el/la ingeniero/a	*engineer*				

(Higher: el/la soldado/a, el/la empresario/a, el/la obrero/a, la construcción)

Cuando era más pequeño, mi padre era soldado en el ejército. Viajábamos mucho. — *When I was younger, my father was a soldier in the army. We used to travel a lot.*

worked abroad a lot — trabajaba mucho en el extranjero

Me gustaría ser escritora de ficción porque me encanta escribir historias. — *I would like to be a fiction writer because I love writing stories.*

Me importa tener un trabajo bien pagado, como el de ingeniero. — *It's important to me to have a well-paid job, like an engineer.*

a job that would make me happy — un trabajo que me haría feliz

Q&A Audio

Question

¿Cuál sería el trabajo de tus sueños?

What would be your dream job?

Simple Answer

Quiero ser médico.

I want to be a doctor.

Extended Answer

Siempre he querido ser médico, por eso voy a estudiar medicina en la universidad. Quisiera ayudar a los demás.

I have always wanted to be a doctor, so I'm going to study medicine at university. I would like to help others.

Grammar — I'm a...

You don't usually use the article 'un(a)' (p.105) when talking about jobs.

Soy pintor(a).
I'm a painter.

You do if you use an adjective.

Soy un buen jardinero.
I'm a good gardener.

Quisiera solicitar... — *I would like to apply for...*

Vocabulary

el puesto	*post, position*	el salario	*salary*	solicitar	*to request, apply for*
buscar	*to look for, fetch*	ganar	*to earn*	cobrar	*to earn*
la oferta	*offer*	pagar	*to pay (for)*	rechazar	*to reject*
aceptar	*to accept*	montar	*to set up*	despedir	*to sack, dismiss*

(Higher: solicitar, cobrar, rechazar, despedir)

You need to use the subjunctive (see p.142) here as the sentence refers to a hypothetical job rather than a job that you know exists.

Quisiera solicitar el puesto de cuidador que encontré en su sitio web. — *I would like to apply for the position of carer that I found on your website.*

Busco un trabajo en la construcción que tenga un salario muy competitivo y días de vacaciones suficientes. — *I am looking for a job in construction that has a very competitive salary and enough days off.*

En el lugar de trabajo — *In the work place...*

Vocabulary

la empresa	*company, business, firm*	el/la jefe/a	*boss, manager*	el laboratorio (Higher)	*laboratory*
la compañía	*company*	el/la compañero/a	*colleague*	la reunión (Higher)	*meeting*
la oficina	*office*	el/la empleado/a	*employee*	atender (Higher)	*to serve, look after (patient, customer)*
el/la director(a)	*director, manager*	el/la cliente	*client, customer*		

La experiencia laboral — *Work experience*

Ayudo en una tienda de ropa en mi tiempo libre. Lo mejor es charlar con los clientes. — *I help in a clothes shop in my free time. The best thing is chatting with customers.*

No tengo empleo, pero a veces paseo al perro de mis vecinos y me pagan. — *I don't have a job, but sometimes I walk my neighbours' dog and they pay me.*

Trabajo en un restaurante los sábados. Me gusta el empleo, pero no gano mucho. — *I work in a restaurant on Saturdays. I like the job, but I don't earn a lot.*

that the employees get discounts — que los empleados reciben descuentos

a hairdresser's — una peluquería

I hope to find another job and earn more money — espero conseguir otro empleo y ganar más dinero

Practice Questions

Q1 *Tao has written about his future career plans.*

WRITING

Cuando era más pequeño, pensaba que me gustaría ser profesor. Mis padres son profesores y aunque encuentran el trabajo interesante, mi padre dice que causa bastante estrés. Ahora he decidido que estudiaré fotografía porque me encantaría tomar fotos de bodas.

Top Tips for Higher Students
✓ Use the subjunctive to say what is important in a future job.
✓ Use impersonal verbs like 'hace falta' to say what is necessary.

Now it's your turn. Write an article for a blog about what you want to do in the future. Mention:

- *your dream job*
- *what you need to do to get your dream job*
- *what made you want your dream job.*

[15 marks]

Higher

Q2 *Read what Padma has written about her family and their jobs, then answer the following questions. Write **P** for Padma, **M** for madre and **H** for hermana.*

READING

Mi madre quería una familia en lugar de una carrera y eso era común para las mujeres de su época. Hoy más mujeres deciden trabajar mientras su pareja cuida a los niños. Por ejemplo, mi hermana es enfermera y su marido se queda en casa con los niños. A mí, me gustaría trabajar y quiero ser policía. Sería un honor proteger mi ciudad y sentirme útil.

a) Who didn't want a career? *[1 mark]*

b) Who works as a nurse? *[1 mark]*

c) Who wants to feel useful? *[1 mark]*

Interview Tip #101 — always dress to *empresa*...

It's perfectly fine to not know what you want to do yet — the examiner doesn't care whether what you say is true as long as it's correct in Spanish. You could tell them you want to be a fire-eater and they'd never know...

Future Study and Work — Vocabulary

Whether you want to be an astronaut or a pet food taster (yes, that's a real job), you still need to learn all this vocab...

Education Post-16

el futuro	*future*
continuar	*to continue*
estudiar	*to study*
el estudio	*study, learning*
el Bachillerato	*Baccalaureate (equivalent to A levels)*
la universidad	*university*
la carrera	*(university) degree course*
la medicina	*medicine*
aprobar	*to pass (test)*
la prueba	*test*
el examen	*exam*
la nota	*grade, mark, note*
el resultado	*result*
la profesión	*profession*
el proyecto	*project, plan*
entrenarse	*to train*

Higher

la formación	*training, education*
el título	*title, (university) degree*
universitario/a	*university*
el derecho	*law (subject of study)*
la traducción	*translation*
la economía	*economics*
conseguir	*to get, obtain*
suspender	*to fail*

For more vocabulary related to subjects you can study, flick back to p.37.

Career Choices and Ambitions

trabajar	*to work*
independiente	*independent, self-sufficient*
el empleo	*work, job, occupation*
el trabajo	*job*
la carrera	*career*
el/la médico/a	*doctor*
el/la enfermero/a	*nurse*
el/la cuidador(a)	*carer*
el/la abogado/a	*lawyer*
el/la ingeniero/a	*engineer*
el/la escritor(a)	*writer*
el/la periodista	*journalist*
el/la pintor(a)	*painter*
el/la peluquero/a	*hairdresser*
el/la policía	*police officer*
la policía	*police (organisation)*
el ejército	*army*
el sueño	*dream*
soñar	*to dream*
el puesto	*post, position*
buscar	*to look for, fetch*
la oportunidad	*opportunity, chance*
la oferta	*offer*
aceptar	*to accept*
el salario	*salary*
ganar	*to earn*
pagar	*to pay (for)*
montar	*to set up*
el negocio	*business*
la empresa	*company, business, firm*
la compañía	*company*
la oficina	*office*
el/la director(a)	*director, manager*
el/la jefe/a	*boss, manager, leader*
el/la compañero/a	*colleague*
el/la empleado/a	*employee*
el/la cliente	*client, customer*
el traje	*suit*
la experiencia	*experience*
laboral	*(of) work, relating to work*
próximo/a	*next*
llegar a (+ infinitive)	*to manage to (+ verb), succeed in (+ verb)*

Higher

el/la soldado/a	*soldier*
el/la empresario/a	*business person, entrepreneur*
el comercio	*commerce, trade, business*
el/la obrero/a	*worker, labourer*
la construcción	*construction (industry)*
solicitar	*to request, apply for*
cobrar	*to earn*
rechazar	*to reject*
emplear	*to employ, use*
despedir	*to sack, dismiss*
el laboratorio	*laboratory*
el/la experto/a	*expert*
profesional	*professional*
hace falta (+ infinitive)	*it's necessary (+ verb)*
la ocasión	*opportunity*
la reunión	*meeting*
la huelga	*strike*
atender	*to serve, look after (patient, customer)*

Revision Summary Test for Section Five

It might feel like it's all work and no play at the moment, but this test will help focus your revision.

- Yep, these questions are **hard** — they'll really help you see **how well you know your stuff**.
- Tackle the **revision summary test** below, or scan the QR code to do it **online**. Use the CGP RevisionHub to **track your progress** and see **which areas need more work**.
- You can find **sample answers** here: www.cgpbooks.co.uk/BuenoExtras

Summary Test

Education Post-16

1) How many university subjects can you name in Spanish? There's 1 in this section (plus 3 for Higher tier).
2) How would you say the sentence below in English? 'Para ir a la universidad, tengo que aprobar una prueba y sacar buenas notas en mis exámenes.'
3) In Spanish, tell your parents that you want to continue your studies and do your A levels.
4) Carmen says: 'Preferiría estudiar una profesión en lugar de hacer una carrera en la universidad.' Translate what she says into English.
5) Your friend doesn't want to go to university. What could they do instead? Tell them in Spanish and give two details.
6) Answer the following question in Spanish: '¿Qué quieres hacer después de los exámenes?'
7) [H] Luis says: 'Aunque suspendí mi primer proyecto universitario, conseguí un resultado muy bueno para mi último.' Translate what he says into English.

Career Choices and Ambitions

8) How many jobs and positions can you list in Spanish? There are 12 in this section (plus 4 for Higher tier). Make sure you list both the feminine and masculine forms.
9) Fernando says: 'Ser jefe de una empresa es mi sueño. Quiero llevar ropa de moda en la oficina.' Translate what he says into English.
10) a) In Spanish, how would you ask someone if they have any work experience?
    b) What would be your answer to this question? Answer in Spanish and give at least one detail.
11) You see an advert that says the following: 'Hemos montado un negocio y buscamos empleados con experiencia en el puesto de director.' What is this advert saying?
12) What's the Spanish for...?
    a) self-sufficient b) offer c) police (organisation) d) suit e) to manage to
13) 'In the future, my job will pay me well and it will give me the opportunity to work with customers.' Say this sentence in Spanish.
14) You're talking to a friend who has recently got a new job. They say: 'Acepté el puesto en el ejército porque el salario es más alto que el que gano ahora.' What does this mean in English?
15) Describe what a family member or friend does for a living in Spanish.
16) Your Colombian friend asks you: '¿En qué carrera te gustaría trabajar en el futuro?' Answer them in Spanish and give at least one reason for your choice.

Higher

17) Aldara says: 'Hizo falta despedir a mi compañero porque siempre rechazó las reglas. Espero que la próxima persona que empleamos sea mejor.' Translate what she says into English.
18) Rafael says: 'No cobramos suficiente dinero, por eso no habrá nadie en la reunión. Continuaremos esta huelga porque la compañía debe atender a sus empleados.' Translate what he says into English.

Quick Quiz

Cinema and TV

Pop on your **3D glasses** because your cinematic revision is about to get real.

Don't forget you can access your online content here: www.cgpbooks.co.uk/Bueno

En el cine — *At the cinema*

Vocabulary

el cine	*cinema*	recomendar	*to recommend*
la película	*film, movie*	preferir	*to prefer*
la escena	*scene (of film)*	pensar	*to think*
la pantalla	*screen*	H el/la protagonista	*protagonist, main character*
el personaje	*character (in book, film)*	H el diálogo	*dialogue*

Me gusta mucho ir al cine porque siempre me divierto. — *I really like to go to the cinema because I always have a good time.*

I can eat lots of popcorn — puedo comer muchas palomitas

Pienso que vale la pena ver películas en la pantalla grande. — *I think it's worth seeing films on the big screen.*

Me encantan las películas que tienen personajes que me hacen reír. — *I love films that have characters who make me laugh.*

solve a mystery — resuelven un misterio

Prefiero las películas de aventura porque son emocionantes. — *I prefer adventure films because they are exciting.*

they scare me less than horror films — me dan menos miedo que las películas de terror

Para mí, los protagonistas deben contar una buena historia y el diálogo tiene que ser divertido. — *For me, the main characters must tell a good story and the dialogue has to be enjoyable.*

Cada escena debería tener sentido. Quiero creer lo que estoy viendo. — *Each scene should have meaning. I want to believe what I'm seeing.*

excellent special effects — efectos especiales excelentes

La última película que vi... — *The last film I saw...*

Q&A Audio

Question

Describe la última película que viste.

Describe the last film you saw.

Simple Answer

El sábado, vi una película de acción. Me gustó mucho.

On Saturday, I saw an action film. I really liked it.

Extended Answer

El fin de semana pasado, vi una película de acción. Se trataba de dos familias que luchaban durante cientos de años.

Last weekend, I saw an action film. It was about two families who were fighting for hundreds of years.

Grammar — I saw...

To say '<u>I saw...</u>' you need the <u>preterite</u> tense. Check how to form it on p.131.

El viernes, <u>vi</u> una película romántica.

On Friday, <u>I saw</u> a romantic film.

<u>Unlike</u> most verbs when they're in the '<u>yo</u>' form of the <u>preterite</u> tense, '<u>vi</u>' <u>doesn't</u> have an <u>accent</u>.

Grammar (Higher only) — 'se trata de'

Use '<u>se trata de</u>' to say what a film is about:

<u>Se trata de</u> unos jóvenes muy ricos.

<u>It's about</u> some very rich young people.

And you can use it in the <u>imperfect</u> to say what a film <u>was</u> about:

<u>Se trataba del</u> amor. ***<u>It was about</u> love.***

Remember — 'de' + 'el' = 'del'.

¿Qué hay en la tele? — *What's on TV?*

Vocabulary

la tele, televisión	*TV, television*	interesar	*to interest*
la serie	*series*	encantar	*to love, delight*
el programa	*programme*	aguantar	*to put up with, stand (tolerate)*
el concurso	*quiz*	el canal (Higher)	*channel*
el anuncio	*advert*	la telenovela (Higher)	*soap opera, TV serial*
la noticia	*news*	el documental (Higher)	*documentary*
actual	*current*		

When 'la noticia' is singular, it means 'a piece of news'. The plural of 'las noticias' is used to mean 'the news' as a TV programme.

¿Qué te gusta ver? — *What do you like watching?*

Suelo ver la televisión en Internet porque es más fácil encontrar los programas que prefiero.
I normally watch TV on the internet because it's easier to find the programmes that I prefer.

I prefer to watch series from other countries — prefiero ver las series de otros países

Me gustan mucho las telenovelas porque hay risas, discusiones, relaciones... ¡Nunca son aburridas!
I really like soap operas because there are laughs, arguments, relationships... They're never boring!

A mi abuela le encantan los concursos porque puede contestar las preguntas.
My grandmother loves quizzes because she can answer the questions.

No aguanto muchos canales porque hay demasiados anuncios.
I can't stand a lot of channels because there are too many adverts.

cartoons — dibujos animados

Practice Questions

Q1 *Translate these sentences into Spanish.*

WRITING

a) *She doesn't like the cinema at all.*
b) *I recommend lots of films to my friends.*
c) *He said that the characters did silly things.*
d) *The scene at the end of the film was very sad.*

[8 marks]

Higher

Q2 *Read Eli's email about TV and choose the correct options below.*

READING

En la televisión británica, creo que hay demasiadas telenovelas. Sin embargo, no hay tantos anuncios como en España. En mi familia, preferimos ver los documentales y las noticias porque nos interesa aprender nueva información sobre el mundo.

a) Eli believes...
A. there are too many soap operas on British TV.
B. there are fewer adverts on Spanish TV.

b) Eli's family...
A. prefer to avoid documentaries
B. are interested in learning about the world.

[2 marks]

GCSE Spanish: The Movie. Now there's a thriller...

I know the TV is calling you, but first check you're confident with all the vocab for this topic. You need to be able to talk about what you watch (or don't watch) and be prepared to give an opinion or two on it.

Quick Quiz

Music

I love music, except when someone decides to share theirs with the rest of the bus. If I'd wanted alternative jazz, I'd have brought my saxophone.

La música — *Music*

When you're using the 'yo' form of 'tocar' in the preterite tense (see p.131), the 'c' changes to 'qu'.

Vocabulary

escuchar	*to listen (to)*	el/la músico/a	*musician*
la canción	*song*	tocar	*to play (an instrument)*
bajar	*to download*	el instrumento	*instrument*
clásico/a	*classical*	la guitarra	*guitar*
alto/a	*loud (volume)*	en vivo (Higher)	*live (e.g. performance, broadcast)*
el concierto	*concert*	la orquesta (Higher)	*orchestra*
el espectáculo	*show, spectacle*	asistir (Higher)	*to attend*
el/la cantante	*singer*		

'asistir' is usually followed by the preposition 'a'.

"Who wants to form a rock band?"

¿Te gusta la música? — *Do you like music?*

Toco el piano desde hace seis años. Espero ser músico cuando sea mayor.
I have been playing the piano for six years. I hope to be a musician when I'm older.

the clarinet — el clarinete
the drums — la batería

Me gusta escuchar la música clásica porque me hace sentir tranquilo.
I like to listen to classical music because it makes me feel calm.

Me encanta la música en vivo porque es una experiencia más emocionante.
I love live music because it's a more exciting experience.

rap music — la música rap
rock music — la música rock
pop music — la música pop

Asistí a un concierto el año pasado y no me divertí. La música estaba demasiado alta y no entendí lo que cantaban las cantantes.
I went to a concert last year and I didn't enjoy myself. The music was too loud and I didn't understand what the singers were singing.

the lyrics — la letra

Me parece genial que puedo bajar muchos tipos de música rápidamente.
It seems great to me that I can download many types of music quickly.

download — descargar

Practice Question

Q1 *Marisol is a famous Spanish singer. Listen to the interview and then answer the questions in English.* LISTENING

Listening Track 10

e.g. *What instrument did Marisol's grandfather teach her to play?* *guitar*

a) What is an advantage that Marisol mentions about listening to music on the internet? *[1 mark]*

b) Why does Marisol like going to concerts? *[1 mark]*

c) What does Marisol say she'll be doing in the coming year? *[1 mark]*

When I stick my headphones on, it's music to my ears...

And that's precisely what that person on the bus should have done. You know who you are. It doesn't matter what music you're into or what instrument you play — just make sure you can discuss it in Spanish.

Sport

Quick Quiz

It's time to get off the sofa and get moving with a page on sport. On your marks, get set, go!

¿Practicas algún deporte? — *Do you practise any sports?*

Vocabulary

el deporte	*sport*	el baloncesto	*basketball*
jugar	*to play*	la temporada	*season (of sport)*
practicar	*to practise*	el partido	*(sports) match*
participar	*to participate*	el equipo	*team*
la carrera	*race*	la natación (Higher)	*swimming*
bailar	*to dance*	la selección (Higher)	*national sports team*
el fútbol	*football*	el torneo (Higher)	*tournament*

Q&A Audio

Question

¿Te gusta hacer deportes?

Do you like playing sports?

Simple Answer

Sí, me gusta jugar al baloncesto porque es emocionante.

Yes, I like playing basketball because it's exciting.

Extended Answer

Sí, me gusta jugar al baloncesto después del colegio porque es emocionante y me ayuda a mantenerme en forma.

Yes, I like playing basketball after school because it's exciting and it helps me keep fit.

Grammar — 'jugar' + 'a' + sport

Use 'jugar a' to say what sports you play. In Spanish, you can't say 'Juego a el fútbol'. So if the sport is a masculine noun (like 'el fútbol'), the 'a' and the article 'el' combine to form 'al'.

Juego al netball. — ***I play netball.***

Juegas al rugby. — ***You play rugby.***

'Jugar' is a stem-changing verb — its stem changes from 'u' to 'ue' in the present tense. See p.128.

Monto a caballo varias veces a la semana. Me gusta porque puedo hacer deporte con mis amigos.

I go horse riding a few times a week. I like it because I can do sport with my friends.

A mí no me interesa la temporada de fútbol, pero veo la Copa Mundial porque mi país suele ganar sus partidos.

The football season doesn't interest me, but I watch the World Cup because my country usually wins its matches.

I play tennis — juego al tenis

the sports centre is near my house — el polideportivo está cerca de mi casa

athletics — el atletismo

the Olympic Games — los Juegos Olímpicos

Practice Question

WRITING

Q1 Write an article for a blog about sports. You should write about 90 words in Spanish. Mention:

- *what sports you play*
- *the advantages of participating in sport*
- *what sport you'd like to try in the future.* *[15 marks]*

Top Tip for Higher Students
✓ Use 'desde hace' to talk about how long you've been doing a sport.

Racing a sibling to the kitchen for snacks is a sport, right?

Always try to give the reasons behind your opinions — those examiners are desperate to know why you do or don't like something. For example, I don't like tennis because my dog keeps stealing the ball...

Quick Quiz

Going Out and Other Hobbies

If cinema, TV, music or sport don't float your boat, you've come to the right place. I can't promise it'll be as exciting as extreme ironing, soap carving or duck herding, but it'll be pretty darn close...

Salir con los amigos — *Going out with friends*

Vocabulary

el tiempo libre	*free time*	el camarero	*waiter*
salir	*to go out, leave*	la camarera	*waitress*
el parque temático	*theme park*	el plato	*plate, dish*
el teatro	*theatre*	la opción	*option*
la escena	*stage (theatre)*	vegetariano/a	*vegetarian*
la entrada	*admission ticket*	vegano/a	*vegan*
gratis	*free (of charge)*	las tapas	*small dishes of food*
el restaurante	*restaurant*	la obra (Higher)	*play (theatre)*
la carta	*menu*	divertir (Higher)	*to amuse, entertain*
la cuenta	*bill*	elegir (Higher)	*to choose*

Q&A Audio

Question

¿Que le gustaría tomar?
What would you like?

Simple Answer

Quiero la sopa, por favor.
I want the soup, please.

Extended Answer

De primer plato, quisiera la sopa y de segundo plato, la paella.
For the starter, I'd like the soup and for main course, the paella.

Grammar — ordering politely

Use '<u>quisiera</u>' to order <u>what you'd like politely</u>. '<u>Quisiera</u>' comes from the verb '<u>querer</u>' (*to want*). See p.136.

<u>Quisiera</u> probar el filete.
<u>I'd like</u> to try the steak.

Me encanta ir a restaurantes, pero a veces es difícil elegir lo que quieres comer.
I love to go to restaurants, but sometimes it's hard to choose what you want to eat.

the dishes can be disappointing — los platos pueden ser decepcionantes

El fin de semana pasado, fui al parque temático con mi hermano mayor. Las entradas costaron mucho dinero, pero nos divertimos muchísimo.
Last weekend, I went to the theme park with my older brother. The admission tickets cost a lot of money, but we had a great time.

the roller coasters were marvellous — las montañas rusas eran estupendas

Mañana mis amigas y yo vamos al teatro a ver una obra sobre un evento histórico.
Tomorrow my friends and I are going to the theatre to see a play about a historical event.

a musical about the war — un musical sobre la guerra

Las actividades — *Activities*

Vocabulary

cantar	*to sing*	el periódico	*newspaper*	cocinar (Higher)	*to cook*
el videojuego	*computer game*	el artículo	*article*	la pintura (Higher)	*painting, paint*
el arte	*art*	la ficción	*fiction*	la obra (Higher)	*work, book*
el dibujo	*drawing, art*	escribir	*to write*	la lectura (Higher)	*reading*
pintar	*to paint*	la novela	*novel*	el género (Higher)	*genre*
leer	*to read*	la historia	*story*	el diario (Higher)	*newspaper*

¿Qué haces en tu tiempo libre? — *What do you do in your free time?*

Hay muchas actividades que me interesan. Prefiero cocinar y hacer pasteles.	*There are lots of activities that interest me. I prefer to cook and make cakes.*
Pinto cuando tengo tiempo libre porque el arte es mi actividad favorita.	*I paint when I have free time because art is my favourite activity.*
A mi hermana le encanta leer. Lee todo tipo de libros, pero su género favorito es la ciencia ficción.	*My sister loves to read. She reads all sorts of books, but her favourite genre is science fiction.*

I have a lot of hobbies — tengo muchos pasatiempos

whenever I can — siempre que puedo

autobiographies — las autobiografías
detective stories — las novelas policíacas

¿Qué piensas? — *What do you think?*

Vocabulary

aburrido/a	*bored, boring*	divertido/a	*fun, enjoyable*
emocionante	*exciting*	favorito/a	*favourite*
estupendo/a	*wonderful, marvellous*	horrible	*horrible*
		imposible	*impossible*
excelente	*excellent*	raro/a	*strange, rare*
increíble	*incredible*	maravilloso/a (Higher)	*wonderful, marvellous*
interesante	*interesting*	decepcionante (Higher)	*disappointing*
genial	*great*	fatal (Higher)	*terrible, awful*
guay	*cool*	extraño/a (Higher)	*strange*

Mikolaj thinks your favourite film is really exciting. Absolutely incredible. Just marvellous. No, really.

Practice Questions

Q1 *Translate these sentences into English.*

READING

a) *La carta tiene mucha variedad. Quiero probar un plato chino.*
b) *Las entradas son gratis para los niños pequeños.*
c) *Leer los periódicos es aburrido y los artículos pueden ser muy raros.*

[6 marks]

Q2 *Look at the two photos below. Talk in Spanish about what is in the photos. You should talk for about a minute and say something about each photo.*

SPEAKING

[5 marks]

It's always good to leave a tip at the end of the ~~meal~~ page...

... but my boss didn't think that my dating advice was particularly appropriate. So I'll leave you with this instead — revision is best done in small, manageable chunks, so don't bite off more than you can chew.

Free-time Activities — Vocabulary

I've found a new hobby — reading all the words on these pages and seeing how many I can remember...

Cinema

el cine	*cinema*
la película	*film, movie*
la escena	*scene (of film)*
el efecto especial	*special effect*
la acción	*action*
la ciencia ficción	*science fiction*
la pantalla	*screen*
el/la director(a)	*director*
el personaje	*character (in book, film)*
ver	*to see, watch*
recomendar	*to recommend*
preferir	*to prefer*
pensar	*to think*

Higher

el/la protagonista	*protagonist, main character*
el diálogo	*dialogue*
romántico/a	*romantic*
la aventura	*adventure*
divertirse	*to enjoy oneself, have a good time*
tratarse	*to be about*

The low special effects budget called for some improvisation...

TV

la tele / televisión	*TV, television*
la serie	*series*
el programa	*programme*
el concurso	*quiz, competition*
la telerrealidad	*reality TV*
el anuncio	*advert*
la noticia	*news*
actual	*current*
la risa	*laugh*
gracioso/a	*funny*
interesar	*to interest*

encantar	*to love, delight, be delightful to*
aguantar	*to put up with, stand (tolerate)*

Higher

el canal	*channel*
la telenovela	*soap opera, TV serial*
el documental	*documentary*
emitir	*to broadcast*

'la noticia' means 'a piece of news'. If you want to talk about the news as a TV programme, you'll need to say 'las noticias'.

Music

escuchar	*to listen (to)*
la música	*music*
la canción	*song*
la letra	*lyrics*
bajar	*to download*
musical	*musical*
clásico/a	*classical*
alto/a	*loud (volume)*
el concierto	*concert*
el espectáculo	*show, spectacle*
el/la cantante	*singer*
la voz	*voice*
el/la músico/a	*musician*

There are two words for 'to play' in Spanish. Use 'jugar' to talk about playing sports (see p.53) and 'tocar' to talk about playing an instrument (see p.52).

tocar	*to play (an instrument), touch*
el instrumento	*instrument*
la guitarra	*guitar*

Higher

en vivo	*live (e.g. performance, broadcast)*
el público	*audience*
la orquesta	*orchestra*
la banda	*(musical) band*
asistir	*to attend*

Sport

el deporte	*sport*
jugar	*to play*
hacer	*to do*
practicar	*to practise*
participar	*to participate*
correr	*to run*
la carrera	*race*
el paso	*pace*
nadar	*to swim*
bailar	*to dance*
dar un paseo	*to go for a walk, stroll*
el fútbol	*football*
el baloncesto	*basketball*
la temporada	*season (of sport, music)*
el partido	*(sports) match*
el equipo	*team*
deportivo/a	*sports*

Higher

la natación	*swimming*
la selección	*national sports team*
el torneo	*tournament*
echar	*to throw, cast*
desde hace + present tense	*to have been + ing for + time*

Going Out

el tiempo libre	*free time*
salir	*to go out, leave*
el parque temático	*theme park*
el teatro	*theatre*
la escena	*stage (theatre)*
la entrada	*entrance, admission ticket*
gratis	*free (of charge)*
el restaurante	*restaurant*
la carta	*menu*
la cuenta	*bill*
el camarero	*waiter*
la camarera	*waitress*
el plato	*plate, dish*
la opción	*option*
vegetariano/a	*vegetarian*
vegano/a	*vegan*
las tapas	*small dishes of food, bar snacks*

H

la obra	*play (theatre)*
divertir	*to amuse, entertain*
elegir	*to choose*

Other Hobbies

la actividad	*activity*
la red	*net (fishing)*
cantar	*to sing*
el videojuego	*computer game*
el arte	*art*
el dibujo	*drawing, art*
pintar	*to paint*
leer	*to read*
el periódico	*newspaper*
el artículo	*article*
la ficción	*fiction*
escribir	*to write*
la carta	*letter*
el correo	*mail, post*
la novela	*novel*
la historia	*story*
el/la autor(a)	*writer, author*
aburrido/a	*bored, boring*
emocionante	*exciting*
estupendo/a	*wonderful, marvellous*
excelente	*excellent*
increíble	*incredible*
interesante	*interesting*
genial	*great*
guay	*cool*
divertido/a	*fun, enjoyable*
favorito/a	*favourite*
horrible	*horrible*
imposible	*impossible*
raro/a	*strange, rare*

Higher

cocinar	*to cook*
la pintura	*painting, paint*
colgar	*to hang (up)*
la obra	*work, book*
la lectura	*reading*
el género	*genre*
el diario	*newspaper*
el contenido	*content, contents*
la sección	*section*
tratar	*to deal with*
soler	*to normally (+ verb), to tend to (+ verb), to usually (+ verb)*
emocionado/a	*excited*
maravilloso/a	*wonderful, marvellous*
decepcionante	*disappointing*
fatal	*terrible, awful*
extraño/a	*strange*

Revision Summary Test for Section Six

Before you whizz off to enjoy your spare time, give this summary test a whirl.

- These questions are **really tricky**, but they'll help you see **how well you know your stuff**.
- Tackle the **revision summary test** below, or scan the QR code to do it **online**. You can **keep track of your progress** online and see **which areas need more work**.
- There are **sample answers** here: www.cgpbooks.co.uk/BuenoExtras

Summary Test

Cinema and TV

1) 'No recomiendo el cine porque muestra demasiados anuncios.' What does this mean in English?
2) In Spanish, say that you love films that have exciting scenes and interesting characters.
3) Describe una película que has visto recientemente.
4) Say this in English: 'Este director siempre hace películas graciosas. Oí muchas risas en el cine.'
5) List the different types of TV programme in Spanish. There are 3 in this section (plus 2 for Higher tier).
6) 'No me interesan los programas de televisión. ¡Todas las series actuales son semejantes!' How would you say this in English?
7) ¿Cuál es tu opinión sobre ver la televisión en Internet?
8) H Txaro says: 'No aguanto los canales que solo emiten la telerrealidad.' What is she saying?

Music

9) Renata says: 'Soy cantante clásica. El mes que viene, voy a cantar una nueva canción en un espectáculo musical.' Translate what she says into English.
10) Aditi asks you about your music tastes. In Spanish, tell her what you like and don't like about music.
11) 'Aprendía a tocar la guitarra, pero era demasiado difícil. Quisiera intentar tocar otro instrumento.' What does this mean in English?
12) Say this in English: 'No me gustaría ir a un concierto. Prefiero escuchar música sin otra gente.'
13) H ¿Qué piensas de la música en vivo?

Sport

14) Answer the following question in Spanish: ¿Practicas algún deporte?
15) 'La temporada de fútbol termina en mayo. Cuando no hay partidos que jugar, doy un paseo todos los días.' What is this person saying?
16) What's the Spanish for...? a) to run b) pace c) to swim d) to dance e) team
17) Iván says: 'Participo en muchos actividades deportivas y gané mi última carrera.' What is he saying?
18) H 'When I am older, I'd like to be part of the national sports team and play in important tournaments.' Translate this sentence into Spanish.

Going Out and Other Hobbies

19) Say these English words in Spanish: a) to go out b) menu c) bill d) waiter / waitress e) dish
20) 'Pido las tapas cuando voy a un restaurante. Hay tantas opciones.' What is this person saying?
21) There are 13 adjectives to describe hobbies (plus 5 for Higher tier). How many can you remember?
22) Galia says: '¿Quieres ir al parque temático este fin de semana?' What does this mean?
23) How would you tell your Cuban friend in Spanish that you think the theatre is a type of art?
24) In Spanish, describe your hobbies.

Higher

25) 'Mi tío escribe artículos para la sección de consejos en un diario. Los leo en mi tiempo libre porque el contenido trata cosas útiles.' How would you say this in English?
26) Describe dos actividades que quieres probar en el futuro.

Celebrations

Quick Quiz

I hope you like surprises because I've secretly been making this page on celebrations for you. I even went to the trouble of giftwrapping it, so do give it a read through.

Head to the CGP RevisionHub for all your online content: www.cgpbooks.co.uk/Bueno

¿Qué celebras? — *What are you celebrating?*

Vocabulary

la celebración	*celebration*	la novia	*bride*
celebrar	*to celebrate*	el novio	*groom*
el cumpleaños	*birthday*	recibir	*to receive*
¡Feliz cumpleaños!	*Happy birthday!*	el regalo	*present, gift*
¡Enhorabuena!	*Congratulations!*	la tarjeta	*written card*
el ambiente	*atmosphere*	celebrarse (Higher)	*to hold (an event)*
la sorpresa	*surprise*	reunir (Higher)	*to gather, bring together*
invitar	*to invite*	reunirse (Higher)	*to get together*
el matrimonio	*marriage*	regalar (Higher)	*to give (as a gift)*
la boda	*wedding*	ofrecer (Higher)	*to offer, present*

Jorge decided the best way to celebrate his birthday was a good old-fashioned siesta.

Me encanta reunirme con mis amigos. — *I love getting together with my friends.*

Celebré mi cumpleaños en familia. Organizaron una fiesta para mi. Fue una sorpresa. Recibí regalos y unas tarjetas. — *I celebrated my birthday with family. They organised a party for me. It was a surprise. I received presents and some cards.*

with my best friends — con mis mejores amigos
on holiday — de vacaciones

Mi prima me invitó a su boda en junio. El ambiente era muy feliz. Les regalé una pintura. — *My cousin invited me to her wedding in June. The atmosphere was very happy. I gave them a painting as a gift.*

was full of joy — estaba lleno de alegría

Q&A Audio

Question

¿Celebraste algo recientemente?

Did you celebrate something recently?

Simple Answer

El mes pasado fui a una boda en la playa.

Last month I went to a wedding on the beach.

Extended Answer

El mes pasado fui a una boda en la playa. Desafortunadamente, el ambiente no era ideal porque ¡todos teníamos demasiado calor!

Last month I went to a wedding on the beach. Unfortunately, the atmosphere wasn't ideal because we were all too hot!

Practice Question

WRITING

Q1 *You are writing a blog post about celebrations. You should write about 90 words in Spanish. Write about:*

- *your favourite event to celebrate*
- *how you celebrated your birthday last year*
- *a celebration you'll be part of in the future.* *[15 marks]*

Top Tip for Higher Students
✓ Use relevant Higher-tier verbs, e.g. 'celebrarse', 'reunirse', and 'regalar'.

I went to a party on the moon — there was no atmosphere...

Celebrations is a really helpful topic for practising your tenses — try writing some sentences about what you did for your last birthday or what you'll do next year. I'm thinking something with a live kazoo band...

Quick Quiz

Customs and Festivals

Festivals are a great way to see into a country's culture. If you get the day off for them, even better....

Los Sanfermines — *The running of the bulls*

One Spanish festival that can be controversial is Los Sanfermines, which takes place in Pamplona each July.

Vocabulary

la tradición	*tradition*	la costumbre	*custom*	la plaza de toros	*bullring*
tradicional	*traditional*	el toro	*bull*	la corrida	*bullfight*

Muchas personas corren por las calles estrechas con los toros peligrosos hasta la plaza de toros.

Many people run through the narrow streets with the dangerous bulls to the bullring.

La corrida de toros es una tradición en España, pero es polémica porque alguna gente piensa que es cruel. Sin embargo, otros creen que es un arte.

Bullfighting is a tradition in Spain, but it's controversial because some people think that it's cruel. However, others believe it's an art.

Las fiestas de Valencia — *The festivals of Valencia*

Vocabulary

la Tomatina	*Spanish tomato festival*	Las Fallas	*Valencian celebration involving burning of papier mâché models*
los fuegos artificiales	*fireworks*		

'La Tomatina' tiene lugar en agosto en Buñol. Los participantes se tiran tomates unos a otros.

'La Tomatina' takes place in August in Buñol. Participants throw tomatoes at each other.

'Las Fallas' se celebran cada marzo en Valencia. Hay cinco días de fuegos artificiales y desfiles. El último día se queman creaciones de papel maché.

'Las Fallas' is celebrated each March in Valencia. There are five days of fireworks and parades. On the last day, they burn papier mâché creations.

El Día de Muertos — *Day of the Dead*

El Día de Muertos is a tradition that happens in Mexico, South America and elsewhere around 1st November.

Vocabulary

la cultura	*culture*	el disfraz	*costume*	la flor	*flower*
cultural	*cultural*	el traje	*costume*	pintarse	*to put on makeup*

El Día de Muertos, las familias limpian y arreglan las tumbas de sus familiares y celebran fiestas.

On the Day of the Dead, families clean and tidy the graves of their relatives and throw parties.

Alguna gente lleva un disfraz de 'la Catrina'. Respetan a los muertos con flores y música mariachi.

Some people dress up as 'la Catrina'. They respect the dead with flowers and Mexican folk music.

share stories — comparten historias

they put makeup on their faces like 'la Catrina' — se pinta la cara como 'la Catrina'

Las fiestas religiosas — *Religious festivals*

Vocabulary

la Semana Santa	*Easter Week*
Nochebuena	*Christmas Eve*
Navidad	*Christmas*
Nochevieja	*New Year's Eve*
el Día de Reyes	*Epiphany, 6th January*
los Reyes Magos	*the Three Kings, the Three Wise Men*

Grammar (Higher only) — the passive

To say that something is done without saying who does it, use 'se' and the 3rd person part of the verb (see p.141).

Se ven los desfiles.
The processions are watched.

La Semana Santa es un evento serio en España. Hay desfiles con música y se llevan pasos por las calles.

Easter Week is a serious event in Spain. There are processions with music, and religious images are carried around the streets.

Muchos españoles celebran el Día de Reyes. Los Reyes Magos traen regalos a los niños.

Many Spaniards celebrate Epiphany. The Three Kings bring gifts to children.

En Navidad, nos damos regalos y comemos juntos.

At Christmas, we give each other presents and we eat together.

During Hanukkah — Durante Janucá
For Diwali — Para Diwali

Q&A Audio

Question
¿Cuál es tu fiesta favorita?
What's your favourite festival?

Simple Answer
Mi fiesta favorita es el Eid al-Fitr. Lo celebro en familia.
My favourite festival is Eid al-Fitr. I celebrate it with family.

Extended Answer
Mi fiesta favorita es el Eid al-Fitr. Visitamos a nuestros familiares y ofrecemos regalos a los niños.
My favourite festival is Eid al-Fitr. We visit our relatives and offer gifts to the children.

Practice Questions

Q1 *Read the following text out loud.* *[5 marks]* SPEAKING

Me interesan las fiestas de España y Sudamérica. Las tradiciones del Día de Muertos son hermosas. La gente celebra las vidas de los muertos. En España, se comen doce uvas a medianoche en Nochevieja. Me gusta celebrar la Nochevieja con mis amigos.

Top Tip for Higher Students
✓ Use relative pronouns like 'lo que' to add more details to your answers.

Now answer the questions below in Spanish. *[10 marks]*

a) ¿Cómo celebras la Nochevieja?
b) ¿Cuál es tu opinión sobre los Sanfermines?
c) ¿Te gustaría ir a una fiesta española?
d) Describe la fiesta favorita que celebras.

Higher

Q2 *In a podcast, Carmen is asking Vicente about festivals in Spain. Fill each gap in the sentences below with **one or two** words.* LISTENING

Listening Track 11

a) ______ is so popular that you need to buy a ticket before attending.
During the ______ the streets are full of people. *[2 marks]*

b) Las Fallas began centuries ago to celebrate the start of ______.
The festival is celebrated with fireworks and ______. *[2 marks]*

Caution — rogue tomatoes approaching at speed...

I'm not sure that being pelted by tomatoes is my idea of fun — I prefer them on pizza. Wacky antics aside, you need to know the details of these festivals for the exams. Have a read over any festivals you're unsure of.

Customs, Festivals and Celebrations — Vocabulary

Grab a hat or vegetable of your choice — it's time to get to grips with the vocab for festivals and celebrations.

Celebrations

la celebración	*celebration*
celebrar	*to celebrate*
el cumpleaños	*birthday*
¡Feliz cumpleaños!	*Happy birthday!*
¡Enhorabuena!	*Congratulations!*
la alegría	*joy, happiness*
el ambiente	*atmosphere, environment*
la sorpresa	*surprise*
invitar	*to invite*
el matrimonio	*marriage*
la boda	*wedding*
la novia	*bride*
el novio	*groom*
recibir	*to receive*
el regalo	*present, gift*
la tarjeta	*written card*

Higher

celebrarse	*to hold (an event)*
sorprender	*to surprise*
reunir	*to gather, bring together*
reunirse	*to get together*
regalar	*to give (as a gift)*
ofrecer	*to offer, present*

Because what's a party without cake and silly hats?

Customs and Festivals

la tradición	*tradition*
tradicional	*traditional*
la costumbre	*custom, tradition*
la fiesta	*party, festival*
los Sanfermines	*festival in Pamplona involving running of the bulls*
el animal	*animal*
el toro	*bull*
la plaza de toros	*bullring*
la corrida	*bullfight*
el/la habitante	*local (person), inhabitant*
la Tomatina	*Spanish tomato festival*
el tomate	*tomato*
tirar	*to throw, pull*
los fuegos artificiales	*fireworks*
Las Fallas	*Valencian celebration involving burning of papier mâché models*
el espectáculo	*show, spectacle*
la cultura	*culture*
cultural	*cultural*
el Día de Muertos	*Day of the Dead (Mexican celebration)*
el disfraz	*costume, fancy dress*
el traje	*costume*
la flor	*flower*
pintarse	*to put on makeup*
el santo	*saint, saint's day*
religioso/a	*religious*
la Semana Santa	*Easter Week, Holy Week*
el desfile	*procession, parade*
el paso	*religious image carried in Holy Week processions*
el cielo	*heaven*
Nochebuena	*Christmas Eve*
Navidad	*Christmas*
Nochevieja	*New Year's Eve*
la uva	*grape*
el Día de Reyes	*Epiphany, 6th January*
los Reyes Magos	*the Three Kings, the Three Wise Men*
real	*royal*
el rey	*king*
la reina	*queen*
la cocina	*cooking*
el baile	*dance*
el flamenco	*flamenco (dance / music from the south of Spain)*
la historia	*story*
el interés	*interest*
especial	*special*
la región	*region*

Higher

la ocasión	*occasion*
el evento	*event*
nacional	*national*
el siglo	*century*
escaparse	*to run away*
el juguete	*toy*
engañar	*to trick, deceive*

Revision Summary Test for Section Seven

The party isn't over just yet — round off the festivities by having a go at this summary test.

- Yep, these questions are **hard** — they'll really help you see **how well you know your stuff**.
- Tackle the **revision summary test** below, or scan the QR code to do it **online**.
  Use the CGP RevisionHub to **track your progress** and see **which areas need more work**.
- You can find **sample answers** here: www.cgpbooks.co.uk/BuenoExtras

Summary Test

Celebrations

1) Monika's birthday is today. What 2 phrases could you say to congratulate her in Spanish?
2) Your friend writes: 'There was a lot of joy in the atmosphere of that celebration.'
   How could they say this in Spanish?
3) List the words in this section that relate to weddings. There are 4 you need to know.
4) '¿Qué haces para celebrar tu cumpleaños?' Translate this question into
   English, then answer it in Spanish, including as much detail as possible.
5) 'Mis padres me dieron una sorpresa. Recibí zapatos nuevos de ellos.' Translate this into English.
6) '¿Has ido a una celebración recientemente?' Translate this question into
   English, then answer it in Spanish. Give as much detail as you can.

H

7) Translate this sentence into Spanish:
   'My parents held a party where all the family got together to surprise my grandparents.'

Customs and Festivals

8) What's the English for...?
   a) el santo b) la Semana Santa c) el desfile d) el paso e) el cielo
9) How many words for Christmas and New Year celebrations can you list in Spanish?
   There are 4 in this section.
10) a) Can you name 4 festivals from Spanish-speaking countries?
    b) Choose one of these festivals and describe it in Spanish, giving as much detail as you can.
11) 'Muchas turistas visitan la región de Valencia durante sus fiestas populares.'
    How would you say this in English?
12) 'Me encantaría visitar Chile para ver sus costumbres y probar la cocina.' Say this in English.
    Then, write about a custom from a Spanish-speaking country you'd like to experience.
13) Write these words in English, then decide which one isn't usually part of Las Fallas celebrations:
    a) las flores b) los fuegos artificiales c) los disfraces d) los tomates
14) 'Day of the Dead traditions are important for many people.' How would you say this in Spanish?
15) Say 'En un baile español que se llama flamenco, se puede ver trajes hermosos.' in English.
16) How would you say these words in Spanish?
    a) inhabitant b) cultural c) royal d) king e) queen f) story
17) Translate this question into English, then answer it in Spanish using complete sentences:
    '¿Cómo celebraste tu tradición favorita el año pasado?'

Higher

18) Translate this into Spanish: 'The Three Kings have been giving toys to children for centuries.'
19) Imagine you're in Pamplona for the Sanfermines festival. Write a description
    in Spanish of what you might see there, including as much detail as possible.

Quick Quiz

Favourite Celebrities

No, I'm sorry — you can't be your own favourite celebrity...

Remember there's also lots of online content here: www.cgpbooks.co.uk/Bueno

Tu famoso favorito — *Your favourite celebrity*

Vocabulary

el/la famoso/a	*celebrity, famous person*	el/la cantante	*singer*	el/la influencer	*influencer*
la actriz	*actor (f), actress*	el/la músico/a	*musician*	el/la deportista (Higher)	*sportsperson*
el actor	*actor (m)*	el/la director(a)	*director*	la banda (Higher)	*(musical) band*
el/la artista	*artist, performer*	el/la jugador(a)	*player*	actuar (Higher)	*to act*
		el/la autor(a)	*writer, author*	el/la aficionado/a (Higher)	*fan*

Mi famosa favorita es una cantante mexicana. Será emocionante verla en vivo. — *My favourite celebrity is a Mexican singer. It'll be exciting to watch her live.*

Uno de mis famosos favoritos es actor en películas de acción. Presenta un programa de entrevistas también. — *One of my favourite celebrities is an actor in action films. He hosts a talk show too.*

he manages a children's charity — dirige una organización benéfica para niños

Soy gran aficionado a un grupo de pop. Estoy aprendiendo todas sus canciones. — *I'm a huge fan of a pop group. I am learning all their songs.*

an indie band — una banda indie

Q&A Audio

Question

¿Qué hace tu famoso favorito?

What does your favourite celebrity do?

Simple Answer

Mi famosa favorita es autora. Escribe libros de ciencia ficción.

My favourite celebrity is an author. She writes science-fiction books.

Extended Answer

Mi famoso favorito es jugador de baloncesto y también es conocido por apoyar a su comunidad local.

My favourite celebrity is a basketball player and he's also known for supporting his local community.

Me gusta esta persona porque... — *I like this person because...*

Vocabulary

la estrella	*star*	seguir	*to follow*	la cara (Higher)	*face, expression*
famoso/a	*famous, well-known*	la voz	*voice*	el estilo (Higher)	*style*
conocido/a	*known, well-known*	de moda	*fashionable*	el talento (Higher)	*talent*
importante	*important, influential*	el carácter	*personality*	el contenido (Higher)	*content*

Me gusta este famoso porque tiene una voz hermosa y unos tatuajes bonitos. Siempre lleva ropa negra. — *I like this celebrity because he has a beautiful voice and some nice tattoos. He always wears black clothes.*

a cool guitar — una guitarra guay

Sigo a mi estrella favorita desde hace dos años porque da buenos consejos y tiene buen estilo. — *I have been following my favourite star for two years because she gives good advice and she has good style.*

she communicates well with her fans — se comunica bien con sus aficionados

Mi famosa favorita es cómica. Sus chistes me hacen reír mucho. — *My favourite celebrity is a stand-up comedian. Her jokes make me laugh a lot.*

Tipos diferentes de famosos — *Different types of celebrities*

The fame had clearly gone to Larry's head.

Una persona famosa que me inspira es científica. Ganó un premio Nobel por sus contribuciones a la medicina.	*One famous person who inspires me is a scientist. She won a Nobel prize for her contributions to medicine.*
Mi famoso favorito cocinaba en la televisión. Parece una persona muy simpática y me gustan las recetas que publica.	*My favourite celebrity used to cook on TV. He seems like a really nice person and I like the recipes that he publishes.*
Hay un influencer que viene de mi pueblo. Es conocido por jugar a videojuegos.	*There's an influencer who comes from my town. He's known for playing computer games.*
Sigo a una famosa que crea contenido en Internet.	*I follow a celebrity who creates content on the internet.*
Mi famoso favorito ha grabado muchos documentales sobre la naturaleza. Siempre son interesantes.	*My favourite celebrity has recorded a lot of nature documentaries. They're always interesting.*

a content creator — un creador de contenido

shares their art on social media — comparte su arte en las redes sociales

broadcasts podcasts each week — emite podcasts cada semana

Grammar — formation of feminine nouns

In Spanish, there are rules for changing masculine nouns (particularly with jobs and positions) to their feminine form. See p.103.

Nouns that end in -o change to -a: **el músico** = **la música**

Nouns that end in -or add -a: **el director** = **la directora**

Nouns ending in -ante, -ente or -ista do not change: **el artista** = **la artista**

When you're talking about what job someone does, you don't use the article, e.g. 'Es cocinero' — 'He's a chef'. However, you do include the article if you use an adjective, e.g. 'Es un buen cocinero' — 'He's a good chef'. See p.105.

Practice Questions

Q1 *You are listening to a podcast where two people are discussing their favourite celebrities. Answer the questions in English.*

LISTENING

Listening Track 12

a) Why is a director Luis's favourite celebrity? *[1 mark]*

b) What did he learn from a magazine? Give **one** detail. *[1 mark]*

c) Give **one** detail of Carla's favourite celebrity's appearance. *[1 mark]*

d) What did her favourite celebrity do recently? *[1 mark]*

Q2 *Write about your favourite celebrity. You should write about 90 words in Spanish. Mention:*

WRITING

- *who your favourite celebrity is*
- *what they have done in their career*
- *why you like them.* *[15 marks]*

Top Tip For Higher Students
✓ Use 'desde hace' to talk about how long your favourite celebrity has been doing something.

Red carpet — good if you're having tomato soup...

If you don't have a favourite celebrity, you can always make someone up. For example, you could describe the mysterious figure who writes your revision jokes, and how your favourite thing is their sparkling wit...

Quick Quiz

Celebrity Life

If I were a celebrity, I'd lead a very humble lifestyle. Now, no photos, please.

La vida de una estrella — *The life of a star*

Vocabulary

la telerrealidad	*reality TV*	el público	*public*
la entrevista	*interview*	la prensa	*press*
la revista	*magazine*	la atención	*attention*
popular	*popular*	reconocer	*to recognise, admit*

(Higher: el público, la prensa, la atención, reconocer)

Los famosos populares suelen participar en las series de telerrealidad. — *Popular celebrities often participate in reality TV series.*

exclusive interviews — entrevistas exclusivas

Muchas estrellas tienen una fuerte presencia en las redes sociales y ahora están compartiendo su vida allí. — *Many stars have a strong presence on social media and they are now sharing their life there.*

they get collaborations — consiguen colaboraciones

Para los famosos, puede ser difícil salir sin ser reconocidos. Muchos quieren evitar la prensa. — *For celebrities, it can be difficult to go out without being recognised. Many want to avoid the press.*

enjoy the attention — disfrutan la atención

Q&A Audio

Question

¿Te gustaría ser una persona famosa?

Would you like to be a famous person?

Simple Answer

Sí, porque mi sueño es ser un músico conocido.

Yes, because my dream is to be a well-known musician.

Extended Answer

No me interesa nada ser una estrella. No me gustaría ni la atención ni la presión.

I'm not interested at all in being a star. I would like neither the attention nor the pressure.

Lo bueno de ser famoso... — *The good thing about being famous...*

Vocabulary

lo bueno	*the good thing*	el dinero	*money*	influir	*to influence*
positivo/a	*positive*	rico/a	*rich, wealthy*	fundar	*to set up, establish*
el éxito	*success*	el respeto	*respect, regard*	merecer	*to deserve, be worthy of*
el premio	*prize, reward, award*	el apoyo	*support, backing*		

(Higher: influir, fundar, merecer)

Lo bueno de ser famoso es que podría abrir las puertas a oportunidades emocionantes. — *The good thing about being famous is that it could open doors to exciting opportunities.*

Es increíble que un famoso tenga el poder de ser una influencia positiva para los jóvenes. — *It's incredible that a celebrity has the power to be a positive influence for young people.*

to change society for the better — cambiar la sociedad para mejor

Los famosos pueden ganar respeto y muchos premios por su trabajo. — *Celebrities can gain respect and lots of awards for their work.*

inspire others with — inspirar a otros con

earn a lot of money for — ganar mucho dinero por

Varios famosos quieren usar su fama para algo bueno y han apoyado causas importantes. — *Various celebrities want to use their fame for something good and have supported important causes.*

Los aspectos negativos — *The negative aspects*

Vocabulary

negativo/a	*negative*	molestarse	*to be offended*
la confianza	*confidence, trust*	la realidad (Higher)	*reality*
mantener	*to keep, maintain*	la soledad (Higher)	*loneliness, solitude*
la imagen	*image*	el comentario (Higher)	*remark, comment*
la presión	*pressure*	la víctima (Higher)	*victim*
criticar	*to criticise*	la vergüenza (Higher)	*embarrassment, shame*

Es posible que un famoso tenga una falta de confianza en otra gente. Por eso, podrían sufrir de soledad.	*It is possible for a famous person to have a lack of trust in other people. Therefore, they may suffer from loneliness.*
Existe presión por mantener siempre la imagen y parecer perfecto.	*There is pressure to always maintain your image and to seem perfect.*
La salud mental de una estrella podría ser afectada por un horario ocupadísimo.	*A star's mental health could be affected by a really busy schedule.*
Los famosos que consiguen atención en Internet pueden ser víctimas de un montón de comentarios intolerantes.	*Celebrities who gain attention on the internet can be victims of a lot of intolerant comments.*

Practice Questions

Q1 *A celebrity is discussing what they do and don't like about being famous.*

SPEAKING

Soy una estrella de la telerrealidad. Grabar mi vida es divertido porque hago muchas actividades diferentes. En cambio, puede ser duro mantener mi imagen todo el día.

Top Tip For Higher Students
✓ Use 'lo mejor' and 'lo peor' to talk about the best and the worst things about being famous.

*Now it's your turn. Imagine you're a celebrity and talk about what you like and dislike about being famous. Aim to talk for **two** minutes.* *[10 marks]*

Higher

Q2 *You are reading a social media post from Tanvir, a famous influencer. Choose the correct option to complete the sentences below.*

READING

Quiero promover mi nuevo libro sobre mi experiencia como influencer. Habla de todas las actividades locas que he grabado y explica cuánto me han ayudado mis aficionados. Además, describo cómo ser influencer ha cambiado mi vida. Aunque todavía me resulta difícil hablar con otra gente, ya tengo mucha más confianza.

a) Tanvir's book is...
A. a novel.
B. an autobiography.
C. a guide book.
[1 mark]

b) He talks about...
A. his fans.
B. his promotion.
C. his family.
[1 mark]

c) Being an influencer has...
A. given him more confidence.
B. made it difficult to talk to others.
C. made him feel happier.
[1 mark]

Astronomers know a thing or two about stars...

Even though the advantages of being famous are attractive to think about (like all the money you'd have to buy a swish home), make sure you learn the disadvantages too. The examiner could ask you about either.

Celebrity Culture — Vocabulary

Show the examiner you've got that star quality by using the celebrity-related vocab on this page.

Favourite Celebrities

el/la famoso/a	*celebrity, famous person*
la personalidad	*celebrity*
la actriz	*actor (f), actress*
el actor	*actor (m)*
el/la artista	*artist, performer*
el/la cantante	*singer*
el/la músico/a	*musician*
el/la director(a)	*director*
el/la modelo	*model*
el/la jugador(a)	*player*
el/la autor(a)	*writer, author*
el/la influencer	*influencer*
el grupo	*group*
la estrella	*star*
famoso/a	*famous, well-known*
conocido/a	*known, well-known*
importante	*important, influential*
seguir	*to follow*
el/la seguidor(a)	*follower*
la voz	*voice*
de moda	*in fashion, fashionable*
el papel	*role, part*

la letra	*lyrics*
la novela	*novel*
el carácter	*personality, character*
listo/a	*clever, intelligent (after ser)*
hermoso/a	*handsome, beautiful*
artístico/a	*artistic*
gracioso/a	*funny*

Higher

el/la deportista	*sportsperson*
la banda	*(musical) band*
la actuación	*performance, acting*
actuar	*to act*
colgar	*to post (photo)*
el/la aficionado/a	*fan*
el/la representante	*representative (agent)*
la cara	*face, expression*
la belleza	*beauty*
el estilo	*style*
el talento	*talent*
el destino	*destiny*
el contenido	*content*
digital	*digital*

Celebrity Life

la telerrealidad	*reality TV*
la entrevista	*interview*
la revista	*magazine*
popular	*popular*
lo bueno	*the good thing*
positivo/a	*positive*
el éxito	*success*
el premio	*prize, reward, award*
el dinero	*money*
rico/a	*rich, wealthy*
el respeto	*respect, regard*
el apoyo	*support, backing*
compartir	*to share*
negativo/a	*negative*
la confianza	*confidence, trust*
mantener	*to keep, maintain*
la imagen	*image, picture*
la presión	*pressure*
criticar	*to criticise*
molestarse	*to be offended*
el comportamiento	*behaviour*
la juventud	*youth*

Higher

el público	*public*
la prensa	*press*
la tendencia	*tendency, trend*
la reacción	*reaction*
la atención	*attention*
conseguir	*to get, obtain*
reconocer	*to recognise, admit*
la influencia	*influence*
influir	*to influence*
la riqueza	*wealth, riches*
fundar	*to set up, establish*
merecer	*to deserve, be worthy of*
la realidad	*reality*
la soledad	*loneliness, solitude*
publicar	*to publish, post (online)*
el comentario	*remark, comment*
la víctima	*victim*
la vergüenza	*embarrassment, shame*

Revision Summary Test for Section Eight

Fame has its ups, downs and everything in between — work through this test to cover it all.

- These questions are **hard**, but they'll really help you see **how well you know your stuff**.
- Tackle the **revision summary test** below, or scan the QR code to do it **online**. You can **track your progress** online and see **which areas need more work**.
- There are **sample answers** for the test here: www.cgpbooks.co.uk/BuenoExtras

Summary Test

Favourite Celebrities

1) Write the English for: a) el/la cantante b) el/la director(a) c) el/la jugador(a) d) el/la autor(a)
2) In Spanish, say what your favourite celebrity does. Give at least two details.
3) There are 4 Spanish adjectives to describe a celebrity's personality in this section. How many can you remember?
4) 'She is famous because she's a very important actress.' Say this in Spanish.
5) In Spanish, describe what your favourite celebrity from your childhood looked like. Give one reason why you liked them.
6) 'Me interesa seguir a los modelos porque puedo ver la ropa que está de moda.' Translate this sentence into English.
7) What's the Spanish for: a) follower b) voice c) role, part d) novel
8) 'My favourite celebrity is really popular on the internet. He makes videos about computer games and he writes songs too.' How would you say this in Spanish?

Higher

9) 'Después de tener una gran discusión con su representante, mi banda favorita ya no es un grupo.' Translate this sentence into English.
10) Imagine you've just met your favourite celebrity. In Spanish, describe how you discovered them and why you like them.

Celebrity Life

11) Write the English for: a) el éxito b) el dinero c) el respeto d) la confianza e) molestarse
12) In Spanish, give one advantage and one disadvantage of being famous.
13) 'La gente critica a los influencers por tener un efecto negativo en la sociedad.' Translate this sentence into English.
14) ¿Qué piensas de las revistas que hablan de los famosos?
15) Say these words in Spanish: a) interview b) support c) behaviour d) youth
16) 'Mis padres odian las series de telerrealidad.' Say this in English.
17) In Spanish, say whether or not you would like to be famous and why.

Higher

18) Sara says: 'The reality of being famous seems difficult to me. You can feel embarrassment due to the articles that journalists publish.' Translate what she says into Spanish.
19) 'Ayer unos deportistas famosos anunciaron a la prensa que fundarán un nuevo estadio.' Say this sentence in English.
20) ¿Crees que los famosos merecen la atención que reciben? ¿Por qué?

Where to Go

Quick Quiz

Caution: reading the next few pages might just give you the travel bug.

Don't forget you can access your online content here: www.cgpbooks.co.uk/Bueno

Vamos de viaje — *We're going on a trip*

Vocabulary

las vacaciones	*holidays*	el extranjero	*abroad*	Sudamérica	*South America*
el viaje	*trip, journey*	el mundo	*world*	H la nación	*nation*
el puente	*long weekend*	España	*Spain*	H hispanohablante	*Spanish-speaking*

El próximo puente, quiero ir de vacaciones al extranjero. — *The next long weekend, I want to go on holiday abroad.*

to another country — a otro país

Todos querríamos ir de vacaciones juntos a Italia. — *We would all like to go on holiday together to Italy.*

France — Francia
Germany — Alemania
the USA — los Estados Unidos

Bashir va a Australia. Será un viaje largo al otro lado del mundo. — *Bashir is going to Australia. It will be a long journey to the other side of the world.*

¿Cómo es el paisaje? — *What's the landscape like?*

Vocabulary

el paisaje	*landscape*	el bosque	*forest, wood*	la costa	*coast*
hermoso/a	*beautiful*	la montaña	*mountain*	la playa	*beach*
tranquilo/a	*calm, tranquil*	el río	*river*	H el monte	*hill, hills, countryside*
el campo	*countryside*	la isla	*island*	H el lago	*lake*

Snowdonia es una región de Gales con muchas montañas. — *Snowdonia is a region of Wales with lots of mountains.*

Vamos a Menorca, una isla que tiene muchas playas de arena. — *We go to Menorca, an island that has many sandy beaches.*

a lot of countryside — mucho monte
beautiful views — vistas preciosas

Hay unos lagos hermosos en el norte de Inglaterra. — *There are some beautiful lakes in the north of England.*

large areas of forest — grandes zonas de bosque

Q&A Audio

Question

¿Adónde vas de vacaciones?
Where do you go on holiday?

Simple Answer

Voy de vacaciones a Irlanda del Norte.
I go on holiday to Northern Ireland.

Extended Answer

Voy de vacaciones a Irlanda del Norte para ver a mis abuelos. Solemos pasar unas semanas allí, en un pueblo cerca del mar.
I go on holiday to Northern Ireland to see my grandparents. We tend to spend a few weeks there, in a village near the sea.

Tom didn't need a beach holiday — his living room worked just fine.

¿Por qué quieres ir allí? — *Why do you want to go there?*

Vocabulary

al aire libre	*in the open air, outdoors*	el sitio	*place, site*
pasarlo bien/mal	*to have a good/bad time*	la arquitectura	*architecture*
disfrutar	*to enjoy*	conocido/a	*known, well-known*
visitar	*to visit*	histórico/a	*historic, historical*

Quiero ir a España porque tiene arquitectura hermosa.	*I want to go to Spain because it has beautiful architecture.*
Cada vez que he ido a Cádiz con mis amigos, lo hemos pasado muy bien.	*Every time I've been to Cádiz with my friends, we have had a really good time.*
Le gustaría ir a Sudamérica para ver una cultura diferente.	*She would like to go to South America in order to see a different culture.*
Espero ir a un sitio conocido como Machu Picchu algún día.	*I hope to go to a well-known site like Machu Picchu one day.*
Vamos a visitar Edimburgo porque es un sitio histórico.	*We are going to visit Edinburgh because it is a historic place.*
Preferiría ir de vacaciones a un país donde se puede pasar mucho tiempo al aire libre.	*I would prefer to go on holiday to a country where you can spend a lot of time outdoors.*

on holiday to Iceland — de vacaciones a Islandia

Rome — Roma
Berlin — Berlín
Athens — Atenas

enjoy the good weather — disfrutar del buen tiempo

Practice Questions

Q1 *Marina and Hugo are telling their Colombian friend about Barcelona. Choose the statement that is mentioned in each pair below.*

LISTENING

Listening Track 13

a) **A.** Barcelona is in the north of Spain.
B. Barcelona has millions of tourists. *[1 mark]*

b) **A.** It's surrounded by the Mediterranean Sea.
B. It's famous for its art and architecture. *[1 mark]*

c) **A.** Marina thinks that there is lots to do outdoors.
B. In July and August, Marina loves spending all day on its beaches. *[1 mark]*

Q2 *You are writing an article about travel for a competition. You should write about 90 words in Spanish. Mention:*

WRITING

- *where you prefer to go on holiday*
- *a recent holiday you went on*
- *what holiday plans you have for this year.* *[15 marks]*

Top Tip for Higher Students
✓ Use the 'we' form of the conditional to talk about what you and your family would like to do.

When do mountains like to go on holiday? Peak season...

I love a beach holiday — there's nothing better. Except the sand makes me feel icky when it gets in my toes. Oh, and I need options for shade too. I also hate getting wet, so I don't like getting too close to the sea...

Quick Quiz

Accommodation and Travel

Now you've chosen where you're going, you need a place to stay and a way to get there...

Busco alojamiento... — *I'm looking for accommodation...*

Vocabulary

el alojamiento	*accommodation*	la instalación	*facility*	reservar	*to book, reserve*
el hotel	*hotel*	el camping	*campsite, camping*	[Higher] el ascensor	*lift, elevator*
la habitación	*room*	la tienda	*tent*	[Higher] la calefacción	*heating*
la recepción	*reception (hotel)*	quedar(se)	*to stay*	[Higher] el lujo	*luxury*

Quisiera quedarme en un camping para cuatro noches. — *I would like to stay on a campsite for four nights.*

for a fortnight — para quince días

Siempre nos quedamos en un hotel de lujo. — *We always stay in a luxury hotel.*

Es esencial encontrar una habitación que tenga cuarto de baño y una cama cómoda. — *It's essential to find a room that has a bathroom and a comfortable bed.*

Me gustaría quedarme en un albergue juvenil para conocer a gente nueva. — *I would like to stay in a youth hostel in order to meet new people.*

to save money — ahorrar dinero

Grammar (Higher only) — I need...

When talking about the features of something you require, use the subjunctive (p.142).

Busco un hotel que tenga piscina. — ***I'm looking for a hotel that has a pool.***

Q&A Audio

Question

¿Qué tipo de habitación le gustaría a usted?

What type of room would you like?

Simple Answer

Me gustaría una habitación con vistas al mar.

I would like a room with sea views.

Extended Answer

Somos una familia de tres, así que necesitamos dos habitaciones — una individual y una doble.

We are a family of three, so we need two rooms — a single and a double.

¿Cuánto cuesta reservar...? — *How much does it cost to book...?*

Vocabulary

costar	*to cost*	el euro	*euro*	caro/a	*expensive*
pagar	*to pay (for)*	alto/a	*high*	barato/a	*cheap*
el precio	*price, cost*	bajo/a	*low*	[H] el costo	*price, cost*

Mi amigo y yo buscamos alojamiento barato. — *My friend and I are looking for cheap accommodation.*

have found a hotel with lower prices — hemos encontrado un hotel con precios más bajos

Una noche en este hotel cuesta ciento diez euros. — *One night in this hotel costs one hundred and ten euros.*

Preferiríamos pagar más para quedarnos en el centro de la ciudad. — *We would prefer to pay more to stay in the city centre.*

a room with modern facilities — una habitación con instalaciones modernas

Cómo llegar allí — *How to get there*

Vocabulary

llegar	*to arrive*	la estación	*station*
viajar	*to travel*	el tren	*train*
volver	*to go back, return*	el destino	*destination*
directo/a	*direct, straight*	la llegada	*arrival*
coger	*to take, catch*	el retraso	*delay*
el coche	*car*	la velocidad	*speed, velocity*
el puerto	*port, harbour*	la distancia	*distance*
el barco	*boat, ship*	la frontera	*border, frontier*
el aeropuerto	*airport*	internacional	*international*
el avión	*plane, aeroplane*	regresar	*to come back, go back, return*
el vuelo	*flight*		

Higher (el destino – regresar)

Viajar en avión me permite llegar a mi destino más pronto. — *Travelling by plane allows me to arrive at my destination sooner.*

Preferiría coger un vuelo directo desde el aeropuerto. — *I would prefer to catch a direct flight from the airport.*

Quieren viajar en barco, pero prefiero ir en tren porque es más rápido. — *They want to travel by boat, but I prefer to go by train because it's faster.*

Vamos a viajar en coche y esperamos llegar a la frontera a las once. — *We are going to travel by car and we hope to arrive at the border at 11 o'clock.*

Catching the high-speed train — Coger el tren de alta velocidad

They hate the delays at the station — Odian los retrasos en la estación

I get seasick — me mareo

Practice Questions

Q1 Read Lucía's diary entry about an upcoming trip and answer the questions below.

READING

En febrero voy de vacaciones a París. Ya he organizado el alojamiento y el transporte. Voy a viajar en tren porque es más barato que viajar en avión y más cómodo que viajar en autobús. Quedarme en un hotel costaría mucho, entonces he reservado un piso pequeño por un precio mejor. Tiene una cocina y un balcón bonito. La estación está muy cerca también.*

*balcón — balcony

a) How will Lucía travel to Paris? *[1 mark]*

b) Give **one** reason why Lucía is going to use that type of transport. *[1 mark]*

c) What type of accommodation will she be staying in? *[1 mark]*

d) Give **two** details about the accommodation. *[2 marks]*

Higher

Q2 Listen carefully to 5 short sentences.
Use your knowledge of Spanish sounds and write down in Spanish exactly what you hear for each sentence. *[10 marks]*

LISTENING

Listening Track 14

I stayed in a bird cage once — I like cheep accommodation...

At least if your flight gets delayed, there's plenty to do. Like eating all the snacks you were meant to save for the plane or having a nap on an uncomfortable seat. Or glancing at your boarding gate over... and over...

Quick Quiz

Getting Around and What to Do

Grab a guidebook because you're about to explore what there is to see and do. Oh, and how to get around. I found out how important that is on my trip to Madrid — but that's a story for another time...

¿Coges el transporte público? — *Do you take public transport?*

Vocabulary

el transporte público	*public transport*	a pie	*on foot*
el billete	*ticket (for transport)*	conducir	*to drive*
la vuelta	*return, trip, ride*	el tráfico	*traffic*
el metro	*underground, tube, metro*	tardar	*to take (time)*
el autobús	*bus*	alquilar (Higher)	*to hire, rent*
montar	*to ride*	caminar (Higher)	*to walk*
la bicicleta, bici	*bicycle, bike*	el camino (Higher)	*way, route, path*

Cogeré el autobús porque será la opción más barata y tardará menos tiempo. — *I will take the bus because it is the cheapest option and it will take less time.*

Fuimos a la playa a pie ya que está cerca de nuestro hotel. — *We went to the beach on foot since it's near our hotel.*

by taxi because our feet were hurting — en taxi porque nos dolían los pies

Cogí el metro porque había mucho tráfico. — *I took the underground because there was a lot of traffic.*

the tram — el tranvía

I couldn't hire a car — no podía alquilar un coche

¿Cuál es la mejor manera de llegar al centro de la ciudad? — *What is the best way to get to the city centre?*

¿Qué te gustaría hacer? — *What would you like to do?*

Vocabulary

la excursión	*trip, excursion*	la plaza	*square*	el/la guía (Higher)	*guide (person)*
el museo	*museum*	el mercado	*market*	la guía (Higher)	*guide book*
el templo	*temple*	el puesto	*stall (market)*	la exposición (Higher)	*exhibition, display*
el castillo	*castle*	el turismo (H)	*tourism*	la torre (Higher)	*tower*

No nos gusta nada más que dar un paseo por los puestos del mercado. — *We like nothing more than to go for a stroll through the market stalls.*

visit historic monuments — visitar monumentos históricos

Vamos a hacer una excursión a las ruinas antiguas de un templo. — *We are going to go on an excursion to the ancient ruins of a temple.*

El guía dice que hay que subir a la torre para ver la ciudad entera. — *The guide says that you have to go up the tower to see the whole town.*

explore the national park — explorar el parque nacional

Quiero ir a una exposición en la plaza mayor del pueblo. — *I want to go to an exhibition in the town's main square.*

Una actividad divertida es... — *An enjoyable activity is...*

Para mí, lo más importante es buscar un parque temático.
For me, the most important thing is to look for a theme park.

to buy a souvenir — comprar un recuerdo
to do water sports — hacer deportes acuáticos

Mañana iremos a un restaurante para probar la comida típica de la región.
Tomorrow we will go to a restaurant to try the region's typical food.

Quieren tomar el sol, pero van a quemarse si no se sientan a la sombra.
They want to sunbathe, but they're going to get sunburnt if they don't sit in the shade.

Cuando estoy de vacaciones, suelo tomar muchas fotos.
When I'm on holiday, I usually take lots of photos.

take my camera — llevar mi cámara
buy some guide books — comprar unas guías

Q&A Audio

Question

¿Qué hiciste durante tus vacaciones?
What did you do during your holiday?

Simple Answer

Fuimos a la playa y fue muy relajante.
We went to the beach and it was very relaxing.

Extended Answer

Pasamos mucho tiempo en la playa porque hacía sol. Tomé el sol y jugué con mis primos.
We spent a lot of time on the beach because it was sunny. I sunbathed and played with my cousins.

Grammar — la foto

Watch out for nouns that don't fit the masculine / feminine rule of ending with an '-o' or '-a' (p.103):

la foto	***the photo***
el agua	***the water***

('water' is actually a feminine noun, but it takes 'el' as its article because 'la agua' is too awkward to pronounce.)

Practice Questions

Q1 *Oleksii is discussing holiday activities with a friend.*

SPEAKING

Cuando voy a un país extranjero, tengo ganas de hacer actividades al aire libre. Iré a Portugal el próximo año. Nadaré en el mar y participaré en clases de baile en la playa.

Top Tip for Higher Students
✓ Use the subjunctive to express something you want to happen, e.g. 'Quiero que haga buen tiempo.'

Now it's your turn. Talk about what you like to do on holiday and what you'd like to see and do on your next one. Aim to talk for about two minutes. *[10 marks]*

Higher

Q2 *You read this extract from a leaflet about Galicia, a region of Spain. Answer the questions below in English.*

READING

La región hermosa de Galicia está en el norte de España. Aquí se puede conocer ciudades como Santiago de Compostela, la capital de la región. Si quieres explorar la ciudad, es posible coger el autobús o montar en bici. Hay una catedral preciosa y varios museos que cuentan la historia de la región. Para disfrutar de la belleza de los edificios, es mejor dar un paseo por las calles.

a) Where is Galicia located? *[1 mark]*

b) Write down two things you can visit in Santiago de Compostela. *[2 marks]*

c) What's the best way to enjoy the architecture in Santiago de Compostela? *[1 mark]*

Time flies when you're on holiday...

If only it went as fast during revision... To help with this, I'd start with learning words that are similar to their English word. That way, you'll have already made a good bit of progress before you start on the trickier ones.

Travel and Tourism — Vocabulary

Welcome to a world of vocab about travel and tourism. There's lots to explore and we hope that you enjoy your stay...

Where to Go

bienvenido/a	*welcome*
las vacaciones	*holidays*
de vacaciones	*on holiday*
el viaje	*trip, journey*
el puente	*long weekend*
el extranjero	*abroad*
el/la extranjero/a	*foreigner*
el/la turista	*tourist*
el mundo	*world*
España	*Spain*
Sudamérica	*South America*
el país	*country*
el paisaje	*landscape*
hermoso/a	*beautiful*
tranquilo/a	*calm, tranquil*
el campo	*countryside*
el bosque	*forest, wood*
la montaña	*mountain*
el río	*river*
la isla	*island*
la costa	*coast*
el mar	*sea*

la playa	*beach*
el calor	*heat, hot*
al aire libre	*in the open air, outdoors*
pasar	*to pass, spend (time), happen*
pasarlo bien/mal	*to have a good/bad time*
disfrutar	*to enjoy*
visitar	*to visit*
el sitio	*place, site*
la capital	*capital (city)*
la arquitectura	*architecture*
conocido/a	*known, well-known*
histórico/a	*historic, historical*
animado/a	*lively*

Higher

la nación	*nation*
hispanohablante	*Spanish-speaking*
precioso/a	*beautiful, precious*
el monte	*hill, hills, countryside*
el lago	*lake*
la arena	*sand*

Accommodation

el alojamiento	*accommodation*
el hotel	*hotel*
la habitación	*room*
cómodo/a	*comfortable*
moderno/a	*modern*
la recepción	*reception (hotel)*
la instalación	*facility*
el camping	*campsite, camping*
la tienda	*tent*
la vista	*view*
quedar(se)	*to stay*
reservar	*to book, reserve*
organizar	*to organise*
ahorrar	*to save (time, money)*

costar	*to cost*
pagar	*to pay (for)*
el precio	*price, cost, value*
el euro	*euro*
el peso	*peso (currency)*
alto/a	*high*
bajo/a	*low*
caro/a	*expensive*
barato/a	*cheap*

Higher

el costo	*price, cost*
la llave	*key*
el ascensor	*lift, elevator*
la calefacción	*heating*
el lujo	*luxury*

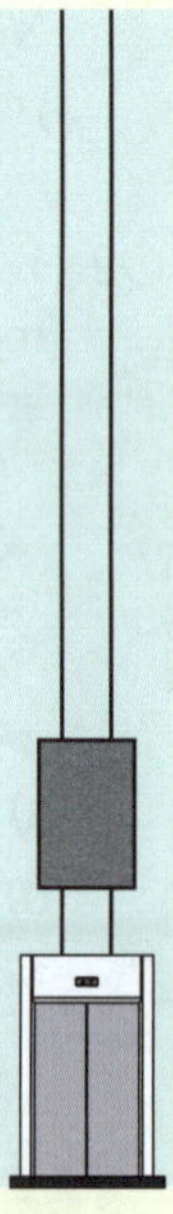

Travel

llegar	*to arrive*
viajar	*to travel*
volver	*to go back, return*
directo/a	*direct, straight*
coger	*to take, catch*
el transporte	*transport*
el coche	*car*
el puerto	*port, harbour*
el barco	*boat, ship*
el aeropuerto	*airport*
el avión	*plane, aeroplane*
el vuelo	*flight*
la estación	*station*
el tren	*train*

la mochila	*rucksack*
la maleta	*suitcase*
la entrada	*entrance*
la salida	*exit, departure*

Higher

el destino	*destination*
la visita	*visit, visitor*
la llegada	*arrival*
el retraso	*delay*
la velocidad	*speed, velocity*
la distancia	*distance*
la frontera	*border, frontier*
internacional	*international*
regresar	*to come back, go back, return*
acostumbrarse a	*to get accustomed, get used to*

Getting Around and What to Do

el transporte público	*public transport*
el billete	*ticket (for transport)*
la vuelta	*return, trip, ride*
perder	*to miss, lose*
el metro	*underground, tube, metro*
el autobús	*bus*
bajar	*to get off, lower*
montar	*to ride*
la bicicleta, bici	*bicycle, bike*
a pie	*on foot*
conducir	*to drive*
el tráfico	*traffic*
tardar	*to take (time)*
rápido/a	*quick, fast*
la excursión	*trip, excursion*
el parque temático	*theme park*
el edificio	*building*
el museo	*museum*
el templo	*temple*
el castillo	*castle*
la plaza	*square*
el mercado	*market*
el puesto	*stall (market)*
el recuerdo	*souvenir*
sacar	*to take out, get, obtain*
el plano	*map*
la cámara	*camera*
la foto	*photo, picture*

perdido/a	*lost*
perderse	*to get lost*
tomar el sol	*to sunbathe*

Higher

alquilar	*to hire, rent*
caminar	*to walk*
el camino	*way, route, path*
atraer	*to attract*
el turismo	*tourism*
el/la guía	*guide (person)*
la guía	*guide book*
la aventura	*adventure*
el deporte acuático	*water sport*
la exposición	*exhibition, display*
la torre	*tower*
la altura	*altitude*
la señal	*sign, signal*
la sombra	*shade, shadow*
quemarse	*to get sunburnt*
quejarse	*to complain*

Souvenirs are a great idea — until you have to pack them...

Revision Summary Test for Section Nine

Get in the holiday mood by trying out this section's summary test. Don't forget your suncream...

- These questions are **really tricky**, but they'll help you see **how well you know your stuff**.
- Tackle the **revision summary test** below, or scan the QR code to do it **online**. You can **keep track of your progress** online and see **which areas need more work**.
- There are **sample answers** here: www.cgpbooks.co.uk/BuenoExtras

Summary Test

Where to Go

1) Translate this into Spanish: 'I want to visit the capital of Spain in order to see its architecture.'
2) Daniela says: 'Muchos turistas viajan a Sudamérica para disfrutar de los sitios históricos conocidos.' How would you say this in English?
3) ¿Qué tipo de paisaje te gusta más? ¿Por qué?
4) 'El mar estaba tranquilo durante mi viaje a la costa de la isla.' Translate this sentence into English.
5) ¿Por qué te gusta ir de vacaciones?
6) In Spanish, how do you say: 'It is important to have a good time when you are on holiday.'
7) 'Pasaron el puente en una ciudad animada.' How would you say this in English?

Higher

8) A guidebook says: 'Esta nación hispanohablante tiene montañas altísimas. Además, uno de los ríos más largos del mundo corre por este país.' Translate this sentence into English.
9) ¿Prefieres las vacaciones en el extranjero o dentro de tu propio país? ¿Por qué?

Accommodation and Travel

10) 'El hotel está cerca. Si sigues esta calle, verás la recepción.' What does this mean in English?
11) In Spanish, say you want to reserve a room for 4 nights. Say 2 features you want the room to have.
12) Julián says: 'En julio, me quedé en un camping en una tienda grande.' What is he saying?
13) List all the Spanish words in this section related to money and prices. There are 10 (plus 1 for Higher tier).
14) 'El tren es el tipo de transporte más directo al aeropuerto.' How would you say this in English?
15) How would you say that you need to take your suitcase and rucksack to the station in Spanish?
16) Imagine you're going on holiday to Cuba. Say how you'll travel there and describe where you'll stay.

Higher

17) 'I'll arrive at my destination late because we have returned to port.' Translate this into Spanish.
18) Belén says: 'Las fronteras internacionales están cerradas, entonces hay un retraso para las llegadas. Espero que el vuelo no tenga que regresar a Madrid.' Translate what she is saying into English.

Getting Around and What to Do

19) In Spanish, how would you say: 'We are going to get off the bus in the main square.'
20) Pablo says: 'El viaje durará menos tiempo si monto en bici o voy a pie en lugar de conducir. El tráfico está muy lento hoy.' Translate what he is saying into English.
21) What do the following Spanish words mean in English?
    a) la entrada b) el billete c) la vuelta d) perder e) el metro f) perderse
22) List all the places of interest from this section in Spanish. There are 7 (plus 1 for Higher tier).
23) 'There are lots of photos from the excursion on my camera.' Translate this sentence into Spanish.
24) Javi says: 'Pasé mucho tiempo en el puesto de recuerdos.' How would you say this in English?
25) Marta says: 'Voy a sacar un plano de la ciudad porque estoy perdida.' What is she saying?

H

26) Describe a problem that you had while you were on holiday.
27) ¿Cómo serían tus vacaciones ideales? ¿A qué destino irías y qué harías allí?

Quick Quiz

Technology

You could sing technology's praises until the cows come home, but that won't be enough in the exams — you'll need to talk about its disadvantages as well.

Head to the CGP RevisionHub for all your online content: www.cgpbooks.co.uk/Bueno

La tecnología — *Technology*

Vocabulary

el ordenador	*computer*	el vídeo	*video*	la ventaja	*advantage*
el móvil	*mobile phone*	el juego	*game*	la desventaja	*disadvantage*
el teléfono	*phone, telephone*	la recepción	*reception*	[H] el dispositivo	*device, gadget*
la tableta	*tablet (e.g. iPad)*	funcionar	*to function, work*	[H] conectar	*to connect, plug in*

Q&A Audio

Question

¿Cómo usas tu móvil?

How do you use your mobile phone?

Simple Answer

Uso mi móvil para mandar mensajes.

I use my mobile phone to send messages.

Extended Answer

Tener un móvil es crucial para mí. Sin mi móvil, no podría ni mandar ni recibir mensajes.

Having a mobile phone is crucial to me. Without my mobile phone, I couldn't send or receive messages.

Grammar — the conditional

To imagine what you 'could do' or 'couldn't do', use the conditional of 'poder' (see p.135) followed by the infinitive.

No podría hacer mis deberes sin un ordenador.

I couldn't do my homework without a computer.

La tecnología es muy útil porque puedes encontrar información rápidamente.

Technology is really useful because you can find information quickly.

and it has improved our quality of life — y ha mejorado nuestra calidad de vida

Sin embargo, una desventaja es que siempre tienes que estar conectado.

However, one disadvantage is that you always have to be connected.

if you lose reception, your device won't work — si pierdes la recepción tu dispositivo no funcionará

Uso mucho la tecnología en mi tiempo libre. Me gusta jugar a juegos en mi portátil y uso mi tableta para ver vídeos.

I use technology a lot in my free time. I like playing games on my laptop and I use my tablet to watch videos.

Practice Question

Q1 *Your friend Indra is talking to you about how her family uses technology. What is her opinion on the following points?*
Write **P** *for a* **positive** *opinion. Write* **N** *for a* **negative** *opinion.*
Write **P + N** *for a* **positive** *and* **negative** *opinion.*

LISTENING

Listening Track 15

a) Her cousins sending her messages *[1 mark]*

b) Her sister playing computer games *[1 mark]*

c) Her brother watching videos *[1 mark]*

d) Watching movies on her tablet *[1 mark]*

So many funny cat videos, so little time...

The thing is, I just find it so easy to get sucked into watching those adorable fluffy hooligans. I watch one video of them getting into mischief, then a recommended one — before I know it, three hours have gone by...

Quick Quiz

The Internet

Ah, the internet — handy for so many things, like that time I looked up how to make a flamingo out of bedsheets. It does have its problems though, so make sure you cover both sides...

¿Qué haces en Internet? — *What do you do on the internet?*

Vocabulary

el Internet	*internet*	comunicar	*to communicate*
la Red	*internet*	descubrir	*to discover*
online	*online*	en línea (Higher)	*online*
el sitio web	*website*	el usuario (Higher)	*user*
la app	*app*	conectarse (a Internet) (Higher)	*to connect (to the internet)*
la página	*page*		
el correo electrónico	*email*	navegar (Higher)	*to surf, browse*
bajar	*to download*	publicar (Higher)	*to publish, post*

No, Marcos... Not that kind of surfing.

Me encanta usar Internet para descubrir nuevas canciones y bajarlas. — *I love using the internet to discover new songs and download them.*

share images — compartir imágenes

Me gustan los sitios web que puedo usar para comunicarme con otra gente. — *I like websites that I can use to communicate with other people.*

Navego por diferentes páginas de arte porque me encanta el dibujo. — *I browse different art pages because I love drawing.*

I receive emails about art classes — Recibo correos electrónicos sobre clases de arte

Q&A Audio

Question

¿Por qué te gusta tu app favorita?

Why do you like your favourite app?

Simple Answer

Mi app favorita es un juego de acción. Lo encuentro divertido.

My favourite app is an action game. I find it fun.

Extended Answer

En mi app favorita hago compras online. Me gusta porque me ha permitido encontrar mucha ropa de segunda mano. Me divierto navegando por artículos diferentes.

On my favourite app I do online shopping. I like it because it has let me find a lot of second-hand clothing. I entertain myself browsing different items.

Las ventajas — *Advantages*

El uso de apps y sitios web nos ayuda en nuestras vidas diarias. — *The use of apps and websites helps us with our daily lives.*

Hay buenas opciones en Internet para investigar un tema que te interesa. — *There are good options on the Internet for researching a topic that interests you.*

Mis padres usan Internet para sus cuentas bancarias porque es más fácil que ir al banco. — *My parents use the internet for their bank accounts because it's easier than going to the bank.*

Gracias a la Red, es más cómodo hacer las compras. Ayer, compré unos regalos en línea y ya están aquí. — *Thanks to the internet, it's more comfortable to do your shopping. Yesterday, I bought some presents online and they're already here.*

easier to find discounts for — más fácil encontrar descuentos para

Grammar — comparisons

In Spanish, you can compare one thing to another using 'más ... que' (more ... than) and 'menos ... que' (less ... than) (see p.120).

Hacer compras por Internet es más rápido que ir a las tiendas.

Doing shopping on the internet is faster than going to the shops.

Los peligros — *Dangers*

Vocabulary

la información	*information*
robar	*to rob, steal*
peligroso/a	*dangerous*
seguro/a	*safe, secure*
el dato	*data, information*
la contraseña	*password*
desconocido/a	*unknown*
la seguridad	*security, safety*
la protección	*protection*

Higher (el dato – la protección)

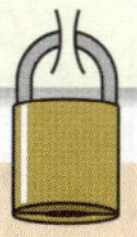

Grammar (Higher only) — the ... thing is that...

In Spanish, you can say 'the good thing' or 'the bad thing' by using 'lo' followed by 'bueno' or 'malo'.

Lo bueno / malo es que... — ***The good / bad thing is that...***

You can do this with any adjective:

Lo mejor / peor es que... — ***The best / worst thing is that...***

Lo peligroso es que... — ***The dangerous thing is that...***

To say 'the most... thing', just add 'más' before the adjective:

Lo más útil es que... — ***The most useful thing is that...***

Lo peor de Internet es que la gente puede usar tu contenido sin tu permiso.

The worst thing about the internet is that people can use your content without your permission.

share your photos with unknown people — compartir tus fotos con gente desconocida

Es fácil perder mucho tiempo en Internet y olvidarse de la vida real.

It's easy to waste a lot of time on the Internet and to forget about real life.

Es importante tener una contraseña segura para proteger tu identidad. Si alguien sabe tu contraseña, puede robar tu información.

It's important to have a secure password to protect your identity. If someone knows your password, they can steal your information.

use your account to post spam — usar tu cuenta para publicar basura

Hacer compras online me molesta porque es difícil saber si me gustará el producto sin verlo en realidad.

Shopping online annoys me because it's difficult to know if I will like the product without seeing it in reality.

the price of delivery is so expensive — el precio de entrega es muy caro

Practice Questions

Q1 *Write a description of ways you use the internet.*
You should write about 90 words in Spanish. Write about:

WRITING

- *how you use the internet*
- *what you used the internet for when you were younger*
- *something you will use the internet for in the future.* *[15 marks]*

Top Tip for Higher Students
✓ Use adverbs, e.g. 'actualmente', 'normalmente', or 'pronto' to give more detail about the time periods that you mention.

Higher

Q2 *You are listening to Alba and Mario discuss internet usage.*
Answer the following questions in English.

LISTENING

Listening Track 16

a) What **two** activities does Mario prefer to going on the internet? *[2 marks]*
b) What does Alba say is the best thing about the internet? *[1 mark]*
c) What does Mario say is a great danger on the internet? *[1 mark]*
d) Why does Alba worry about junk email? *[1 mark]*

Spiders love the internet — they're always on the web...

There are lots of ways to say what you love or what annoys you, like 'me encanta comunicar con mis amigos en Gobbledegook'. OK, maybe not that exactly, but I'm sure you get the point... Just try to keep it varied.

Quick Quiz

Social Media

If you want something to break up the endless social media scrolling, these pages are just the ticket...

Las redes sociales — *Social networks*

Vocabulary

la red	*network*	mandar	*to send*
social	*social*	el contenido (Higher)	*content*
la cuenta	*account*	el blog (Higher)	*blog*
el seguidor	*follower*	colgar (Higher)	*to post (photo)*
compartir	*share*	comentar (Higher)	*to comment*
subir	*to upload*	el comentario (Higher)	*comment*
popular	*popular*	charlar (Higher)	*to chat*
el mensaje	*message*	la reacción (Higher)	*reaction*
enviar	*to send*	el emoticón (Higher)	*emoji®*

Grammar (Higher only) — colgar (to post)

'Colgar' (to post) is a stem-changing verb (see p.128) that changes in the present tense:

Cuelgo las fotos que hago en mi blog.
I post the photos that I take on my blog.

Mis amigos cuelgan fotos en mi página.
My friends post photos on my page.

Hoy hay muchas apps de las redes sociales. Permiten al usuario hablar con otras personas y ver su contenido.

Nowadays there are many social networking apps. They allow the user to talk with others and to view their content.

to gain followers — ganar seguidores

Las redes sociales están cambiando la forma en la que nos comunicamos. Usamos reacciones e imágenes para expresarnos.

Social networks are changing the way in which we communicate. We use reactions and images to express ourselves.

Uso las redes sociales para... — *I use social networks to...*

Q&A Audio

Question

¿Usas las redes sociales?
Do you use social networks?

Simple Answer

Sí, comparto fotos con mis amigos en las redes sociales.
Yes, I share photos with my friends on social networks.

Extended Answer

Sí, las uso para encontrar nuevos cantantes porque muchos lanzan sus canciones en ellas. Sin embargo, intento poner un límite al tiempo que paso en las redes sociales.
Yes, I use them to find new singers because many release their songs on them. However, I try to put a limit on the time that I spend on social media.

Me encanta usar las redes sociales para hablar con mis amigos que viven lejos de mí.

I love using social networks to talk to my friends who live far away from me.

my cousins who live in Canada — mis primos que viven en Canadá

Uso mi cuenta para charlar con personas que comparten mis intereses. Además, cuelgo fotos de la comida que he preparado porque me gusta cocinar.

I use my account to chat with people who share my interests. Also, I post photos of food that I've prepared because I like cooking.

I've met in a game — he conocido en un juego

Paso demasiado tiempo en las redes sociales porque me pierdo leyendo comentarios.

I spend too much time on social media because I get lost reading comments.

when I could go out with my friends — cuando podría salir con mis amigos

Los problemas de las redes sociales — *The problems of social media*

Vocabulary

el contacto	*contact*	el ciberacoso	*cyberbullying*
contestar	*to answer, reply, respond*	la víctima	*victim*
guardar	*to keep, save*	la tendencia	*tendency, trend*

Higher

Una red antisocial

Gracias a las redes sociales, puedo seguir noticias mundiales y tendencias. Sin embargo, a veces es difícil apagar mi móvil.

Thanks to social networks, I can follow world news and trends. However, sometimes it's difficult to switch off my phone.

I always have someone I can chat to — siempre tengo alguien con quien puedo charlar

Por una parte, puedo ver una variedad de vídeos en las redes sociales. Por otra parte, la mayoría de los vídeos tienen muchos anuncios.

On the one hand, I can watch a variety of videos on social media. On the other hand, the majority of the videos have a lot of adverts.

I waste time looking at useless things — pierdo tiempo mirando cosas inútiles

'Pierdo' comes from 'perder', which is a stem-changing verb. See p.128.

Las redes sociales son útiles pero pueden ser preocupantes. Por ejemplo, el ciberacoso causa mucho daño a las víctimas.

Social networks are useful but they can be worrying. For example, cyberbullying causes a lot of hurt to victims.

Practice Questions

Q1 *Your Spanish friend asks you the questions below about your thoughts on social media. Reply to the questions out loud in Spanish.*

SPEAKING

a) ¿Cómo usas las redes sociales?

b) ¿Cuánto tiempo pasas en las redes sociales?

c) ¿Por qué te gusta tu red social favorita?

d) ¿Por qué es importante la tecnología? *[8 marks]*

Top Tip for Higher Students
✓ Use 'lo más útil es que...' or 'lo más divertido es que...' to describe why you like social media in extra detail.

Q2 *Toni has written a blog post about spending time on the internet and social networks. Read their comments and then answer the questions below in English.*

READING

Mucha gente dice que los jóvenes pasan demasiado tiempo en Internet, pero yo no estoy de acuerdo. En mi familia mis padres pasan mucho más tiempo en Internet que mis hermanos. Uso las redes sociales bastante. Como vivo lejos de mis amigos del colegio y no puedo verlos por las tardes, hablamos por nuestros móviles. Sin embargo, me molesta cuando tengo que esperar mucho tiempo para recibir una respuesta a mis mensajes.

a) In Toni's family, who spends the most time on the internet? *[1 mark]*

b) What does Toni use social media for? *[1 mark]*

c) What disadvantage of using social media does Toni give? *[1 mark]*

Update your status to 'revising' and give this vocab a like...

If you want to look really impressive, you can change the language settings on your social media apps to Spanish — you can keep your profiles updated and revise at the same time. Sounds like a win-win to me.

Media and Technology — Vocabulary

Sorry, your search for 'siesta' does not match any results. You might find some of these other words useful, though...

Technology

la tecnología	*technology*
moderno/a	*modern*
eléctrico/a	*electric*
el ordenador	*computer*
el móvil	*mobile phone*
el teléfono	*phone, telephone*
la tableta	*tablet (e.g. iPad)*
el teclado	*keyboard*
la pantalla	*screen, monitor*
el vídeo	*video*
el juego	*game*
el videojuego	*computer game*
la recepción	*reception (e.g. radio)*
funcionar	*to function, work*
apagar	*to turn off*
encender	*to turn on*
servir	*to serve*
la ventaja	*advantage, benefit*
la desventaja	*disadvantage*

Higher

el dispositivo	*device, gadget*
digital	*digital*
la radio	*radio*
el portátil	*laptop*
el diseño	*design*
el sistema	*system*
la memoria	*memory*
el volumen	*volume*
el sonido	*sound*
conectar	*to connect, plug in*
instalar	*to install*
cargar	*to charge (phone)*
la línea	*line (phone)*

The Internet

el Internet	*internet*
la Red	*internet*
los medios de comunicación	*media*
online	*online*
el sitio web	*website*
la app	*app*
la página	*page*
el correo electrónico	*email*
bajar	*to download*
comunicar	*to communicate*
descubrir	*to discover*
la información	*information*
robar	*to rob, steal*
el peligro	*danger*
peligroso/a	*dangerous*
seguro/a	*safe, secure*

Higher

en línea	*online*
el usuario	*user*
conectarse (a Internet)	*to connect (to the Internet)*
navegar	*to surf, browse*
publicar (en Internet)	*to publish, post (online)*
la investigación	*research*
investigar	*to research*
el dato	*data, information, fact*
la contraseña	*password*
desconocido/a	*unknown*
la seguridad	*security, safety*
la protección	*protection*
apropiado/a	*appropriate, suitable*

Social Media

la red	*network*
social	*social*
la cuenta	*account*
el seguidor	*follower*
el/la joven	*teenager, young person*
compartir	*to share*
subir	*to upload*
popular	*popular*
la conversación	*conversation*
el mensaje	*message*
enviar	*to send*
mandar	*to send*
el contacto	*contact*
contestar	*to answer, reply, respond*
guardar	*to keep, save*
grabar	*to record*

Higher

el contenido	*content*
el blog	*blog*
colgar	*to post (photo)*
comentar	*to comment*
el comentario	*remark, comment*
el diálogo	*conversation*
charlar	*to chat*
la reacción	*reaction*
el emoticón	*emoji*
el ciberacoso	*cyberbullying*
la víctima	*victim*
la tendencia	*tendency, trend*

Revision Summary Test for Section Ten

Another test? I'm just going to try the 'turn it off and on again' trick on my brain...

- These questions are **hard**, but they'll really help you see **how well you know your stuff**.
- Tackle the **revision summary test** below, or scan the QR code to do it **online**. You can **track your progress** online and see **which areas need more work**.
- There are **sample answers** for the test here: www.cgpbooks.co.uk/BuenoExtras

Summary Test

Technology

1) How many words for technological devices and equipment can you remember from this section? There are 6 you need to know (plus 3 for Higher tier).
2) ¿Cómo y cuándo usas la tecnología?
3) Write the Spanish for:
   a) modern b) electric c) reception d) to function e) to turn on f) to serve
4) What's the technology like at your school? Write about it in Spanish.
5) In Spanish, give at least one advantage and one disadvantage of technology.

H

6) Translate these sentences into Spanish: 'I bought a new laptop with more memory. I love the design and the sound quality. However, installing apps takes a long time.'

The Internet

7) Translate this sentence into English: 'Uso mi correo electrónico y diferentes sitios web para comunicarme con otra gente y mirar páginas interesantes.'
8) In Spanish, give two ways that you use the internet. Include as much detail as you can.
9) a) List as many words as you can think of that are related to internet security. There are 5 you need to know (plus 5 for Higher tier).
   b) Use some of these words to write about potential dangers online.
10) 'There are lots of fun online games that you can play with friends.' Say this in Spanish.

H

11) Translate these sentences into English: 'Necesitaba hacer más investigación para un proyecto de geografía. Navegué por Internet para encontrar la información necesaria.'

Social Media

12) Dolores says: 'There are too many young people that worry about being popular and having lots of followers.' Translate this sentence into Spanish. In Spanish, say whether you agree and why.
13) Which words can you think of from this section that would relate to sending messages and posting content online? There are 8 you need to know (plus 9 for Higher tier).
14) '¿Cómo usas las redes sociales? ¿Cuáles son las ventajas y desventajas?' Translate these questions into English, then answer them in Spanish, giving as much detail as you can.

Higher

15) Marcos says: 'Mis compañeros de clase piensan que las tendencias de las redes sociales son las más importantes del mundo. Para mí, es una idea tonta'. Translate this into English.
16) En español, escribe lo que piensas sobre la cuestión del ciberacoso.

Quick Quiz

At Home

Home is where the heart is — and where the marks are — so you need to be able to describe it.

¿Cómo es tu casa? — *What's your house like?*

Don't forget you can access your online content here: www.cgpbooks.co.uk/Bueno

Vocabulary

vivir	*to live*	el salón	*living room*
la casa	*house*	el baño	*bathroom*
el piso	*flat, apartment*	la cocina	*kitchen*
la planta	*floor*	el jardín	*garden*
agradable	*pleasant, nice*	la escalera	*stairs, ladder*
cómodo/a	*comfortable*	la pared	*(interior) wall*
el cuarto	*room*	la puerta	*door*
el dormitorio	*bedroom*	la ventana	*window*
la habitación	*bedroom*	la cama	*bed*

Grammar — there is / are

To say what there is in your house, use 'hay'. This word stays the same regardless of whether the thing you're talking about is singular or plural.

En mi casa, hay un salón.
In my house, there is a lounge.
Hay seis cuartos.
There are six rooms.

Vivo en una casa muy agradable. Hay una cocina grande con muchas ventanas y tengo mi propio dormitorio también.

I live in a really nice house. There's a big kitchen with a lot of windows and I have my own bedroom too.

but I share my bedroom with my brother — pero comparto mi dormitorio con mi hermano

Vivimos en un piso pequeño con dos habitaciones. Está en la tercera planta y mi cuarto favorito es el salón.

We live in a small flat with two bedrooms. It's on the third floor and my favourite room is the living room.

I hate how many stairs there are — odio cuántas escaleras hay

Me gustaría vivir en una casa moderna.

I'd like to live in a modern house.

Q&A Audio

Question

¿Cómo sería tu casa ideal?

What would your ideal house be like?

Simple Answer

Mi casa ideal sería muy grande.

My ideal house would be really big.

Extended Answer

Mi casa ideal tendría una piscina de lujo y un jardín enorme. Quisiera tener el espacio para invitar a todos mis amigos.

My ideal house would have a luxury swimming pool and a huge garden. I would like to have the space to invite all of my friends over.

Un día típico — *A typical day*

Vocabulary

despertarse	*to wake (up)*
levantarse	*to get up*
lavarse	*to have a wash*
vestirse	*to get dressed*
cambiarse	*to get changed*
dormirse	*to fall asleep*

Grammar — reflexive verbs

These verbs are reflexive — they say what you do to yourself. To use them, remove the reflexive pronoun (se), conjugate the verb as normal and put the reflexive pronoun back in front of the verb in its correct form (see p.137).

Me duermo a las diez de la noche. ***I fall asleep at 10 pm.***

Some of these verbs are stem-changing. See p.128.

Cada mañana, me despierto a las siete y luego me lavo.

Every morning, I wake up at seven o'clock and then I have a wash.

I always get dressed quickly — siempre me visto rápidamente

Después de volver del colegio me cambio y hago mis deberes.

After returning from school, I get changed and I do my homework.

I shower — me ducho

Las tareas — *Chores*

Vocabulary

la tarea	*chore*	limpiar	*to clean*	sacar	*to take out*
hacer	*to do, make*	lavar	*to wash*	la basura	*rubbish, junk*
ayudar	*to help*	pasear	*to take for a walk*	H cocinar	*to cook*
preparar	*to prepare*	el perro	*dog*	H arreglar	*to tidy*

Cada mañana hago mi cama. También ayudo a preparar el desayuno.	*Every morning, I make my bed. I also help to prepare breakfast.*
Después de la cena, tengo que lavar los platos y quitar la mesa.	*After dinner, I have to wash the dishes and clear the table.*
Los fines de semana paseo al perro, pero durante la semana mis padres lo hacen.	*On weekends I take the dog for a walk, but during the week my parents do it.*
Una tarea que no me gusta hacer es sacar la basura.	*One chore I don't like doing is taking out the rubbish.*

I put the dishwasher on — pongo el lavavajillas

tidy my bedroom — arreglar mi dormitorio

organising my clothes — ordenar mi ropa

Practice Questions

Q1 You are writing a blog about your house.
You should write about 90 words in Spanish. Mention:

- *what the house you live in is like*
- *what chores you did last week*
- *what your dream house would be like.* *[15 marks]*

WRITING

Top Tip for Higher Students
✓ Use possessive adjectives to describe your house, e.g. 'en la casa nuestra' or 'en el dormitorio mío'.

Q2 Your pen-pal from Colombia sends you this email about their typical day at home.
Read the passage and then write the correct letter for each question.

READING

Me encanta despertarme a las seis porque la casa está tranquila. Cuando me levanto, me visto y hago mi cama. Intento hacer mis deberes por la tarde, y a veces mis padres me ayudan. Cada noche, tengo que hacer una tarea. Anoche limpié el baño y ¡eso era horrible!

a) They love...
A. falling asleep late **B.** waking up early **C.** waking up late *[1 mark]*

b) In the afternoon, they...
A. do their homework **B.** wash the dishes **C.** get dressed *[1 mark]*

c) Last night, they...
A. made their bed **B.** cleaned the bathroom **C.** helped their parents *[1 mark]*

Ben treats revision like a chore — don't be like Ben...

To get to grips with this home vocab, you could try walking around your home and saying the room or part of the house in Spanish as you walk through it. Your family may think you're strange, but it might just help...

Quick Quiz

The Local Area

Ah, my local area. It's not much, but it's home. You'll need to say more than that to impress your examiner though, so crack on with pulling together some *100% truthful* details about your region.

Háblame de tu región — *Talk to me about your region*

Vocabulary

la región	*region*	el barrio	*neighbourhood, district*
el campo	*countryside*	la zona	*area, zone*
la ciudad	*city, town*	industrial	*industrial*
el pueblo	*village, small town*	principal	*main, principal*
el centro	*centre*	la comunidad	*community*

Simón lives in 'the zone'.

Vivo en la zona industrial de una ciudad. No está en el centro, pero hay mucho ruido. — *I live in the industrial area of a city. It isn't in the centre, but there is a lot of noise.*

there are options for shopping — hay opciones para hacer compras

Mi pueblo está en el campo. Es muy bonito pero no hay muchos sitios para visitar. — *My village is in the countryside. It's very pretty, but there aren't many places to visit.*

Q&A Audio

Question

¿Dónde vives?

Where do you live?

Simple Answer

Vivo en un pueblo en Cumbria.

I live in a village in Cumbria.

Extended Answer

Vivo en un pueblito en el campo. Preferiría vivir en una ciudad porque hay más que hacer. Aquí solo hay bosques.

I live in a little town in the countryside. I would prefer to live in a city because there is more to do. Here there are only forests.

Grammar — adding 'ito'

In Spanish, you can add bits onto the ends of nouns and adjectives to change their meanings. Adding 'ito/a/os/as' makes the word smaller or cuter. Find out more on p.104.

En mi barrio hay... — *In my neighbourhood, there is...*

Vocabulary

se puede	*one can, you can*	el café	*café*	el estadio	*stadium*
el ayuntamiento	*town hall*	el gimnasio	*gym*	la iglesia	*church*
la biblioteca	*library*	la piscina	*swimming pool*	la mezquita	*mosque*
el parque	*park*	el banco	*bank, bench*	la sinagoga	*synagogue*

En mi barrio, hay un gran parque, un gimnasio y dos cafés. — *In my neighbourhood, there's a big park, a gym and two cafés.*

a famous restaurant — un restaurante famoso

Mi ciudad tiene varios edificios hermosos. Aquí se puede visitar una biblioteca muy antigua. — *My city has various beautiful buildings. Here one can visit a really ancient library.*

a historic mosque — una mezquita histórica

Me gustaría ver una nueva piscina en mi pueblo. — *I'd like to see a new swimming pool in my village.*

more green spaces — más espacios verdes

¡Vamos de compras! — *Let's go shopping!*

Vocabulary

el centro comercial	*shopping centre*	el producto	*product*	el zapato	*shoe*
la tienda	*shop*	la marca	*make, brand*	el reloj	*clock, watch*
cerrar	*to close*	la ropa	*clothes, clothing*	la venta (Higher)	*sale*
comprar	*to buy*	la moda	*fashion*	la cola (Higher)	*queue*
vender	*to sell*	la camiseta	*T-shirt*	cobrar (Higher)	*to charge (money)*
		el pantalón	*trousers*	devolver (Higher)	*to return, give back*

Los fines de semana me gusta ir de compras con mis amigos. Normalmente compramos caramelos y vemos una película en el cine.

On weekends, I like to go shopping with my friends. Normally we buy sweets and see a movie at the cinema.

Prefiero ver la ropa en una tienda. Cuando hago las compras online, los artículos nunca son mi talla exacta y tengo que devolverlos.

I prefer to see clothes in a shop. When I do online shopping, the items are never my exact size and I have to return them.

Las tiendas locales están cerrando porque mucha gente va a los centros comerciales más grandes. Creo que es triste para la comunidad.

The local shops are closing because many people are going to the bigger shopping centres. I think it's sad for the community.

Practice Questions

Q1 Read aloud the following text. *[5 marks]*

SPEAKING

> *Mi región es bastante grande. Vivo en un pueblo industrial. Creo que mi pueblo necesita más parques. Me gusta ir al centro comercial. Mañana voy de compras con mi hermana.*

Top Tip for Higher Students
✓ Use the subjunctive mood correctly, e.g. 'Es decepcionante que solo tenga un parque.'

Answer the questions below out loud in Spanish.

a) Describe tu pueblo.
b) ¿Qué no te gusta de tu pueblo?
c) ¿Qué se puede hacer en tu región?
d) ¿Qué piensas de los centros comerciales? *[10 marks]*

Higher

Q2 Ridwan is writing to you about what his region is like.
Read the passage and then answer the questions below in English.

READING

> *La gente dice que no hay mucho que hacer en mi región. Es cierto que aquí no hay muchas tiendas y las que tenemos cobran mucho por sus productos. En cambio, hay que reconocer los edificios maravillosos que tenemos aquí. Por ejemplo, yo podría pasar un día entero en el museo de arte porque me parece muy interesante.*

a) What is generally said about where Ridwan lives? *[1 mark]*
b) What does Ridwan say about existing shops in his local area? Give **one** detail. *[1 mark]*
c) What is **one** positive thing that Ridwan says about his local area? *[1 mark]*

Why do trousers come in pairs? They're pantalonely...

'La ropa' is always a singular noun even when the English word is plural. So 'my clothes are sad' would be 'mi ropa está triste' rather than 'mis ropas están tristes'. Might want to give your poor clothing a pep talk...

Quick Quiz

Directions and Weather

The vocab on these pages will help you get by in Spain... and when you're in your exam.

¿Dónde está? — *Where is it?*

Vocabulary

aquí	*here*	la calle	*street*
allí	*there, over there*	la esquina	*corner (of a street)*
cerca	*close, near, nearby*	el kilómetro	*kilometre*
lejos	*far (away)*	el metro	*metre*
delante	*in front, ahead*	hacia (Higher)	*towards*
detrás	*behind*	fuera (Higher)	*outside*
entre	*between, among*	situado (Higher)	*situated, located*

Grammar — 'estar' for locations

In Spanish, there are two verbs for 'to be' — 'ser' and 'estar'. To describe where things are, you need to use 'estar' — see p.130. You can also use 'estar situado' to say where something is situated.

El ayuntamiento está entre la biblioteca y el banco. — *The town hall is between the library and the bank.*

Mi casa no está lejos del centro del pueblo. Está en la esquina de la calle. — *My house isn't far from the town centre. It's on the corner of the street.*

Hay un café delante del parque. Está fuera de la ciudad. — *There's a café in front of the park. It's outside of the city.*

quite close to here — bastante cerca de aquí

¿Cómo se llega a...? — *How do you get to...?*

Vocabulary

andar	*to walk*	el norte	*north*	encontrar	*to find*
tomar	*to take*	el sur	*south*	el lugar	*place, position*
la izquierda	*left*	el este	*east*	cruzar (H)	*to cross*
la derecha	*right (direction)*	el oeste	*west*	el camino (H)	*way, route, path*

Toma la salida de la derecha y el parque temático no está muy lejos. — *Take the right exit and the theme park isn't too far.*

Follow the road — Sigue la carretera

Si te pierdes, anda hacia el centro donde verás una iglesia alta. — *If you get lost, walk towards the centre where you'll see a tall church.*

El estadio está al oeste de la ciudad. Es muy fácil encontrarlo. — *The stadium is to the west of the city. It's very easy to find it.*

Ese camino te lleva en la dirección equivocada. Ve a la izquierda y el centro comercial está allí. — *That path leads you in the wrong direction. Go left and the shopping centre is there.*

Grammar — giving instructions

To give instructions, use the imperative. See how to form it on p.143.

Cruza la calle y luego sigue las señales. — ***Cross the street and then follow the signs.***

Toma la segunda salida a la derecha. — ***Take the second exit on the right.***

Ve en esta dirección — está cerca. — ***Go in this direction — it's nearby.***

Hace buen / mal tiempo — *The weather is good / bad*

Vocabulary

el tiempo	*weather*	el calor	*heat, hot*	la temperatura	*temperature*
el clima	*climate*	el viento	*wind*	el grado	*degree*
hace (+ noun)	*it is (+ weather noun)*	la lluvia	*rain*	frío/a (adj.)	*cold*
el sol	*sun*	llover	*to rain*	fresco/a	*cool*

Q&A Audio

Question

¿Qué tiempo hace donde vives?

What's the weather like where you live?

Simple Answer

De momento hace mucho frío.

It's very cold at the moment.

'frío' can be used as an adjective (e.g. 'No me gusta el tiempo frío.') or as a noun with the verb 'hacer' (e.g. 'Hace frío hoy.')

Extended Answer

Hoy hace mucho sol en el sur, pero mañana habrá nubes. Eso me parece genial, porque prefiero el tiempo cuando no hace demasiado calor.

Today it's very sunny in the south, but tomorrow there will be clouds. This seems great to me, because I prefer the weather when it's not too hot.

Esta semana lloverá en el este del país, pero hará sol aquí.	*This week it will rain in the east of the country, but it will be sunny here.*
Ayer hizo mal tiempo en mi región. Había un viento fresco.	*Yesterday the weather was bad in my region. There was a cool wind.*
Espero que haga sol esta primavera. No me gusta la lluvia.	*I hope that it's sunny this spring. I don't like the rain.*
El verano pasado pasé mal las vacaciones debido a las temperaturas altas.	*Last summer I didn't enjoy the holidays due to the high temperatures.*

Grammar — hace + noun

To describe the weather in English, you often use 'to be', e.g. 'it's sunny'. In Spanish, you have to use the verb 'hacer' instead:

Hace sol / viento / frío.

It's sunny / windy / cold.

Remember you can put the verbs into different tenses too.

Practice Questions

Q1 *A tour guide is giving you directions to different places in a city you're visiting. Listen to the description of where each place is and choose the correct letter from the box for each question.*

LISTENING — Listening Track 17

A. *Behind* **B.** *To the left of* **C.** *To the right of* **D.** *On the corner of*

a) The town hall is ... the park.
b) The shopping centre is ... the cinema.
c) The clothes shop is ... this street.
d) The gym is ... the swimming pool. *[4 marks]*

Higher

Q2 *Translate these sentences into Spanish.*

WRITING

a) *My friend's house isn't far from mine.*
b) *We will ask for the right way.*
c) *Last autumn it barely rained.*
d) *Cold temperatures are the best.*

[8 marks]

Don't let revision rain on your parade...

I'd recommend writing out verb tables for both 'ser' and 'estar'. You'll end up using them a lot when you talk about directions and the weather. Of course, it'd be typical if you got nice weather during your exams...

Where People Live — Vocabulary

These pages should point you in the right direction for all the vocab you'll need to describe where you live.

The Home

vivir	*to live*
la casa	*house*
el piso	*flat, apartment, floor (of building)*
la planta	*floor*
el/la vecino/a	*neighbour*
el/la dueño/a	*owner, landlord*
describir	*to describe*
agradable	*pleasant, nice*
cómodo/a	*comfortable*
el espacio	*space, room*
el cuarto	*room*
el dormitorio	*bedroom*
la habitación	*bedroom*
el salón	*living room*
el baño	*bathroom*
la cocina	*kitchen*
el jardín	*garden*
el estudio	*study, studio*
la escalera	*stairs, ladder*
bajar	*to go down*
subir	*to go up*
la pared	*(interior) wall*
la puerta	*door*
la ventana	*window*
la mesa	*table*
la cama	*bed*

despertar	*to wake (someone) (up)*
despertarse	*to wake (up)*
levantarse	*to get up*
lavarse	*to have a wash*
vestir	*to dress*
vestirse	*to get dressed*
cambiarse	*to get changed*
quitarse	*to take off (clothes)*
dormir	*to sleep*
dormirse	*to fall asleep*
la tarea	*chore*
hacer	*to do, make*
ayudar	*to help*
preparar	*to prepare*
limpiar	*to clean*
lavar	*to wash*
pasear	*to take for a walk*
el perro	*dog*
sacar	*to take out*
la basura	*rubbish, junk*

Higher

el hogar	*home*
el rincón	*corner (inside shape, house)*
acostar	*to put to bed*
acostarse	*to go to bed*
cocinar	*to cook*
arreglar	*to tidy*

The Local Area — Places

la región	*region*
el campo	*countryside, pitch, field (sport)*
la ciudad	*city, town*
el pueblo	*village, small town*
bonito/a	*pretty, nice, beautiful*
el centro	*centre, middle*
las afueras	*outskirts, suburbs*
el barrio	*neighbourhood, district*
la zona	*area, zone*
industrial	*industrial*
principal	*main, principal*
la comunidad	*community*
se puede	*you can (general), one can*
el edificio	*building*
el ayuntamiento	*Spanish town council, city council, town hall*
la plaza	*square*
el puente	*bridge*

la biblioteca	*library*
el parque	*park*
el café	*café*
el restaurante	*restaurant*
el cine	*cinema*
el teatro	*theatre*
el gimnasio	*gym*
la piscina	*swimming pool*
el hospital	*hospital*
el banco	*(financial) bank, bench*
la estación	*station*
el estadio	*stadium*
la iglesia	*church*
la mezquita	*mosque*
la sinagoga	*synagogue*

Higher

el/la ciudadano/a	*citizen, member of the public*
la construcción	*building*
la fuente	*fountain*

The Local Area — Shopping

el centro comercial	*shopping centre*
el supermercado	*supermarket*
la tienda	*shop*
abierto/a	*open, unlocked*
cerrado/a	*closed*
cerrar	*to close*
la(s) compra(s)	*shopping*
ir de compras	*to go shopping*
el cliente	*client, customer*
la caja	*till (in shop)*
la bolsa	*bag*
la tarjeta	*bank card*
comprar	*to buy, purchase*
gastar	*to spend (money)*
costar	*to cost*
vender	*to sell*
el producto	*product*
el artículo	*product, item*
la marca	*make, brand*

el tamaño	*size, dimension*
la ropa	*clothes, clothing*
la moda	*fashion*
de moda	*in fashion, fashionable*
la camisa	*shirt*
la camiseta	*T-shirt*
el pantalón	*trousers*
el vestido	*dress*
la falda	*skirt*
el zapato	*shoe*
el reloj	*clock, watch*

Higher

la sección	*department (in store)*
la cola	*queue*
la venta	*sale*
el descuento	*discount*
los gastos	*expenses, costs, spending*
cobrar	*to charge (money)*
devolver	*to return, give back*

Directions and Weather

la dirección	*address, direction*
aquí	*here*
allí	*there, over there*
cerca	*close, near, nearby*
lejos	*far (away)*
delante	*in front, ahead*
detrás	*behind*
entre	*between, among*
la calle	*street*
la esquina	*corner (of a street)*
la carretera	*road*
el kilómetro	*kilometre*
el metro	*metre*
perderse	*to get lost*
andar	*to walk*
tomar	*to take*
la izquierda	*left*
la derecha	*right (direction)*
el norte	*north*
el sur	*south*
el este	*east*
el oeste	*west*
encontrar	*to find*
el lugar	*place, position*
el tiempo	*weather*
el clima	*climate*
hace (+ noun)	*it is (+ weather noun or adjective)*

el sol	*sun*
el calor	*heat, hot*
el viento	*wind*
la lluvia	*rain*
llover	*to rain*
la temperatura	*temperature*
el grado	*degree (temperature)*
frío/a (adj.)	*cold*
fresco/a	*cool*
la estación	*season (of the year)*
la primavera	*spring*
el verano	*summer*
el otoño	*autumn*
el invierno	*winter*

Higher

hacia	*toward, towards*
fuera	*outside, out*
situado/a	*situated, located*
cruzar	*to cross*
el camino	*way, route, path*
la nube	*cloud*

Ah... The perfect weather for a walk.

Revision Summary Test for Section Eleven

I'm sure you're all fired up to go and get your chores done now, but have a go at this test first.

- These questions are **really tricky**, but they'll help you see **how well you know your stuff**.
- Tackle the **revision summary test** below, or scan the QR code to do it **online**. You can **keep track of your progress** online and see **which areas need more work**.
- There are **sample answers** here: www.cgpbooks.co.uk/BuenoExtras

Summary Test

At Home

1) How many nouns can you remember that relate to rooms and parts of a house? There are 14 in this section (plus 1 for Higher tier).
2) In Spanish, write about what you like and dislike about your house.
3) Translate this sentence into Spanish: 'My bedroom has a comfortable bed and a small table.'
4) a) List the verbs from this section to do with a typical routine. There are 10 (plus 2 for Higher tier).
   b) Use some of these words to describe in Spanish what you typically do after school.
5) '¿Qué haces para ayudar en casa?' Translate this question into English, then answer it in Spanish.

Higher

6) Translate this sentence into English: 'Nuestros vecinos nos han dicho que querían alquilar una casa nueva, pero desafortunadamente el dueño de la casa los rechazó.'
7) In Spanish, describe two characteristics you would like your house to have.

The Local Area

8) En español, y con frases completas, describe tu barrio. ¿Qué hay? ¿Qué te gusta?
9) 'Vivo en la zona principal de mi ciudad. Aquí se pueden encontrar un estadio famoso y un parque grande.' Translate these sentences into English.
10) List the 3 religious buildings that appear in this section.
11) Write the Spanish for: a) pitch b) industrial c) town hall d) café e) bench
12) In Spanish, describe a time you went shopping, including as much relevant vocabulary as you can.
13) List the 9 nouns from this section to do with clothes.
14) Translate these words and give their opposites in Spanish: a) closed b) to save (money) c) to buy

Higher

15) '¿Cómo mejorarías tu región?' Translate this question into English and answer it in Spanish.
16) Translate these sentences into Spanish: 'To celebrate the building of a new section in the supermarket, there will be big discounts. However, the queues will be really long.'

Directions and Weather

17) 'Para llegar al hospital, toma la carretera a la izquierda.' Translate this sentence into English.
18) a) In Spanish, give all the directions on a compass.
    b) List the words in this section that describe an object's position. There are 7 (plus 2 for Higher tier).
19) How would you say in Spanish that the gym is on the corner of the street, to the right of the theatre?
20) '¿Qué tiempo hace hoy?' Translate this question into English, then answer it in Spanish.
21) What's the English for...?
    a) la dirección b) el kilómetro c) el metro d) andar e) el clima
22) 'Mañana hará calor. Las temperaturas van a subir a los 32 grados.' What's tomorrow's forecast?
23) In Spanish, write about your favourite season of the year. Include as much detail as you can.

Higher

24) Translate this sentence into Spanish: 'My friend got lost on the route towards my house, which is situated outside the city. She waited in an obvious place to be able to find her easily.'
25) Pick two locations in your town, and in Spanish, say how to get from one to the other.

Quick Quiz

Environmental Problems

It's time to talk about the issues that affect the environment — serious stuff.

El medioambiente — *The environment*

Remember there's also lots of online content here: www.cgpbooks.co.uk/Bueno

Vocabulary

el problema	*problem*	contaminar	*to pollute*	el aumento	*increase, rise*
destruir	*to destroy, ruin*	tirar	*to throw*	cortar	*to cut (up)*
el bosque	*forest, wood*	el plástico	*plastic*	emitir	*to emit, give off*
el daño	*harm, damage*	la basura	*rubbish, junk*	el humo	*smoke, fumes*
la contaminación	*pollution*	la energía	*energy, power*	el recurso	*resource*

(Higher: el aumento, cortar, emitir, el humo, el recurso)

El mundo ha perdido muchos de sus bosques. Se cortan árboles para producir más recursos. — *The world has lost many of its forests. Trees are cut down to produce more resources.*

El uso de ciertos combustibles contamina el aire. — *The use of certain fuels pollutes the air.*

En mi barrio... — *In my neighbourhood...*

Q&A Audio

Question

¿Qué problemas con el medioambiente hay en tu barrio?

What environmental problems are there in your neighbourhood?

Simple Answer

En mi barrio las calles están llenas de basura.

In my neighbourhood the streets are filled with rubbish.

Extended Answer

La contaminación acústica es un gran problema en el pueblo donde vivo. También hay muchas obras porque el pueblo está creciendo.

Noise pollution is a big problem in the town where I live. There are also lots of building works because the town is growing.

En mi región los ríos están sucios. La gente tira plástico y basura a ellos. — *In my region the rivers are dirty. People throw plastic and rubbish in them.*

smell awful — huelen fatal

Vivo en una zona industrial. Las fábricas aquí usan mucha energía. — *I live in an industrial area. The factories here use a lot of energy.*

emit a lot of fumes — emiten muchos humos

Practice Question

SPEAKING

Q1 *Look at the two photos below. Talk in Spanish about what is in the photos. You should talk for about a minute and say something about each photo.*

Top Tip for Higher Students
✓ Start a relative clause by using relative pronouns, e.g. 'lo cual' or 'donde', to add more detail to your sentences.

[5 marks]

Pollution is rubbish...

You'll get fifteen minutes of prep time before the speaking exam to read the questions and jot down some notes. Also, don't forget to mention both photos in your photo card question — you'll lose marks if you don't.

Quick Quiz

Environmental Impacts

Now you've seen some problems the environment faces, I've got a page for you about their impacts.

Los efectos — *The effects*

Vocabulary

la causa	*cause*	el río	*river*	el impacto	*impact*
la naturaleza	*nature*	el olor	*smell, odour*	desaparecer	*to disappear*
la especie	*species*	el cambio climático	*climate change*	contribuir	*to contribute*
la planta	*plant*	preocupar	*to worry*	el incendio	*fire*
el cielo	*sky*	debido (a)	*due (to)*	el desastre	*disaster*

Higher: el impacto, desaparecer, contribuir, el incendio, el desastre

El daño a la Tierra — *The damage to Earth*

Parece que no hay espacio suficiente para toda la basura que producimos. Sin embargo, si creamos más vertederos, podrían afectar a nuestros ríos.	*It seems that there isn't enough space for all the rubbish that we produce. However, if we create more landfills, they could affect our rivers.*
El uso excesivo de productos químicos puede matar muchos cultivos y plantas.	*The excessive use of chemical products can kill many crops and plants.*
Los científicos creen que la destrucción de los bosques contribuye al cambio climático. Si no actuamos, el nivel del mar va a aumentar aún más.	*Scientists believe that the destruction of forests contributes to climate change. If we don't act, the sea level will rise even more.*
Algunas personas dicen que no habrá recursos suficientes para las generaciones del futuro si seguimos usándolos al ritmo actual.	*Some people say that there won't be enough resources for future generations if we keep using them at the current rate.*
Me preocupo que más especies desaparecerán si no dejamos de destruir los hábitats.	*I worry that more species will disappear if we don't stop destroying habitats.*

Grammar — the inflectional/proper future

To talk about what things will be like in the future, you can use the inflectional future tense. See p.134.

Pienso que el cambio climático afectará a todos. — ***I think that climate change will affect everyone.***

Practice Question

Q1 *Translate these sentences about environmental impacts into English.*

READING

a) *Construir más zonas industriales aumenta el uso de energía.*
b) *La contaminación del aire puede causar enfermedades graves.*
c) *Hemos perdido muchas especies debido al daño causado a los bosques.*
d) *Según varios estudios recientes, el clima está cambiando.*

[8 marks]

This page will have a positive impact on your Spanish...

The inflectional future tense is really handy for talking about your predictions for the future. It's worth making a verb table for all the future endings — then they'll all be in one place for when you need them.

Protecting the Environment

Quick Quiz

Time to round off these environment pages by looking at the ways we can protect it. Lovely stuff.

Proteger al medioambiente — *Protecting the environment*

Vocabulary

proteger	*to protect*	limpiar	*to clean*	conservar	*to conserve*
ayudar	*to help*	reducir	*to reduce*	fundar	*to set up*
resolver	*to solve, resolve*	apagar	*to turn off*	la campaña	*campaign*
salvar	*to save, rescue*	la organización	*organisation*	la manifestación	*protest*
reciclar	*to recycle*	en contra	*against*	efectivo/a	*effective*
recoger	*to pick up, tidy up*	a favor	*in favour*	el asunto	*matter, issue*

Higher (conservar – el asunto)

¿Qué podemos hacer? — *What can we do?*

Q&A Audio

Question

¿Qué haces para proteger el medioambiente?

What do you do to protect the environment?

Simple Answer

Nunca compro bolsas nuevas y reciclo mi papel.

I never buy new bags and I recycle my paper.

Extended Answer

Intento no utilizar bolsas nuevas sino reciclar las viejas. Mi padre y yo vamos al centro de reciclaje para reciclar el vidrio. Además, camino al colegio para conservar la energía y reducir el uso de combustible.

I try not to use new bags but rather recycle old ones. My dad and I go to the recycling centre to recycle glass. Also, I walk to school to conserve energy and to reduce fuel use.

Apoyo a organizaciones que quieren salvar nuestros bosques y reducir la deforestación.

I support organisations that want to save our forests and reduce deforestation.

Estoy participando en una campaña de ahorro de energía. Apagaré las luces de casa para reducir la cantidad de energía que uso. Si todos hacen este cambio pequeño, podría tener un gran impacto.

I'm participating in an energy-saving campaign. I'll switch off the lights at home to reduce the amount of energy I use. If everyone makes this small change, it could have a big impact.

El mes pasado mi hermano mayor fue a una manifestación en contra de la moda rápida.

Last month my older brother went to a protest against fast fashion.

Practice Question

Q1 *Listen to Carmen talk about what her town is doing to protect the environment. Answer the following questions in English about what she says.*

LISTENING

Listening Track 18

a) i) What are the people of her town going to do in March? *[1 mark]*

ii) Why is Carmen in favour of this idea? *[1 mark]*

b) i) What have the town council asked young people to do? *[1 mark]*

ii) What does Carmen suggest everyone does instead? *[1 mark]*

I once met a 'green' comedian — he only used recycled material...

You'll get more marks in the exams if you give reasons for your answers. Try adding 'porque' to your sentences to add extra detail, e.g. 'mi hermano no hizo sus deberes porque no quería cortar más árboles'.

Quick Quiz

Social Issues

And the problems don't end there — you still have social issues to get through.

La falta de comida y el paro — *Food shortages and unemployment*

Vocabulary

la sociedad	*society*	el hambre	*hunger*	la economía	*economy*
la gente	*people*	la falta	*lack, shortage*	H la preocupación	*worry, concern*
el tema	*issue, subject*	el paro	*unemployment*	H la pobreza	*poverty*

Quiero que todo el mundo tenga acceso a la comida porque es un derecho básico. El hambre debería importarnos.

I want everyone to have access to food because it is a basic right. Hunger should matter to us.

we need it to survive — la necesitamos para sobrevivir

El paro es una preocupación muy grave porque sin empleo es difícil vivir bien.

Unemployment is a very serious concern because without a job it's difficult to live well.

it can affect people's mental health — puede afectar la salud mental de la gente

El delito — *Crime*

Vocabulary

la violencia	*violence*	H el conflicto	*conflict*	H cometer	*to commit (crime)*
el delito	*crime*	H amenazar	*to threaten*	H la culpa	*blame, fault*

El problema del delito es grave en mi barrio. Un grupo de ladrones robó a mi vecino el mes pasado pero por suerte la policía encontró a los culpables.

Crime is a serious problem in my neighbourhood. A group of thieves stole from my neighbour last month but luckily the police found the culprits.

Una manera en que podemos reducir la violencia es dar a la gente espacios seguros para expresar sus emociones y sentimientos.

One way that we can reduce violence is to give people safe spaces to express their emotions and feelings.

Las diferencias sociales — *Social differences*

Vocabulary

la diferencia	*difference*	Higher: la discriminación	*discrimination*
justo/a	*fair, just*	Higher: la igualdad	*equality*
comparar	*to compare*	Higher: la libertad	*freedom*

Grammar — the verb 'should'

To say what someone should do, use '<u>deber</u>' in the conditional followed by the <u>infinitive</u>.

<u>Deberías</u> dar tu apoyo.
<u>You should</u> give your support.

La discriminación es un problema grave. Muchas personas son juzgadas por el color de su piel, su sexualidad o su género. Deberíamos trabajar juntos para crear un mundo igual.

Discrimination is a serious problem. Many people are judged for the colour of their skin, their sexuality or their gender. We should work together to create an equal world.

Los muy ricos tienen vidas de lujo en comparación con la gente más pobre. No parece justo.

The very rich have lives of luxury compared to poorer people. It doesn't seem fair.

Ayudar a la sociedad — *Helping society*

Vocabulary

importar	*to matter, be important*	el apoyo	*support, backing*	elegir (Higher)	*to choose, elect*
mejorar	*to improve, make better*	la actitud	*attitude*	la solución (Higher)	*solution, answer*
dar	*to give*	la felicidad	*happiness*	el beneficio (Higher)	*benefit*

Q&A Audio

Question

¿Qué haces para apoyar tu comunidad?

What do you do to support your community?

Simple Answer

Los lunes ayudo en un club deportivo del colegio.

On Mondays I help out in a sports club at school.

Extended Answer

Llevo un año ayudando en un banco de alimentos. Estoy agradecido de poder apoyar a la gente porque siento que estoy ayudando a mejorar la situación.

I've been helping out in a food bank for a year. I'm grateful to be able to support people because I feel like I'm helping to improve their situation.

Dar apoyo a las organizaciones benéficas es una solución para mejorar la sociedad.	*Giving support to charitable organisations is one solution to improve society.*
Participo en un club juvenil cerca de mí. Es una idea genial porque ofrece muchos beneficios a los jóvenes.	*I'm participating in a youth club near me. It's a great idea because it offers a lot of benefits to young people.*
Los fines de semana ayudo a los ancianos de mi comunidad. Para mí es importante traerles felicidad especialmente cuando tanta gente sufre de soledad.	*At the weekend I help the elderly in my community. It's important to me to bring them happiness, especially when so many people suffer from loneliness.*

Practice Questions

Q1 *Write a description of social problems relevant to you. You should write about 90 words in Spanish. Write about:* WRITING

- *a social problem that exists where you live*
- *something that you've done in the past to make a difference in your area*
- *something that people should do to improve a social problem in your area.* *[15 marks]*

Top Tip for Higher Students
✓ Use the plural form of the conditional, e.g. 'deberíamos...' (we should...).

Higher

Q2 *In an interview, Juan is talking about social problems in his area. Fill each gap in the sentences below with **one** word.* LISTENING

Listening Track 19

a) Many people are affected by ______.
Others could help by supporting the appropriate ______. *[2 marks]*

b) In schools, ______ is an issue.
It is important that each student has equal ______. *[2 marks]*

I know — it's *justa* lot to take in sometimes...

Don't worry about all the tricky vocab here. You can always make it easier by sorting the vocab into smaller topics (e.g. jobs, food, crime, equality and helping people), then learning the words just one topic at a time.

The Environment and Social Issues — Vocabulary

This vocab list is made from 100% re-usable material. Give it a thorough read as you'll need to recycle it later...

Environmental Problems

el medioambiente / el medio ambiente	*environment, natural world*
el problema	*problem*
grave	*serious, grave*
causar	*to cause*
producir	*to produce, cause*
aumentar	*to increase*
destruir	*to destroy, ruin*
el bosque	*forest, wood*
el árbol	*tree*
el daño	*harm, damage*
la contaminación	*pollution*
contaminar	*to pollute, contaminate*
tirar	*to throw*
el plástico	*plastic*
la basura	*rubbish, junk*
limpio/a	*clean*
sucio/a	*dirty*
la fábrica	*factory*
construir	*to build*
el ruido	*noise*
el aire	*air*
la luz	*light, electricity*
la energía	*energy, power*
usar	*to use*
el uso	*use*

Higher

el planeta	*planet*
el entorno	*environment, surroundings*
los alrededores	*surrounding area, vicinity*
el aumento	*increase, rise*
crecer	*to grow, increase*
existir	*to exist*
cortar	*to cut (up)*
el suelo	*ground, floor*
emitir	*to emit, give off*
el humo	*smoke, fumes*
químico/a (adj.)	*chemical*
fabricar	*to manufacture, produce*
las obras	*roadworks, building works*
utilizar	*to use*
el recurso	*resource*
el gas	*gas*
la piedra	*stone, rock*
la madera	*wood*
el oro	*gold*
el vidrio	*glass*

Environmental Impacts

la causa	*cause*
el efecto	*effect*
la naturaleza	*nature*
la especie	*species*
la planta	*plant*
la tierra	*earth, land, ground*
el cielo	*sky*
el río	*river*
el cambio climático	*climate change*
el fuego	*fire*
el olor	*smell, odour*
seco/a	*dry*
roto/a	*torn*
preocupar	*to worry, be a worry*
preocuparse por	*to worry about*
debido (a)	*owing (to), due (to)*
la prueba	*trial, proof*
la cifra	*figure, number, amount*
el/la científico/a	*scientist*

H

el impacto	*impact*
la consecuencia	*consequence*
como consecuencia	*in consequence, as a result*

Higher

acuático/a	*water, aquatic*
desaparecer	*to disappear*
matar	*to kill*
sufrir	*to suffer*
contribuir	*to contribute*
abandonar	*to abandon, leave (a place)*
el cultivo	*crop*
el incendio	*fire*
quemar	*to burn*
huele (a)	*it smells (of)*
el desastre	*disaster*
natural	*natural*
sobrevivir	*to survive*
advertir	*to warn*
negar	*to deny, refuse*
negarse a (+ infinitive)	*to refuse to*
la fuente	*source*
el factor	*factor*
el nivel	*level*

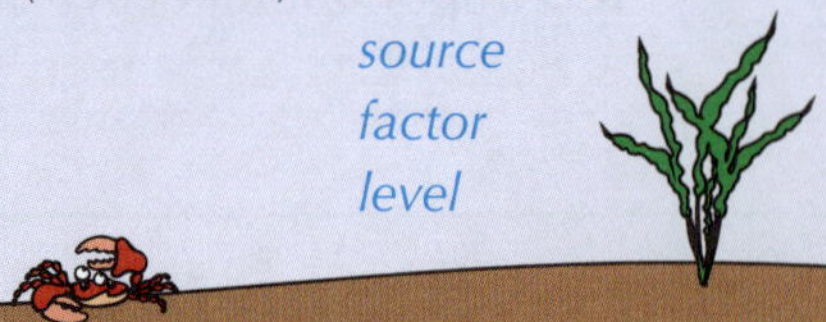

Protecting the Environment

proteger	*to protect*
ayudar	*to help*
la ayuda	*help*
resolver	*to solve, resolve*
el cambio	*change*
la acción	*action, act*
salvar	*to save, rescue*
reciclar	*to recycle*
recoger	*to pick up, collect, tidy up*
limpiar	*to clean*
reducir	*to reduce*
apagar	*to turn off, extinguish*
parar	*to stop (person, vehicle)*
responsable	*responsible*
práctico/a	*practical, useful*
la organización	*organisation*
público/a	*public*
en contra	*against*
a favor	*in favour*
en cambio	*on the other hand, whereas*

Higher

conservar	*to conserve, preserve*
puro/a	*pure, clean*
fundar	*to set up, establish*
la iniciativa	*initiative*
la campaña	*campaign*
la manifestación	*protest*
la responsabilidad	*responsibility*
el público	*public*
la esperanza	*hope*
profundo/a	*deep, profound*
mundial	*world(wide)*
consciente	*conscious, aware*
efectivo/a	*effective*
la cuestión	*issue, matter, question*
el asunto	*matter, issue, affair*
la clave	*key, crucial thing*
el motivo	*reason, motive*

Social Issues

la sociedad	*society*
el partido	*(political) party*
votar	*to vote*
la gente	*people*
el tema	*issue, subject, matter*
el aspecto	*aspect*
la ventaja	*advantage, benefit*
la desventaja	*disadvantage*
el hambre	*hunger*
la falta	*lack, shortage*
el paro	*unemployment, strike*
la economía	*economy*
la industria	*industry*
deber	*to have to, must*
la violencia	*violence*
el delito	*crime*
la diferencia	*difference*
justo/a	*fair, just*
pobre	*poor, unfortunate, without money*
rico/a	*rich, wealthy*
comparar	*to compare*
importar	*to matter, be important*
mejorar	*to improve, make better*
dar	*to give*
el apoyo	*support, backing*
la actitud	*attitude*
la felicidad	*happiness*

Higher

la población	*population*
el gobierno	*government*
la política	*politics, policy*
el documento	*document*
el informe	*report*
elegir	*to choose, elect*

Higher

el límite	*limit*
la dificultad	*difficulty, obstacle*
la preocupación	*worry, concern*
enorme	*enormous, vast*
temer	*to fear*
luchar	*to fight, struggle*
la soledad	*loneliness, solitude*
la pobreza	*poverty*
económico/a	*cheap, inexpensive, economic*
el comercio	*commerce, trade, business*
el impuesto	*tax*
la paz	*peace*
el conflicto	*conflict*
violento/a	*violent*
amenazar	*to threaten*
cometer	*to commit (crime)*
investigar	*to investigate*
la investigación	*investigation*
la culpa	*blame, fault*
entregarse	*to turn yourself in*
el derecho	*right (legal)*
la ley	*law, rule*
la autoridad	*authority*
el estado	*state, condition*
la discriminación	*discrimination*
igual	*equal, same, alike*
la igualdad	*equality*
la libertad	*freedom*
dirigir	*to direct, manage*
desarrollar	*to develop*
el desarrollo	*development*
la solución	*solution, answer*
el beneficio	*benefit*

Revision Summary Test for Section Twelve

And as if by magic, it's another summary test. See, I told you you'd need to recycle that vocab...

- Yep, these questions are **hard** — they'll really help you see **how well you know your stuff**.
- Tackle the **revision summary test** below, or scan the QR code to do it **online**. Use the CGP RevisionHub to **track your progress** and see **which areas need more work**.
- You can find **sample answers** here: www.cgpbooks.co.uk/BuenoExtras

Summary Test

Environmental Problems

1) 'In my city there are many factories. The air doesn't seem clean, the sky is never clear and there is always a lot of noise.' Translate this into Spanish.
2) Describe un problema con el medioambiente en tu región que te preocupa.
3) In Spanish, write about one thing that people do that harms the environment.
4) Translate these sentences into English: 'Las obras en los alrededores de mi barrio emiten muchos gases y mucho humo que contaminan el aire. También producen demasiado ruido.' (H)

Environmental Impacts

5) In Spanish, describe the impact of an environmental problem that concerns you.
6) Write down the Spanish for... :
   a) fire b) smell c) dry d) torn e) proof f) figure g) scientist
7) Translate this into Spanish: 'One of the main causes of climate change is that energy use is increasing.'
8) Lin says: 'Si negamos los efectos del cambio climático, tendrán un impacto aun más enorme. Habrá un aumento del nivel del mar y como consecuencia mucha tierra desaparecerá.' Translate what he says. (Higher)
9) En tu opinión, ¿qué pasará con el medioambiente en el futuro? (Higher)

Protecting the Environment

10) List the 10 verbs (plus 2 for Higher tier) related to protecting the environment from this section.
11) What are two things you would like to do to help the environment? Write your answer in Spanish.
12) Translate this sentence into English: 'Apoyo a una organización pública que salva animales en peligro.'
13) Write about something you've done in the past to protect the environment.
14) Translate this into English: 'La esperanza es la clave de la iniciativa que dirijo. Quiero que la gente sea consciente de su responsabilidad por el planeta de una manera positiva porque es más efectivo.' (H)

Social Issues

15) List the 5 nouns (plus 4 for Higher tier) for the social issues covered in this section.
16) In Spanish, describe a social problem in your area and how you think it could be improved.
17) 'It's important to vote for parties that improve aspects of society that matter to you.' Translate this sentence into Spanish.
18) Write down the English for the following words:
    a) la ventaja b) la desventaja c) la economía d) rico/a e) la actitud f) la felicidad
19) In Spanish, write about something you've done recently to help your community.
20) Raúl says: 'El paro y la falta de oportunidades laborales son temas graves. Tenemos que dar más dinero a varias industrias para crear más empleos.' Translate what he says into English.
21) ¿Cuál es el problema social del mundo que más te importa? ¿Por qué? (Higher)
22) 'It isn't fair that so many people have to struggle to be equal to others. Equality and freedom of expression are rights that every person should have.' Translate this sentence into Spanish. (Higher)

Nouns

Quick Quiz

Nouns are the words for people and objects — they're like the building blocks of a language.

Every Spanish noun is masculine or feminine...

1) Whether a word is masculine, feminine or plural affects lots of things.
2) Articles (words for 'the' and 'a') change depending on the noun's gender, and so do any adjectives which describe it.
3) If you see a word with 'el' or 'un' before it, it's usually masculine. 'La' or 'una' in front of a word means it's feminine.
4) If you don't have these clues, you can look at a word's ending to help you guess.

When you learn a new noun, learn its gender too.

el árbol alto (m) *the tall tree*
la casa alta (f) *the tall house*

Most masculine nouns end in:
-o -l -n -r -s -ta -aje -ma -pa

Most feminine nouns end in:
-a -ción -sión -tad -tud -dad -umbre

Languages, days of the week, months, rivers, seas and mountains are also masculine in Spanish.

5) You can't tell whether a noun ending in 'e', 'ista' or 'z' is masculine or feminine — you just have to learn them.

el coche *the car* la gente *the people*

...and some nouns can be both

1) Words for people often have a masculine and a feminine form. If the masculine noun ends in 'o', drop the 'o' and add 'a' to make it feminine.

Don't forget to change the article too.

el ingeniero → *la ingeniera (engineer)*

2) Nouns with other endings follow a different pattern. Here are a few examples:

Masc. ending	To make it feminine...	Example
-ante, -ente, -ista	no change	el turista *tourist (male)* → la turista *tourist (female)*
-or	add -a	el cuidador *carer (male)* → la cuidadora *carer (female)*

Making nouns plural

1) Some nouns in Spanish end in a vowel. To make them plural, just add 's' — 'una cama' (*one bed*) becomes 'dos camas' (*two beds*).
2) There are some exceptions to this rule though:

Noun ending	To make it plural...	Example
consonant except 'z'	add 'es'	una flor (*one flower*) → dos flores (*two flowers*)
'z'	drop the 'z' and add 'ces'	un disfraz (*one costume*) → dos disfraces (*two costumes*)
'(i)ón'	drop the accent and add 'es'	un avión (*one plane*) → dos aviones (*two planes*)

Grammar Questions

Write 'el' or 'la' for each of these words. Then write each one in the plural form with 'los' or 'las'.

1. zapato **2.** camisa **3.** tradición **4.** color **5.** vez **6.** mitad [H: **7.** monte **8.** dificultad **9.** ciudadano **10.** huelga **11.** impresión **12.** siglo]

Some words are re-noun-ed for not playing by the rules...

It's annoying when Spanish breaks its own rules but you just have to learn the exceptions. Some nouns ending in 'a' are masculine, like 'el día' (day), and others ending in 'o' are feminine, like 'la foto' (photo).

Quick Quiz

Forming Nouns

In Spanish, you can make adjectives into nouns and even use the infinitive as a noun. Fancy stuff...

You can turn some adjectives into nouns

See p.117 for more on adjectives and their uses.

1) In English, adding the suffix '-ity' to an adjective can turn it into a noun. For example, 'secure' becomes 'security'.
2) You can form nouns from some adjectives in Spanish by adding the suffix '-idad'. For adjectives ending in a vowel, you often remove the ending and add '-idad'. If the adjective ends in a consonant, just add '-idad'.

oportuno → oportun- → la oportunidad
opportune — *opportunity*

H real → real- → la realidad
real — *reality*

3) You can also form the Spanish words for languages by adding an article to the masculine form of nationality adjectives.

español *Spanish (person, object)* — el español *Spanish (language)*

4) Adding an article also turns nationality adjectives into nationality nouns.

un inglés *an English person* — los ingleses *the English (people)*

When a masculine singular nationality has an accent on its final syllable, it loses the accent in the feminine or plural form. See p.117 for more.

Verbs can be used as nouns too

The infinitive is the form of the verb you'd find in a dictionary, e.g. 'hablar' (to speak, talk).

1) In Spanish, the infinitive form of a verb can be used as a noun. It's usually equivalent to the '-ing' form in English.

Andar es bueno para la salud. — *Walking is good for your health.*
Me encanta bailar por la tarde. — *I love dancing in the evening.*

2) When you use an infinitive as a noun, it's always masculine and usually singular. You'll need to make sure any adjectives you use agree.

Repasar es necesario para aprobar la prueba. — *Revising is necessary in order to pass the test.*

Add '-ito/a' to nouns to say 'little'

You can take off the final 'o' or 'a' from some nouns and add '-ito/a' instead to make something seem smaller or show affection.

Me encanta este pueblito.
I love this little town.

Grammar Questions

Translate the following sentences into **Spanish**.

1. I like eating Mexican food.
2. French is a fun language.
3. Smoking is prohibited.
4. The Spanish are friendly.
5. Being famous is complicated. (H)
6. Renting a car is expensive. (H)

N'awww I love a tip-ito at the end of a page...

Nouns appear absolutely everywhere, so you need to be able to recognise all the weird and wonderful ways they're formed. You can also make nouns seem smaller with '-ito/a' — just make sure the gender agrees.

Articles

Quick Quiz

Articles are words like 'a' and 'the'. Where there's a noun, there's usually an article introducing it.

El, la, los, las — *the*

1) 'El', 'la', 'los' and 'las' are definite articles. They all mean 'the'.
2) The definite article changes depending on the gender of the noun, and whether it's singular or plural.

	Masculine	Feminine
Singular	el	la
Plural	los	las

3) Use 'el' before feminine nouns that start with a stressed 'a'.

El agua está fría. — *The water is cold.*

4) When the masculine definite article 'el' is placed after the prepositions 'a' and 'de', it becomes 'al' and 'del'.

Al final del día... — *At the end of the day...*

For more on prepositions, see p.110.

5) Sometimes you need a definite article in Spanish where you wouldn't use one in English:

a) With nouns used in a general sense:	No me gusta el café.	*I don't like coffee.*
b) In front of the days of the week and times:	los lunes a las seis	*Mondays at six o'clock*
c) In front of weights and measurements:	dos euros el kilo	*two euros a kilo*
d) When you use a person's title:	¿Cómo está el señor Gómez?	*How is Mr Gómez?*

Higher

6) There's a neuter article 'lo' for things that aren't masculine or feminine.

lo mejor / peor es que... — *the best / worst thing is that...*

When you use 'lo' in front of an adjective, the adjective has to be in the masculine form — see p.117.

Un, una, unos, unas — *'a' and 'some'*

1) 'Un' and 'una' are indefinite articles. They both mean 'a'.
2) 'Un' is used for masculine words and 'una' is used for feminine words.

un gato — *a cat*
una casa — *a house*

3) When you make 'un' or 'una' plural, they become 'unos' and 'unas' — they mean 'some' or 'a few'.

unos gatos — *some cats*
unas casas — *some houses*

4) Watch out, though — 'a' is left out...
   a) ...after the verb 'ser' when talking about someone's occupation or nationality: → Soy estudiante. — *I'm a student.*
   b) ...after a negative verb: → No tengo perro. — *I haven't got a dog.*

Grammar Questions

Translate these sentences into **Spanish**.

1. I ate a chicken sandwich.
2. The water runs fast.
3. She is an English teacher.
4. He wants some chips.
5. I play basketball on Thursdays.
6. It took a few hours.

AHHHHHHHHHH — a stressed 'a'...

When you learn a noun, it's a really good idea to learn its gender at the same time because then you'll always know which articles you need. Now bear with me a second while I check on our ol' pal 'a' here...

Quick Quiz

Subject Pronouns

Subject pronouns are handy little words that save you from needing to repeat nouns all the time.

Yo, tú, él, ella — *I, you, he, she*

1) Pronouns are words that replace nouns — like 'you' or 'them'. You use them to avoid repeating nouns.
2) Subject pronouns replace the subject of a sentence. The subject is the noun doing the action.

Khadija went to the beach and she sat on the sand.

In English, the pronoun 'she' replaces Khadija's name. 'She' is a subject pronoun because it replaces the subject of the sentence — Khadija.

3) You don't normally include subject pronouns in Spanish sentences — but you still need to know them.

I	yo	**we**	nosotros/as
you (inf., sing.)	tú	**you (inf., pl.)**	vosotros/as
he/it	él	**they (masc.)**	ellos
she/it	ella	**they (fem.)**	ellas
you (form., sing.)	usted	**you (form., pl.)**	ustedes

The masculine 'they' form is also used for groups made up of masculine and feminine nouns.

There's also 'se' which means 'one'. It's used in phrases like 'se puede' (you (general) can, one can). It uses the third person singular form of the verb. See p.141 for more impersonal verbs.

Remember there are four ways to say 'you' in Spanish — see p.10 for more.

Fui a la playa y comí un helado. *I went to the beach and I ate an ice cream.*

You don't need the pronoun 'yo' here as the first person verb forms 'fui' and 'comí' show that the person speaking ('I') is doing the action.

4) You can use the indefinite pronoun 'alguien' (*someone*) to talk about an unidentified person.

Alguien cerró la puerta.
Someone closed the door.

¿Alguien dijo algo?
Did someone say something?

You can use subject pronouns for emphasis

Although you don't usually need subject pronouns in Spanish, they help emphasise exactly who does what:

¿Qué queréis hacer el fin de semana que viene? *What would you (inf., pl.) like to do next weekend?*

Yo quiero ir de compras, pero él quiere ir al cine.
*I want to go shopping, but **he** wants to go to the cinema.*

You include the pronouns here to emphasise who wants what. They're used in Spanish in cases when extra stress is put on pronouns in English.

¿Quieren visitar el museo? *Do they / you (form., pl.) want to visit the museum?*
Yo sí, pero ella no. ***I** do, but **she** doesn't.*

Remember that if you're using 'ustedes', you need the 'they' form of the verb.

Grammar Questions

Write down the Spanish subject pronoun you'd use to replace each of these subjects.

1. Mosi (m) y Jorge (m)
2. el señor Pérez y usted
3. Alberto (m) y Tania (f)
4. Tidam (m) y tú (m)
5. tu tío (m)
6. Biyu (f) y yo (f)
7. Miranda (f)
8. Nico (m)

Poor subject pronouns — they feel a bit left out in Spanish...

Not seeing subject pronouns is a bit unnatural at first, but if you get into the habit of checking the verb endings you'll be used to it in no time. Remember to only use them if you're emphasising who's doing the action.

Object Pronouns

Quick Quiz

Now you've got to grips with subject pronouns, it's time for object pronouns — what a treat.

Me, te, los, las — *me, you, them*

1) Object pronouns replace the object of a sentence. This is the thing having the action done to it.

2) Use direct object pronouns when you're talking about who or what an action is done to.

me	me
you (inf., sing.)	te
him/it/you (form., sing)	lo
her/it/you (form., sing)	la
them (m/f)/you (form., pl.)	los/las

H

us	nos
you (inf., pl.)	os

Cruz lava el coche. Cruz lo lava.
Cruz washes the car. Cruz washes it.

The pronoun usually goes before the verb and it needs to agree with the noun it replaces.

Me, te, les — *to me, to you, to them*

1) If you want to talk about doing something 'to' or 'for' someone, you need an indirect object pronoun.

El niño da la flor a su abuela. → El niño le da la flor.
The boy gives the flower to his grandmother. → *The boy gives the flower to her.*

2) These pronouns are the same ones you use with the verb 'gustar' when you say you like something. This is because 'me gusta el chocolate' literally means 'chocolate is pleasing to me'.

me	me
you (inf., sing.)	te
him/her/it/you (form., sing.)	le
them/you (form., pl.)	les

H

us	nos
you (inf., pl.)	os

Getting the order right

1) Object pronouns normally come before the verb, but they can go before or after the verb if it's an infinitive (p.127) or a present participle (p.138).

Often you need to add an accent to keep the right pronunciation.

Lo quiero ver. **OR** Quiero verlo.
I want to see it.

Le estamos hablando. **OR** Estamos hablándole.
We're talking to him.

2) With commands, the pronoun is tacked on to the end.

Escríbeme, por favor. *Write to me, please.*

Grammar Questions

Translate these sentences into **Spanish**, replacing the words in bold with the correct pronouns.

1. She breaks **the window**.
2. I drink **the water**.
3. He bought **her** a skirt.
4. I will send **them** an email.

H
5. I gave **you (inf., pl.)** the cat.
6. He told **us** the secret.

Getting the order right — most important for takeaways...

My ex-friend forgot to order poppadoms once. With ordering object pronouns, keep in mind that they usually go before the verb, but for infinitives, they can go before *or* after. For commands, just stick 'em on the end.

Quick Quiz

More Pronouns

I know, I know — it's another batch of pronouns. But it's the last two pages. I pinky promise.

Algo, alguno, ninguno — *something, one, none*

'Algo', 'alguno' and 'ninguno' are indefinite pronouns.

1) You can use the pronoun 'algo' to talk about an unidentified object.

¿Dijiste algo a alguien? *Did you (inf., sing.) say something to someone?*

'Alguien' ('someone') is another indefinite pronoun. See p.106 for more.

2) When you use 'alguno' to replace a singular noun, it can mean 'one' or 'any'. For plural nouns, it means 'some (of them)'. 'Ninguno' can mean 'none' or 'no one'.

Vi a algunos. *I saw some (of them).*

Ninguno de ellos lo tiene. *None of them has it.*

3) For feminine nouns, you need 'alguna(s)' or 'ninguna(s)'.

Que — *that, who*

1) 'Que' can mean 'that' or 'who' — it's a relative pronoun. You can use it to start a relative clause, which is a way of adding detail to a sentence.

2) 'Que' can be used to refer to the subject of a clause — the person or thing doing the action:

Allí está el hombre que vive en nuestra calle. *There's the man who lives on our street.*

Higher

3) 'Que' can also refer to the object of a clause — the person or thing something is done to:

¿Dónde está el pan que compré ayer? *Where's the bread that I bought yesterday?*

4) After prepositions, like 'con', 'a' and 'de', use 'el / la que' or 'el / la cual' for 'that / which'. When talking about plural nouns, you need to use 'los / las que' or 'los / las cuales' instead.

el mercado del cual compro flores
the market from which I buy flowers

los cafés a los que fui ayer
the cafés that I went to yesterday

5) If you're talking about a general idea instead of a specific subject, you need 'lo que'.

Van a venir, lo que es maravilloso. *They're going to come, which is wonderful.*

6) You can also use 'cuando' (when) and 'donde' (where) as relative pronouns.

Suelo ir a la playa cuando hace calor.
I usually go to the beach when it's hot.

la tienda donde compré las uvas
the shop where I bought the grapes

Some pronouns change after certain prepositions

Watch out — 'mí' needs an accent, but 'ti' doesn't.

Higher

1) The words for 'me' and 'you' (inf., sing.) become 'mí' and 'ti' after prepositions like 'a' (to), 'para' (for), and 'sobre' / 'de' (about).

me	mí	**us**	nosotros/as
you (inf., sing.)	ti	**you (inf., pl.)**	vosotros/as
him/her	él/ella	**them (m/f)**	ellos/as
you (form., sing.)	usted	**you (form., pl.)**	ustedes

Lo hice para ti. *I made it for you (inf., sing.).*

2) You can use these pronouns after the preposition 'a' to put extra emphasis on who you're talking about.

Me dio la pizza a mí. *He gave the pizza **to me**.*

3) You can't say 'con mí' or 'con ti' in Spanish — you need 'conmigo' and 'contigo' instead.

Está conmigo. *He's with me.*

Using pronouns to ask questions

Pronouns for asking questions are called 'interrogative pronouns'.

1) Normally, you can use '¿Qué...' to ask a question that starts with 'What...' in English.

¿Qué te gustaría hacer? *What would you (inf., sing.) like to do?*

2) Use '¿Cuál(es)...' when you'd use 'Which...' or 'Which one(s)...' in English. But remember — sometimes you need '¿Cuál...' when you'd actually use 'What...' in English — see p.8.

¿Cuál es mejor? *Which (one) is better?*

¿Cuál es su apellido? *What is his surname?*

3) '¿Cuánto(s)/a(s)...' means 'How much...' or 'How many...'.

¿Cuánta agua hay? *How much water is there?*

4) '¿Quién...' means 'Who...'. It changes to 'Quiénes...' when you're referring to more than one person.

¿Quién es? *Who is it?*

Higher: You often use '¿Quién(es)...' with prepositions.

¿Con quién? *With whom?*

Esto, eso — *this, that*

If you don't know the gender of the noun you're replacing, or you want to talk about something more generally, you can use demonstrative pronouns like 'esto' and 'eso'.

'Esto' and 'eso' are invariable, which means they don't change to agree with a noun's gender.

No me gusta esto. *I don't like this.*

¿Qué es eso? *What's that?*

H: Use 'aquello' instead of 'eso' when the object is farther away.

¿Qué es aquello? *What's that (thing)?*

El mío, el tuyo — *mine, yours*

Higher

1) 'El mío', 'el tuyo', etc. are possessive pronouns. You use them to say 'mine' or 'yours'.

2) Possessive pronouns agree in gender and number with the noun they're replacing.

Possessive pronoun	Masc. sing.	Fem. sing.	Masc. pl.	Fem. pl.
mine	el mío	la mía	los míos	las mías
yours (inf., sing.)	el tuyo	la tuya	los tuyos	las tuyas
his/hers/its/yours (form., sing.)	el suyo	la suya	los suyos	las suyas
ours	el nuestro	la nuestra	los nuestros	las nuestras
yours (inf., pl.)	el vuestro	la vuestra	los vuestros	las vuestras
theirs/yours (form., pl.)	el suyo	la suya	los suyos	las suyas

Kwesi really didn't want to admit that the bread was his...

¿Es su casa? *Is it their house?*
No, la suya es más alta. *No, theirs is taller.*

¿Es tu pan? *Is it your (inf., sing.) bread?*
No, el mío está allí. *No, mine is there.*

Grammar Questions

Translate these sentences into **English**.

1. ¿Cuál es tu color favorito?
2. Leeré el libro que me dio.
3. ¿Has comido algo?
4. Eso no es verdad.
H: **5.** La tuya está aquí.
6. Cociné para ti.
7. Irían contigo.
8. Querré aquello.

I gotta hand it *tuya* — you're a pro at pronouns...

I know it looked like the rest of the book was just going to be about pronouns, but I never break my promises. Now go and reward yourself with a quick break, then onwards and upwards with more delicious grammar.

Quick Quiz

Prepositions

Prepositions are very useful words that you can use to talk about direction, time or location.

Use these words to say where something is

Don't forget to use 'estar' (see p.130) to say where something is.

al lado de	*to the side of*	contra	*against, opposite*	dentro de (Higher)	*inside of*
delante de	*in front of*	encima de	*on top of*	fuera de (Higher)	*outside of*
entre	*between, among*	desde	*from, since*	hacia (Higher)	*toward(s)*

A — *to, at*

To say '<u>to</u>' in Spanish, you <u>normally</u> say '<u>a</u>'. But you can sometimes also use '<u>a</u>' to mean '<u>at</u>'.

Va a Hull. *She's going to Hull.*

Vine a la fiesta. *I came to the party.*

a las seis *at six o'clock*

En — *in, on*

You can <u>normally</u> use '<u>en</u>' when you want to say '<u>in</u>'. You can also use '<u>en</u>' to say '<u>on</u>'.

You don't need 'on' for days of the week.

En Leeds... *In Leeds...*

Lo vi en la tele. *I saw it on TV.*

El lunes... *On Monday...*

De — *of, from*

'<u>De</u>' usually means '<u>of</u>' or '<u>from</u>'. You can also use '<u>de</u>' to say what something's <u>made of</u> or <u>who</u> something <u>belongs to</u>.

un vaso de agua *a glass of water*

Es de oro. *It's made of gold.*

la casa de Xavi *Xavi's house*

Hasta — *up to, as far as, until*

You can use '<u>hasta</u>' to say '<u>up to</u>' or '<u>as far as</u>'. It can also mean '<u>until</u>'.

Solo va hasta Kent. *It only goes as far as Kent.*

Está abierto hasta las dos. *It's open until two o'clock.*

Sobre — *on top of, over, about*

For '<u>on top of</u>', use '<u>sobre</u>'. You can also use '<u>sobre</u>' when you want to say '<u>over</u>' or '<u>about</u>'.

Está sobre el armario. *It's on top of the wardrobe.*

Vuela sobre el mar. *It flies over the sea.*

Discuten sobre sus planes. *They argue about their plans.*

Grammar Questions

Use what you know about prepositions to translate these sentences into **Spanish**.

1. We talked about the weather.
2. The train goes as far as Spain.
3. I saw it on the wall.
4. They're from Valencia.
5. The dog ran towards me. (H)
6. I live outside of the city. (H)

Not a *de* goes by where I don't use a preposition...

You can add 'de' to some adverbs to make useful location prepositions, e.g. 'cerca' (*close, near, nearby*) can become 'cerca de' (*close to, near to*). You also have 'detrás de' (*behind*), which is perfect for pantomimes.

Prepositions with Verbs and Nouns

Quick Quiz

Prepositions aren't just for describing where something is — you'll often see them before an infinitive or noun and after certain verbs. When they follow a verb, they can change its meaning.

Some prepositions are followed by an infinitive...

1) 'Para' followed by an infinitive means 'to' or 'in order to'.

Veo la tele para descansar. *I watch TV to relax.*

2) The preposition 'sin' means 'without'. Use it with an infinitive when you want to say 'without -ing'.

Salió sin decir una palabra más. *He left without saying another word.*

Higher

3) You can use 'antes de' + infinitive to say 'before -ing'.

Compré la entrada antes de llegar al cine. *I bought the ticket before arriving at the cinema.*

4) If you want to say 'after -ing', use 'después de' + infinitive.

Después de terminar el examen, iré a una fiesta. *After finishing the exam, I will go to a party.*

...and some are followed by a noun

In some verb phrases, the preposition is followed by a noun.

Voy de vacaciones en julio. *I'm going on holiday in July.*

H

Los trabajadores están en huelga. *The workers are on strike.*

Verb phrase	Meaning
ir de vacaciones	to go on holiday
estar de acuerdo	to be in agreement
preocuparse por (+ noun)	to worry about
estar en huelga (H)	to be on strike
huele a (+ noun) (H)	it smells of...

Some verbs are followed by a preposition

1) Sometimes you need to use a preposition after the verb. The preposition can change the verb's meaning:

Verb	Verb + preposition	Example sentence
llegar (*to arrive*)	llegar a (*to manage to, succeed in*)	Llegué a encontrarlo. (*I managed to find it.*)
dejar (*to let, leave*)	dejar de (*to stop -ing*)	He dejado de leerlos. (*I've stopped reading them.*)
volver (*to go back, return*)	volver a (*to do again*)	Volví a mirarlo. (*I looked at it again.*)
H tratar (*to treat, deal with*)	tratar de (*to try to*)	Trataré de hacerlo rápido. (*I'll try to do it quickly.*)

2) The verb that comes after the preposition is always an infinitive.

Grammar Questions

Translate these sentences into **English**.

1. Hablé sin pensar.
2. Vuelven a hacer la tarea.
3. Ha dejado de fumar.
4. Juego para ganar.
H **5.** Cerraré la puerta antes de salir.
H **6.** Trato de beber más agua.

Let's pretend there's a joke about prepositions here...

I enjoyed writing the last one so much that I think my creative juices might have run dry. While I grab a top up, try learning these verb phrases with specific examples — they'll be easier to remember in a sentence.

Quick Quiz

'Por', 'Para' and the Personal 'a'

'Por' and 'para' each have multiple uses. But don't fret — they're listed below to help you.

Use 'por' to...

1) ...say 'around'. El museo está por aquí. *The museum is around here.*

2) ...say 'because of'. No salí por el mal tiempo. *I didn't go out because of the bad weather.*

3) ...say 'by'. Fue pintada por un artista famoso. *It was painted by a famous artist.*

4) ...say 'for' or 'on behalf of'. Vivió allí por un año. *He lived there for a year.*

5) ...say 'through'. Entré por la puerta. *I came through the door.*

You usually use 'por' to talk about the past, but sometimes you need it for the future, e.g. 'Estaré en Galicia por dos años'.

Use 'para' instead...

Using 'para' with an infinitive helps you say 'in order to' (see p.111).

1) ...in future time phrases like 'for X number of days' or 'for / by X time'. Quiero el coche para un día. *I want the car for one day.*

2) ...when you're talking about destinations. el tren para Bilbao *the train for Bilbao*

3) ...to say who something is for. El artista la pintó para su cliente. *The artist painted it for his client.*

H 4) ...to give your opinion. Para mí, es importante. *For me, it's important.*

The personal 'a'

You need an extra 'a' before the word for any human being or pet after every single verb.

Estoy buscando a Ozan.
I'm looking for Ozan.

BUT

Estoy buscando un libro.
I'm looking for a book.

You don't usually use the personal 'a' after 'tener' or 'ser'.

Grammar Questions

Translate these sentences into **English**.

1. Ahora llega el tren para París.
2. Lo haré para mañana.
3. La salida está por aquí.
4. Yo andaba por el campo.
H **5.** Lo guardaban para sus hijos.
H **6.** Salían raramente por el calor.

Decide whether you need a personal 'a' in each of these sentences.

7. Vieron ___ la película ayer.
8. Conocía ___ mucha gente.
9. Sacará ___ la basura.
10. Visito ___ mi abuelo.
H **11.** Iban a ver ___ las mascotas.
H **12.** Eso mata ___ las plantas.

Don't confuse the personal 'a' with the preposition 'a'...

The preposition 'a' is used in sentences with an indirect object, like 'doy la guitarra al caballo' (I give the guitar to the horse). The personal 'a' is used when the human being or pet you're talking about is a direct object.

Conjunctions

Quick Quiz

Conjunctions help you link your ideas together to make longer, more complex sentences.

Y — *and*

1) 'Y' means 'and' — you use it just like you would in English.

Me gusta jugar al fútbol. *I like playing football.*	AND	Me gusta jugar al rugby. *I like playing rugby.*	=	Me gusta jugar al fútbol y al rugby. *I like playing football and rugby.*

2) 'Y' changes to 'e' before a word starting with 'i' or 'hi'.

Hablo español e inglés. *I speak Spanish and English.*

O — *or*

1) 'O' means 'or'.

Juego al fútbol los sábados. *I play football on Saturdays.*	OR	Juego al rugby los sábados. *I play rugby on Saturdays.*	=	Juego al fútbol o al rugby los sábados. *I play football or rugby on Saturdays.*

2) When 'o' comes just before a word starting with 'o' or 'ho', it changes to 'u'.

Cuesta siete u ocho euros. *It costs seven or eight euros.*

Pero — *but*

1) 'Pero' means 'but'.

Me gusta el fútbol. *I like football.*	BUT	No me gusta el rugby. *I don't like rugby.*	=	Me gusta el fútbol, pero no me gusta el rugby. *I like football, but I don't like rugby.*

H 2) When 'but' means 'but rather', it becomes 'sino'.

No es español, sino francés. *He isn't Spanish, but (rather) French.*

Porque — *because*

There's more about 'porque' and opinions on p.12.

'Porque' means 'because'. It helps you give opinions:

Me gusta esta comida porque está rica. *I like this food because it's tasty.*

Other conjunctions you need to know

You usually use 'ni' with a negative verb to say 'neither...nor...'. See p.140 for more on negatives.

que	*that*	en cambio	*on the other hand, whereas*	como	*as*
si	*if*	aunque	*although, even though*	H (no) ni... ni...	*nor, neither ... nor*
sin embargo	*however*	mientras	*while, whilst*	H para que	*so that, in order that*

Grammar Questions

Translate these sentences into **Spanish**, deciding which conjunctions you need to use.

1. Geography is fun, but it's hard.
2. I like history because it's easy.
3. As I'm ill, I'll stay at home.
4. If it's hot, I go to the beach.
5. I speak French and Italian.
6. Do you prefer blue or green?

You don't want to sound like a robot, so start using conjunctions...

I don't want to stop you from doing it in your free time, but an exam is probably the wrong place to start.

Nouns, Articles & Linking Words — Grammar List

There's a lot to take in from this section so I've popped the essentials on these next two pages — I'm nice like that.

Nouns

Common endings for masculine nouns are:
-o, -l, -n, -r, -s, -ta, -aje

Common endings for feminine nouns are:
-a, -ción, -sión, -tad, -tud, -dad, -umbre

For nouns ending in 'e' or 'ista', see p.103.

Some masculine nouns can be made feminine:

el médico → **la** médica	*doctor (m/f)*
el escritor → la escritora	*writer (m/f)*
un inglés → una inglesa	*English person (m/f)*
el periodista → **la** periodista	*journalist (m/f)*
el cantante → **la** cantante	*singer (m/f)*
el cliente → **la** cliente	*client, customer (m/f)*

There are different ways to make singular nouns plural:

el gato → **los** gatos	*cat(s)*
la amistad → **las** amistades	*friendship(s)*
la actriz → **las** actrices	*actor(s) (f)*
la estación → **las** estaciones	*station(s)*
el corazón → **los** corazones	*heart(s)*

Some nouns can be formed from adjectives:

activo → la actividad	*activity*
español → **el** español	*Spanish (language)*

You can also use the infinitive of a verb as a noun:
Reciclar es importante. *Recycling is important.*

Add -ito/a to make a noun seem smaller:
la cosa → la cosita *thing → little thing*

Articles

Articles (words like 'the' and 'a') introduce nouns. They change depending on the noun's gender and whether it's singular or plural.

Definite articles:

el	*the (m, sing.)*
la	*the (f, sing.)*
los	*the (m, pl.)*
las	*the (f, pl.)*

Indefinite articles:

un	*a, an (m, sing.)*
una	*a, an (f, sing.)*
unos	*some (m, pl.)*
unas	*some (f, pl.)*

The masculine singular article 'el' changes when combined with the prepositions 'a' or 'de':
a + el → al
de + el → del

H: The article 'lo' can be used to talk about general things, e.g. 'lo bueno' (*the good thing*).

Emphatic Pronouns

Use subject pronouns after the preposition 'a' for emphasis.

Higher:

(a) mí	*(to) me*
(a) ti	*(to) you (inf., sing.)*
(a) él / ella	*(to) him / her*
(a) usted / ustedes	*(to) you (form., sing./pl.)*
(a) nosotros/as	*(to) us*
(a) vosotros/as	*(to) you (inf., pl.)*
(a) ellos / ellas	*(to) them (m/f)*

Subject Pronouns

Subject pronouns replace the subject of the sentence.

yo	*I*
tú	*you (inf., sing.)*
él	*he, it (m)*
ella	*she, it (f)*
usted	*you (form., sing.)*
nosotros/as	*we*
vosotros/as	*you (inf., pl.)*
ellos	*they (m)*
ellas	*they (f)*
ustedes	*you (form., pl.)*

Higher: Some subject pronouns change after certain prepositions.
con + mí → conmigo *with me*
con + ti → contigo *with you (inf., sing.)*

Direct Object Pronouns

Direct object pronouns replace the person or thing the action is being done to.

me	*me*
te	*you (inf., sing.)*
lo	*him, it (m), you (form., sing.)*
la	*her, it (f), you (form., sing.)*
los	*them, you (form., pl.) (m)*
las	*them, you (form., pl.) (f)*
nos (H)	*us*
os (H)	*you (inf., pl.)*

Indirect Object Pronouns

Indirect object pronouns replace the person or thing being indirectly affected by the action.

me	*(to) me*
te	*(to) you (inf., sing.)*
le	*(to) him, her, it, you (form., sing.)*
les	*(to) them, you (form., pl.)*
nos (H)	*(to) us*
os (H)	*(to) you (inf., pl.)*

Indefinite Pronouns

Indefinite pronouns refer to nouns that are general and unspecific.

alguien	*someone*
algo	*something*
alguno	*one*
algunos	*some (of them)*
ninguno	*no one, none*
todo	*everything, all of it*
H los/las demás	*the others (m/f)*

Demonstrative Pronouns

These demonstrative pronouns replace things in a sentence that are unspecific. They don't have to agree in gender or number.

esto	*this*
eso	*that*
H aquello	*that (thing)*

Prepositions with Verbs and Nouns

Some prepositions are followed by an infinitive:

para (+ infinitive)	*in order to (+ verb)*
sin (+ infinitive)	*without (+ -ing)*
H antes de (+ infinitive)	*before (+ -ing)*
H después de (+ infinitive)	*after (+ -ing)*

Some verb phrases use a preposition + noun:

ir de vacaciones	*to go on holiday*
estar de acuerdo	*to be in agreement*
preocuparse por	*to worry about*
H estar en huelga	*to be on strike*
H huele a (+ noun)	*it smells of...*

The meaning of some verbs changes when they're followed by a preposition:

E.g. llegar → llegar a
to arrive → *to manage to, succeed in*

Relative Pronouns

Relative pronouns introduce extra information to a sentence. 'Que' can mean 'who' (if you're referring to someone) or 'that' (if you're referring to something).

que *who, that*

E.g. Es el vecino que cuidó a mi gato.
He's the neighbour who took care of my cat.

Higher

After prepositions, you use 'el/la que', 'los/las que', 'el/la cual' or 'los/las cuales' to say 'that / which'.

el/la que los/las que *that / which*
el/la cual los/las cuales

E.g Lo vi durante el evento al que asistí.
I saw it during the event that I attended.

If you're talking about a general idea, you need 'lo que'.

lo que *what, that which*

E.g. La carta nunca llegó, lo que era una sorpresa.
The letter never arrived, which was a surprise.

You can use 'cuando' and 'donde' as relative pronouns.

cuando *when* donde *where*

Possessive Pronouns

Possessive pronouns show what belongs to who.

Higher

el/la mío/a los/las míos/as	*mine*
el/la tuyo/a los/las tuyos/as	*yours (inf., sing.)*
el/la suyo/a los/las suyos/as	*his, hers, its,* *yours (form., sing./pl.), theirs*
el/la nuestro/a los/las nuestros/as	*ours*
el/la vuestro/a los/las vuestros/as	*yours (inf., pl.)*

Conjunctions

y	*and*
o	*or*
pero	*but*
porque	*because*
que	*that*
si	*if*
por eso	*so, therefore*
sin embargo	*however*
en cambio	*on the other hand*
aunque	*although, even though*
mientras	*while, whilst*
como	*as*
Higher: para que	*so that, in order that*
Higher: sino	*but (rather), except*
Higher: (no) ni...(ni)...	*nor, neither...nor*

Remember — the personal 'a' is different to the preposition 'a'. See p.112 for more.

Prepositions

a	*to, at*	al lado de	*to the side of*
al	*to the (m, sing.)*	delante de	*in front of*
en	*in, on*	entre	*between, among*
de	*of, from*	contra	*against, opposite*
del	*of the (m, sing.)*	debajo de	*underneath, below*
hasta	*up to, as far as, until*	encima de	*on top of*
sobre	*on top of, over, about*	desde	*from, since*
con	*with*	durante	*during*
por	*around, because of, by, for, through*	según	*according to*
para	*for*	sin	*without*
		H dentro de	*inside of*
		H fuera de	*outside of*
		H hacia	*toward(s)*

Revision Summary Test for Section Thirteen

If more grammar ar-tickles your fancy, this test will let you show off everything you've learnt.

- These questions are **hard**, but they'll really help you see **how well you know your stuff**.
- Tackle the **revision summary test** below, or scan the QR code to do it **online**. You can **track your progress** online and see **which areas need more work**.
- There are **sample answers** for the test here: www.cgpbooks.co.uk/BuenoExtras

Summary Test

Nouns and Articles

1) Write either 'm' or 'f' to show whether each noun is masculine or feminine.
a) azúcar b) canción c) pájaro d) papel e) playa f) árbol g) falda h) clase
2) Make these nouns feminine: a) el periodista b) el médico c) un alemán d) el pintor
3) Make each of these nouns plural — don't forget to include 'los' or 'las':
a) examen b) mes c) sábado d) enfermedad e) estación f) actriz g) camisa
4) Translate these sentences into Spanish: a) Reading is interesting. b) Singing is really boring.
5) Choose the correct article in bold to complete each of these sentences: a) **El** / **La** agua está limpia.
b) **Los** / **Las** chicas juegan al fútbol. c) Dame **un** / **una** bolígrafo, por favor.
6) Fill in the gaps with 'a' or 'de' combined with the correct definite article ('el' or 'la'):
a) Voy ...... restaurante. b) Salió ...... biblioteca. c) Le gustaría ir ...... fiesta. d) al lado ...... río
7) Translate the following into Spanish: a) I'm a teacher. b) I don't have a cat. c) Are you Spanish?

Pronouns

8) List all the Spanish subject pronouns in this section. There are 12 you need to know.
9) Rewrite these sentences, replacing the words in bold with the correct direct object pronoun.
a) Buscaba **la caja**. b) Estudio **las ciencias**. c) Vi **al músico**. d) He encontrado **mis zapatos**.
10) Now rewrite these sentences, replacing the words in bold with the correct indirect object pronoun.
a) Di los libros **a los alumnos**. b) Envié la carta **a mi tía**. c) Hablará **a sus amigos** mañana.
11) Translate these sentences into Spanish using the correct indefinite pronouns.
a) I have something in my eye. b) Did they buy some (of them)? c) None of them made dinner.
12) What type of pronoun is the word 'que'? How would you say 'que' in English?
13) Translate these sentences into Spanish using the correct interrogative pronouns.
a) Who called you (inf., sing.)? b) What did they do yesterday? c) Which one is worse?
14) Translate these sentences into Spanish using the correct demonstrative pronouns.
a) I never wanted this. b) I'd like to do that. c) Have you read this? d) That doesn't seem fair.

Higher

15) Complete each sentence by circling the correct option:
a) Ese pan es para **tú** / **ti**. c) Pensaba en **ella** / **suya**. e) ¿Las uvas son para **me** / **mí**?
b) A **ellos** / **él** le gustan mucho. d) ¿Vamos **contigo** / **con tú**? f) Hablábamos de **ti** / **tú**.
16) Translate these sentences into English: a) ¿Es la tuya o la mía? b) Puse el vuestro en la cocina.

Prepositions and Conjunctions

17) Fill in the gaps with the correct preposition in Spanish: a) Queremos las bicis ...... una semana.
b) Pagué treinta euros ...... el vestido. c) La vi ...... la tele. d) Me preguntaron ...... este tema.
18) Translate these sentences into English: a) Entré en la casa por la ventana. b) Fui al café de Diego.
c) Destruí la carta sin leerla. d) Van a quedarse hasta noviembre. e) Bailé mucho durante la fiesta.
19) What do these verbs mean in English? a) dejar de b) llegar a c) volver a d) preocuparse por
20) Choose the correct conjunction in bold, then translate these sentences into English:
a) Es una fiesta tradicional **y** / **e** importante. b) Comí esas naranjas **porque** / **pero** me encantan.

H

21) Translate these sentences into English: a) Leo antes de acostarme. b) Lo haré después de cenar.
22) Say what the conjunction 'sino' means in English, then give a sentence in Spanish that uses it.

Adjectives

Quick Quiz

Jazz up your work with some flashy describing words — and collect more marks while you're at it.

Adjectives describe things

1) In Spanish, adjectives have to agree with the noun they refer to, even if they aren't right next to it.
2) This means the adjective changes depending on the gender of the noun and whether it's singular or plural.
3) Adjectives that end in 'o' in the masculine singular form change the 'o' to 'a' in the feminine form. When plural, the adjective ends in 'os' (masculine) or 'as' (feminine).

el chico alto — *the tall boy*

la chica alta — *the tall girl*

los chicos altos — *the tall boys*

las chicas altas — *the tall girls*

4) Adjectives with certain endings follow different rules:

Ending	Example	Masc. sing.	Fem. sing.	Masc. pl.	Fem. pl.
-e	triste (*sad*)	triste	triste	tristes	tristes
-ista	optimista (*optimistic*)	optimista	optimista	optimistas	optimistas
-z	feliz (*happy*)	feliz	feliz	felices	felices
-és	francés (*French*)	francés	francesa	franceses	francesas
-ol	español (*Spanish*)	español	española	españoles	españolas

When you look up a Spanish adjective in the dictionary, it will be in the masculine singular form.

Nationality adjectives that end in consonants add an ending in the feminine and plural forms. If they have an accent in the masculine singular, they drop it in the feminine and plural.

You can add -able to some verb stems to make adjectives

For some verbs that end in '-ar', you can add the suffix '-able' to the verb stem to form an adjective.

aceptar (*to accept*) ⟶ aceptable (*acceptable*)

Spanish adjectives with this ending often end in '-able' in English too.

'ser' and 'estar' can change an adjective's meaning

1) Adjectives that follow 'ser' describe a permanent trait.
2) Adjectives that follow 'estar' describe someone at a given moment.
3) Some adjectives change their meaning completely depending on whether they follow 'ser' or 'estar':

For more on using 'ser' and 'estar' with adjectives, see p.90.

Dilip es listo. — *Dilip is clever.*
Dilip está listo. — *Dilip is ready.*

Mis primos son aburridos. — *My cousins are (always) boring.*
Mis primos están aburridos. — *My cousins are (feeling) bored.*

Grammar Questions

Translate these phrases into **Spanish**, making sure the adjectives agree.

1. the happy dog
2. a vegan salad
3. the blue car
4. a recyclable bottle
5. the German sister
6. an avoidable problem
7. The group is tired.
8. Is she ready?

Adjectives agree (and I'm sure you do too) that this page is great...

Don't let unfamiliar adjectives catch you out — learn how different endings change depending on the noun.

Quick Quiz

More Adjectives

Adjectives are really useful for saying what's yours and for pointing things out. For example, this is *my* delicious muffin and it is certainly not *yours*... Sorry. I'm just protective of my snacks.

Most adjectives go after the word they describe

1) In Spanish, most adjectives go after the noun (the word they describe).
2) But that's not always the case — some adjectives always go in front of the noun they're describing, like these ones:

Es un vestido bonito.
It's a nice dress.

mucho/a	*much, a lot*	alguno/a	*a/an, some*	pocos/as	*few, not many*	próximo/a	*next*
muchos/as	*many, lots of*	ninguno/a	*no, not...any*	primero/a	*first*	último/a	*last, final*
otro/a	*other, another*	tanto/a	*so much + noun*	segundo/a	*second*	cada	*each, every*
otros/as	*other*	tantos/as	*so many + noun*	tercero/a	*third*		
		poco/a	*little, not much*				

algunos parques — *some parks*

tanta gente — *so many people*

pocas casas — *few houses*

Some adjectives change before masculine nouns...

primer	*first (m) (pre-noun)*	mal	*bad (m) (pre-noun)*	gran	*big, great (pre-noun)*
tercer	*third (m) (pre-noun)*	algún	*a/an, any (m) (pre-noun)*		
buen	*good (m) (pre-noun)*	ningún	*no, not...any (m) (pre-noun)*		

1) Some adjectives lose the final 'o' when they go in front of a masculine noun.
2) 'Alguno' and 'ninguno' drop the final 'o' and add an accent.
3) 'Grande' is the only adjective that drops 'de' in front of both masculine and feminine words.

el tercer libro — *the third book*

un buen día — *a good day*

No hay ningún taxi libre. — *There's no taxi free.*

un gran paso — *a great step*

una gran señora — *a great lady*

...and some change their meaning depending on their position

Adjective	Before the noun...	After the noun...
grande	un gran hombre *a great man*	un hombre grande *a big man*
único	el único edificio *the only building*	el edificio único *the unique building*
nuevo	un nuevo coche *a new (to owner) car*	un coche nuevo *a newly-made car*
viejo	un viejo amigo *an old (long-standing) friend*	un amigo viejo *an old (elderly) friend*
antiguo	un antiguo templo *a former temple*	un templo antiguo *an ancient temple*

"I should've checked that advert more carefully..."

Mi, tu, nuestro — *my, your, our*

'Mi', 'tu', 'nuestro' etc. are possessive adjectives.

1) Words like 'my' and 'your' show possession. In Spanish they go before the noun and have to agree with the noun they're describing — not the owner. You only need to learn the forms in brackets if you're doing Higher tier (see below).

Possessive	Masc. sing.	Fem. sing.	Masc. pl.	Fem. pl.
my	mi (mío)	mi (mía)	mis (míos)	mis (mías)
your (inf., sing.)	tu (tuyo)	tu (tuya)	tus (tuyos)	tus (tuyas)
his/her/its/your (form., sing.)	su (suyo)	su (suya)	sus (suyos)	sus (suyas)
our	nuestro	nuestra	nuestros	nuestras
your (inf., pl.)	vuestro	vuestra	vuestros	vuestras
their/your (form., pl.)	su (suyo)	su (suya)	sus (suyos)	sus (suyas)

'Su(s)' can mean 'his', 'her', 'its', 'their' and 'your' (formal). Use the rest of the sentence to work out which of these it is.

mi libro *my book*
su perro *his dog*

H 2) The forms in brackets are long-form adjectives. You use them for emphasis and put them after the noun:

el gato nuestro *our cat*

The 'our' and 'your (inf., pl.)' forms are the same in the short and long forms.

Este, ese — *this, that*

'Este', 'ese' and 'aquel' are demonstrative adjectives.

1) Use 'este' to say 'this'. It's an adjective, so it changes to agree with the noun. When the noun is feminine, use 'esta', and when it's plural, use 'estos' (masculine) or 'estas' (feminine).

este tigre *this tiger* | esta leche *this milk* | estos huevos *these eggs* | estas mesas *these tables*

2) Use 'ese' to say 'that' in English. Use 'esa' for feminine nouns, and 'esos' or 'esas' for plural nouns.

ese tigre *that tiger* | esa leche *that milk* | esos huevos *those eggs* | esas mesas *those tables*

Higher

3) 'Aquel' also means that. It's used for things that are further away — in English, you might say 'that over there'.

4) 'Aquel' changes to 'aquella' in the feminine form and 'aquellos' and 'aquellas' for the plural forms.

aquel tigre — *that tiger (over there)*
aquella leche — *that milk (over there)*
aquellos huevos — *those eggs (over there)*
aquellas mesas — *those tables (over there)*

Indefinite adjectives describe words in a more general way

1) 'Otro' (*other, another*), 'todo' (*all, the whole*), 'alguno' (*some*), 'ninguno' (*no, not any*) and 'mismo' (*same*) are all examples of indefinite adjectives. They change to agree with the noun.

2) 'cada' (*each, every*), is also an indefinite adjective, but it never changes to agree with what it's describing.

otro tigre — *another tiger*
algunos tigres — *some tigers*
cada tigre — *each tiger*

Grammar Questions

Translate these phrases into **Spanish**, making sure the adjectives go in the right place.

1. the first day
2. few products
3. each family
4. no plate
5. their books
6. those films
H **7.** my pen (long form)
H **8.** that apple over there

Someone must really like tigers...

Possessive adjectives show who something belongs to, and demonstrative adjectives show where something is compared to where you are. Indefinite adjectives generally describe how much of something there is.

Quick Quiz

Comparative and Superlative Adjectives

Comparative and superlative adjectives help you compare one thing to another. Marvellous.

Más, menos — *more, less*

'More' is a comparative. 'The most' (Higher only) is a superlative.

1) In Spanish you can't say 'cheaper' or 'cheapest' — you have to say 'more cheap' or 'the most cheap'.

Este piso es barato. *This flat is cheap.* → Este piso es más barato. *This flat is cheaper.* → H Este piso es el más barato. *This flat is the cheapest.*

2) To say 'less cheap' or 'the least cheap', use 'menos'.

Este piso es barato. *This flat is cheap.* → Este piso es menos barato. *This flat is less cheap.* → H Este piso es el menos barato. *This flat is the least cheap.*

H 3) To say 'the most / least' if the word you're describing is feminine, use 'la más / menos'. For plural words, use 'los/las más / menos'.

Zeynab es la más baja. *Zeynab is the shortest.*

Más / menos ... que — *more / less ... than*

1) Use 'más ... que' (more ... than) and 'menos ... que' (less ... than) to compare two things directly.
2) If you want to say something is 'more than...' followed by a number, use 'más de'.
3) To say two things are as young or old or brilliant as each other, use 'tan ... como' (as ... as).

Catalina es más tranquila que Minho, pero ella es tan tranquila como Daniel. *Catalina is more calm than Minho, but she is as calm as Daniel.*

There are some exceptions...

All these comparatives and superlatives add 'es' for the plural forms.

bueno	*good*	→ mejor	*better*	→	el mejor	*the best*
malo	*bad*	→ peor	*worse*	→	el peor	*the worst*
viejo	*old (people only)*	→ mayor	*older*	→	el mayor	*the oldest*
joven	*young (people only)*	→ menor	*younger*	→	el menor	*the youngest*

(Higher: el mejor / el peor / el mayor / el menor)

If the noun is feminine or plural, you'll need to change the 'el' to 'la', 'los' or 'las'.

Sara es mayor que Javier. *Sara is older than Javier.*

H Aya es la mayor. *Aya is the oldest.*

Grammar Questions

Translate these sentences into **Spanish** — watch out for the irregular adjectives though.

1. This page is easier.
2. I am as tall as my father.
3. Faiza is older than Emilio.
4. Books are better than films.
H **5.** Today is the worst day.
H **6.** She is the youngest.

Making comparisons is the best thing ever...

Comparatives have to agree with what they're describing. So to say 'The horse and the bird are angrier' in Spanish, you say 'El caballo y el pájaro son más enojados' because 'the horse and the bird' is a plural phrase.

Adverbs

Quick Quiz

Adverbs describe how you do something, like cooking terribly — even my toast gets incinerated...

Adverbs describe how actions are done

1) If you wanted to describe how you run, you could say 'I run slowly' — 'slowly' is an adverb of manner.
2) In English, you add '-ly' to the adjective 'slow' to make 'slowly'.
3) It's similar in Spanish — to form an adverb of manner, you add '-mente' to the end of the adjective. However, you need to make sure the adjective is in the feminine form first.

lento (*slow*) ⟶ lenta (*feminine form of 'slow'*) + -mente ⟶ lentamente (*slowly*)

4) With adjectives that don't end in 'o', you can just add '-mente'.

fácil (*easy*) + -mente ⟶ fácilmente (*easily*)

You can also use the Higher tier word 'despacio' to say slowly, e.g. 'Escribes despacio'. It's irregular and doesn't add -mente or change its ending.

5) Unlike with adjectives (see p.117), adverbs don't need to agree. This is because they're describing an action, not the person doing the action.
6) Adverbs of manner come after the verb.

Comemos rápidamente.	*We eat quickly.*
Habla alegremente.	*She speaks happily.*
Estudio tranquilamente.	*I study calmly.*
Contestan correctamente.	*They answer correctly.*

Some adverbs are formed differently

You don't say 'I sing goodly' in English, and you can't say 'buenamente' in Spanish either.

bueno/a *good* ⟶ bien *well*
malo/a *bad* ⟶ mal *badly*

Canto bien.	*I sing well.*
Canto mal.	*I sing badly.*

Letting Andrea choose the music was a big mistake...

Some adverbs describe possibility

Adverbs of certainty describe how possible something is. They normally come before the verb.

probablemente	*probably*
completamente	*completely*
quizás	*perhaps, maybe*
claro	*of course, clearly*

Probablemente seré profesor.
I will probably be a teacher.

Quizás visitaré.
I'll maybe visit.

Grammar Questions

Turn these adjectives into adverbs, then translate the **adverb** into **English**.

1. positivo **2.** directo **3.** social **4.** diferente **5.** exacto **6.** perfecto **7.** posible **8.** tradicional

H: **9.** evidente **10.** estricto **11.** nacional **12.** efectivo

Adverbs are stubborn — they never agree with anything...

Though I guess that makes them a bit easier than adjectives. Just remember to use the adjective's feminine form if you're forming an adverb with an adjective and '-mente' and you'll be an adverbs expert in no time.

Quick Quiz

Adverbs and Adverbial Phrases

And here's another page on adverbs — these ones say where or when something is happening.

Adverbs can tell you where something is done...

Adverbs of place say where things happen. They come after the verb in a phrase or sentence.

aquí	*here*	lejos	*far (away)*	dentro (Higher)	*inside, within*
allí	*there, over there*	detrás	*behind*	abajo (Higher)	*down, below, downstairs*
cerca	*close, near, nearby*	delante	*in front, ahead*	arriba (Higher)	*above, upstairs*

Mi tía trabaja aquí. *My aunt works here.* (*there* — allí)

Está muy cerca. *It's very near.* (*far away* — lejos)

...or when it's happening

Adverbs of time say when or how often something is done. They can come at the beginning or end of a sentence, or after the verb they describe.

ya	*already*	después	*after, afterwards*	a veces	*sometimes*
ahora	*now, these days*	luego	*then, later*	pronto (Higher)	*soon, early*
de momento	*at the moment*	siempre	*always, forever*	todavía (Higher)	*still, yet*
antes	*before, beforehand*	nunca	*never*	jamás (Higher)	*never*

Ya tengo un reloj. *I already have a watch.*

Siempre veo la tele. *I always watch TV.*

Adverbial phrases work like adverbs

Adverbial phrases can often be used like adverbs and describe how, when or where something is happening. They are placed at the beginning or end of a sentence, or after the verb they describe.

aparte de	*besides, apart (from)*	por fin	*finally, at last*	por la noche	*at night*

Aparte de leer me gusta jugar a los videojuegos. *Apart from reading, I like to play videogames.*

Por fin gané una carrera. *I finally won a race.*

Me lavo por la noche. *I have a wash at night.*

Grammar Questions

Translate these phrases into **Spanish**.

1. My shoes are here.
2. I want to leave now.
3. Sometimes I travel.
4. We live far away.
5. I can finally sleep.
6. The shop is over there.

Por fin — it's time for a tip about adverb placement...

Adverbs of manner and adverbs of place come after the verb they describe, while adverbs of certainty usually come before the verb. Adverbs of time can go at the beginning or end of a sentence, or come after the verb.

Comparative and Superlative Adverbs

Quick Quiz

You can use similar techniques to those you learned on p.120 to compare how people do things.

Comparative adverbs compare how people do actions

1) To say that something is done 'more ...ly', use 'más ... que'.

Pilar trabaja más alegremente que Hani.	*Pilar works more happily than Hani.*

2) If you want to say that something is done 'less ...ly', use 'menos ... que'.

Hani trabaja menos alegremente que Pilar.	*Hani works less happily than Pilar.*

3) To say that someone does something 'as ... as' someone else, use 'tan ... como'.

Pilar trabaja tan alegremente como Hani.	*Pilar works as happily as Hani.*

Paula and Alazne found that pizza always helped them work more happily.

Superlative adverbs say who does something the 'most ...ly'

Higher

To say someone does something 'the most ...ly', follow this pattern. Remember to change 'el' to 'la' if the subject is feminine, 'los' if it's a masculine plural subject, and 'las' for a feminine plural subject.

Ligaya es la que trabaja más alegremente.	*Ligaya is the one who works the most happily.*
Hugo es el que baila menos rápidamente.	*Hugo is the one who dances the least quickly.*

Watch out for irregulars...

bien	*well*	→	mejor	*better*	→ (H) el que mejor...	*the one who ... the best*
mal	*badly*	→	peor	*worse*	→ (H) el que peor...	*the one who ... the worst*

Juego mejor que él.	*I play better than him.*
Nado peor que Lin.	*I swim worse than Lin.*

Higher

Él es el que peor cocina.	*He's the one who cooks the worst.*
Ellas son las que mejor actúan.	*They are the ones who act the best.*

In Spanish, irregular superlative adverbs come straight after the 'que' and before the verb.

Grammar Questions

Complete the sentences in **Spanish** so that they match the words in the brackets.

1. Wafa come .... yo. (more quickly than)
2. Yo pinto .... ella. (better than)
3. Luis baila .... tú. (as well as)

Higher

4. Alba (f) es .... habla .... (the most calmly)
5. Ellos son .... conducen. (the best)
6. Inoke (m) es .... corre. (the worst)

Superlative Simon — the ultimate superhero...

For regular comparative adverb structures, remember to sandwich the adverb in between 'más / menos / tan' and 'como / que'. For irregular comparative adverb structures, just stick the adverb straight before the 'que'.

Quick Quiz

Quantifiers and Intensifiers

You can use this page to say you've had enough of Spanish adjectives and adverbs...

Quantifiers say how many or how much

1) Just saying 'I have apples' is boring. Use quantifiers to say you have lots of apples — or too many.
2) Quantifiers go before the noun, and most change their endings to agree with it, just like adjectives do.

mucho(s)	*much, a lot (many)*	tanto(s)	*so much (so many) + noun*
poco(s)	*little, not much (few, not many)*	bastante(s)	*quite a lot, enough*
demasiado(s)	*too much/many + noun*		

Tengo muchos deberes.
I have a lot of homework.

Escribes pocas cartas.
You (inf., sing.) write few letters.

Tienen bastantes zapatos.
They have enough shoes.

3) You don't just have to use these quantifiers with nouns — you can also use them with verbs. When you use them with verbs, they work like adverbs, so they go after the verb and don't change their endings.

Hablas demasiado. *You (inf., sing.) talk too much.*

Comen mucho. *They eat a lot.*

Intensifiers strengthen what you're saying

1) You can use intensifiers like 'very' and 'quite' to add detail to what you're saying.

2) Intensifiers go before the word they're modifying, but their endings don't change at all.

muy	*very, really*	tan	*so*	bastante	*quite*	demasiado	*too*

Simón está muy feliz. *Simón is very happy.*

Comemos bastante bien. *We eat quite well.*

Adding 'ísimo' makes adjectives stronger

1) If you add 'ísimo/a/os/as' to an adjective, it's like adding 'really' — it makes the meaning stronger.
2) The ending of 'ísimo' changes like other regular adjectives to agree with the noun it describes.

Su voz es hermosísima. *Her voice is really beautiful.*

Él es divertidísimo. *He is really funny.*

Grammar Questions

Rewrite each sentence, changing the quantifier or intensifier so it's used correctly.

1. Hay demasiado gatos aquí.
2. Es interesante bastante.
3. Tengo muchas amigos.
4. Tan hablan rápidamente.
5. Es un libro mucho bueno.
6. Hay una playa buenísimo.

I personally can't get enough of quantifiers and intensifiers...

But I think I've got too many apples. Remember — you only need to change a quantifier to agree if it's used with a noun. Quantifiers that are used with verbs don't need to agree and intensifiers don't change either.

Adjectives and Adverbs — Grammar List

If you've been thinking 'my nouns and verbs need extra details', then this list of adjectives and adverbs is a real treat.

Adjectives

Adjectives often change to match the gender and number of what they're describing. Many feminine adjectives change an '-o' ending to '-a'.

bueno/a	*good*
malo/a	*bad*
H ambos/as	*both*
H propio/a	*own (pre-noun)*

For more on adjective agreement, see p.117.

Other adjectives only change to become plural.

grande	*big, large*	alegre	*cheerful*

Some adjectives change when they go in front of a masculine singular noun.

buen	*good (pre-noun)*	gran	*big, great (pre-noun)*
mal	*bad (pre-noun)*		

An adjective's position can change its meaning.

único/a	*only (pre-noun), unique (post-noun)*
nuevo/a	*new, another (pre-noun), new, newly-made (post-noun)*
viejo/a	*old, long-standing (pre-noun), old, elderly (post-noun)*
antiguo/a	*former (pre-noun), old, ancient (pre- and post-noun)*

Possessive Adjectives

mi	*my*	nuestro/a/os/as	*our*
tu	*your (inf., sing.)*	vuestro/a/os/as	*your (inf., pl.)*
su	*his, her, its, your (form.), their*		

Higher:

mío/a/os/as	*mine*
tuyo/a/os/as	*your (inf., sing.)*
suyo/a/os/as	*his, her, its, your (form.), their*
nuestro/a/os/as	*our*
vuestro/a/os/as	*your (form., pl.)*

These Higher words are long-form possessive adjectives.

Demonstrative Adjectives

este/a	*this*	ese/a	*that*	H aquel/la	*that*
estos/as	*these*	esos/as	*those*	H aquellos/as	*those*

Indefinite Adjectives

cada	*each, every*	alguno/a	*a/an, any*
otro/a	*other, another*	ningún	*no, not...any (pre-noun)*
todo/a	*all, the whole*	ninguno/a	*no, not...any*
mismo/a	*same*		
algún	*a/an, any (pre-noun)*		

Only use 'algún' and 'ningún' with singular masculine nouns.

Adverbs

Most adverbs are formed by adding '-mente' to the feminine form of an adjective.

rápidamente	*quickly*
normalmente	*normally*
probablemente	*probably*
H actualmente	*now, at present*
H desafortunadamente	*unfortunately*
H afortunadamente	*fortunately*

Adverbs don't need to change to agree — they stay the same.

Others don't follow this pattern.

también	*also, too, as well*	aun	*even*
además	*also, as well, besides*	H incluso	*even, including*

Adverbs of manner describe how something is done.

bien	*well*	mal	*badly*	así	*like this/that*

Adverbs of certainty describe how likely something is.

quizás	*perhaps, maybe*

Adverbs of place describe where something happens.

aquí	*here*	H abajo	*down, below, downstairs*
detrás	*behind*	H arriba	*upstairs, above*
H dentro	*inside, within*		

Adverbs of time show when or how often something occurs.

ya	*already*	casi	*almost, nearly*
siempre	*always, forever*	Higher: pronto	*soon, early, quick*
por fin	*finally, at last*	Higher: todavía	*still, yet*
entonces	*then, so*	Higher: jamás	*never*
aún	*still*	Higher: enseguida	*straight away*
solo	*only, just*	Higher: apenas	*hardly, barely*

Comparative & Superlative Adjectives and Adverbs

más (...que)	*more (...than), adj. / adv. + er (...than)*
más de (+ number)	*more than (+ num)*
menos (...que)	*less (...than), fewer (...than)*
menos de (+ number)	*less than (+ num)*
tan...como	*as...as*
mejor	*better, best*
peor	*worse, worst*
H el/la/los/las mejor(es)	*the best*
H el/la/los/las peor(es)	*the worst*

Quantifiers & Intensifiers

Quantifiers say how much of something there is.

mucho(s)	*much, a lot (many)*
poco(s)	*little, not much (few, not many)*
demasiado(s)	*too much (many)*
tanto(s)	*so much (many)*
bastante(s)	*quite a lot, enough*

Intensifiers add detail to adjectives.

muy	*very, really*	bastante	*quite*
tan	*so*	demasiado	*too*

Revision Summary Test for Section Fourteen

Ah, another section down. You know what that means — a lovely summary test to have a crack at.

- These questions are **really tricky**, but they'll help you see **how well you know your stuff**.
- Tackle the **revision summary test** below, or scan the QR code to do it **online**.
  You can **keep track of your progress** online and see **which areas need more work**.
- There are **sample answers** here: www.cgpbooks.co.uk/BuenoExtras

Summary Test

Adjectives

1) Add the adjective in brackets to each phrase so that it agrees with the noun.
   a) las chicas (feliz) b) el hombre (optimista) c) los exámenes (difícil) d) una bebida (fresco)
2) Turn these verbs into adjectives using '-able': a) emplear b) aceptar c) separar
3) Translate each sentence into Spanish. Decide whether each sentence needs 'ser' or 'estar'.
   a) She is feeling sick. b) His parents are uptight. c) I think that football is boring.
4) Rewrite each sentence, putting the adjective in brackets into the right position.
   a) Quiero pantalones. (esos) c) Es una casa. (gran) e) Es mi móvil. (primer)
   b) Es la película. (tercera) d) Es una casa. (grande) f) Hay tiendas. (muchas)
5) Translate these sentences into Spanish using long-form possessive adjectives.
   a) I really like your dress. b) Her shoes are in that box over there.

Adverbs

6) Turn these adjectives into adverbs: a) sencillo b) estupendo c) malo d) fácil e) bueno
7) Choose the adverb or adverbial phrase in these sentences, then translate each sentence into English.
   a) Casi he terminado el libro. c) A veces voy al teatro. e) Quizás beberé café.
   b) Me encantaría estudiar allí. d) El coche llegó por fin. f) Hago mi cama por la mañana.
8) Rewrite each sentence so that the adverbs are in the correct position.
   a) Es divertido independientemente viajar. b) Lejos vivo de mi colegio. c) Está ahora trabajando.
9) Fill in the gaps by choosing the most appropriate adverb from each list.
   a) Vamos a hacer las compras .... (apenas / enseguida / jamás)
   b) Han limpiado todos los cuartos, ... el baño. (incluso / ya / solo)

Comparatives and Superlatives

10) Correct the mistakes in these sentences.
    a) Carmen habla más rápidamente como Dani. c) Odio estudiar. Estudio más mal que tú.
    b) Mi prima es tan directa que mi tía. d) Monika puede cantar mayor que yo.
11) Translate each sentence into Spanish: a) Raúl is older than his sister. b) We write better than them.
12) Translate these sentences into Spanish:
    a) Jorge (m) is the most ambitious. c) Those girls are the youngest of the class.
    b) Paula (f) is the one who paints the worst. d) They are the ones who run the slowest.

Quantifiers and Intensifiers

13) Complete each sentence by adding the quantifier or intensifier in brackets.
    a) Es una asignatura .... divertida. (quite) c) Mi amigo estudia .... (too much)
    b) Tengo .... videojuegos. (so many) d) .... gente vive en este pueblo. (few)
14) For each sentence, say if the bold word is a quantifier (Q) or intensifier (I), then translate the sentence.
    a) La fiesta fue **muy** emocionante. c) El café está **demasiado** caliente.
    b) Tenemos **tanta** comida. d) Has puesto **bastante** leche en el vaso.
15) Translate these sentences into Spanish, adding the ending in brackets to form the adjective.
    a) Paella is really good. (-ísima) b) The castle is really big. (-ísimo)

Verbs in the Present Tense

Quick Quiz

As a reward for all your hard work, I've bought you a present in the form of a tense. You lucky thing.

Verbs are actions

1) A verb is an action word like 'speak', 'eat' and 'live'.
2) Verbs can be put into different tenses, such as the future or past. For example, 'Yesterday, I ate a pie'.
3) To use a verb, you need to know its infinitive — the form you find in a dictionary, e.g. 'hablar' (*to speak*).

Forming the present tense

1) Regular verbs in Spanish end in '-ar', '-er' or '-ir'. To form the present tense of these regular verbs, you need to find the stem. To do this, remove the last two letters from the infinitive.

Infinitive	Remove last two letters	Stem
hablar	-ar	habl-

2) Then add the endings below to the stem.

-ar verbs

I speak	hablo	hablamos	we speak
you (inf., sing.) speak	hablas	habláis	you (inf., pl.) speak
he/she/it/you (form., sing.) speak(s)	habla	hablan	they/you (form., pl.) speak

Cantan. *They sing.*

Grita. *He shouts.*

Some verb forms change the spelling in their stem to avoid changing the pronunciation.

-er verbs

I eat	como	comemos	we eat
you (inf., sing.) eat	comes	coméis	you (inf., pl.) eat
he/she/it/you (form., sing.) eat(s)	come	comen	they/you (form., pl.) eat

Cojo. *I catch.*

Depende. *It depends.*

-ir verbs

I live	vivo	vivimos	we live
you (inf., sing.) live	vives	vivís	you (inf., pl.) live
he/she/it/you (form., sing.) live(s)	vive	viven	they/you (form., pl.) live

Abren. *They open.*

Escribe. *She writes.*

When to use the present tense

For another way to say what you're doing now, see p.138-139.

1) Use the present tense for actions taking place now... Hablo español. *I speak / I'm speaking Spanish.*
2) ...or for things that take place regularly. Canto todos los días. *I sing every day.*
3) You can also use it for things that are about to happen. Mañana voy al cine. *Tomorrow I'm going to the cinema.*

Grammar Questions

Put each of these infinitives into the present tense. The form of the verb is given in brackets.

1. bailar (yo)
2. beber (nosotros)
3. discutir (ustedes)
4. romper (ellas)
5. aprender (él)
6. nadar (vosotros)
7. escribir (tú)
8. visitar (ellos)

As the old saying goes, there's no tense like the present...

If you want full marks, you'll need to know the present tense inside out, back to front and top to bottom.

Quick Quiz

Irregular Verbs in the Present Tense

My irregular verb senses are tingling... It must be time to look at some rule breakers.

Some verbs are stem-changing

These are also called 'radical-changing verbs'.

Adva was excited about all types of stem changes.

1) A stem-changing verb is a verb that changes its spelling in the present tense.
2) Usually, the 'e' in the stem changes to 'ie', or the 'o' or 'u' changes to 'ue'. Some verbs change the 'e' in their stem to 'i'.
3) The stem changes in every form apart from the 'we' and 'you (inf., pl.)' forms.

pensar — to think (e to ie)	
I think	pienso
you (inf., sing.) think	piensas
he/she/it/you (form., sing.) think(s)	piensa
we think	pensamos
you (inf., pl.) think	pensáis
they/you (form., pl.) think	piensan

Even though their stems change, their endings are regular.

These verbs also change their 'e' to 'ie'...

cerrar	*to close*	despertarse	*to wake up*
comenzar	*to begin*	querer	*to want, love*
empezar	*to begin*	preferir	*to prefer*

encontrar — to find (o to ue)	
I find	encuentro
you (inf., sing.) find	encuentras
he/she/it/you (form., sing.) find(s)	encuentra
we find	encontramos
you (inf., pl.) find	encontráis
they/you (form., pl.) find	encuentran

These verbs also change their 'o' or 'u' to 'ue'...

doler	*to hurt*	jugar	*to play*
dormir	*to sleep*	llover	*to rain*
poder	*to be able to*	volver	*to return*

pedir — to ask for (e to i)	
I ask for	pido
you (inf., sing.) ask for	pides
he/she/it/you (form., sing.) ask(s) for	pide
we ask for	pedimos
you (inf., pl.) ask for	pedís
they/you (form., pl.) ask for	piden

These verbs also change their 'e' to 'i'...

You also drop the 'u' in the present tense 'I' form of seguir — 'sigo'.

decir	*to say, tell*	servir	*to serve*
repetir	*to repeat*	seguir	*to follow*
vestirse	*to get dressed*	H elegir	*to choose, elect*

Some stem-changing verbs follow a different pattern

1) In some stem-changing verbs, the stem only changes its spelling in the 'I' form. All the other forms of the verb follow the same pattern as regular verbs in the present tense.

poner — to put (add g)	
I put	pongo

Pongo mis dibujos sobre la mesa. *I put my drawings on the table.*

conocer — to know (c to zc)	
I know	conozco

Conozco a unas personas aquí. *I know a few people here.*

2) Here are a couple of examples of verbs that follow a similar pattern to 'poner'...

salir — to go out, leave	salgo	*I go out, I leave*
traer — to bring	traigo	*I bring*

'Traer' is a little different — the 'e' changes to 'i' as well.

3) ...and here are some that follow a similar pattern to 'conocer':

conducir — to drive	conduzco	*I drive*
H ofrecer — to offer	ofrezco	*I offer*

'Hacer', 'ir' and 'tener'

In Spanish, the verbs '<u>to do / make</u>', '<u>to go</u>' and '<u>to have</u>' are irregular.

hacer — to do, make	
I do, make	hago
you (inf., sing.) do, make	haces
he/she/it/you (form., sing.) do(es), make(s)	hace
we do, make	hacemos
you (inf., pl.) do, make	hacéis
they/you (form., pl.) do, make	hacen

Only the 'I' form is irregular in the present tense.

Hago mis deberes. *I do my homework.*

Lo hago sonreír. *I make him smile.*

All of the present tense forms of 'ir' are irregular.

ir — to go	
I go	voy
you (inf., sing.) go	vas
he/she/it/you (form., sing.) go(es)	va
we go	vamos
you (inf., pl.) go	vais
they/you (form., pl.) go	van

The verb 'dar' (to give) follows the same pattern as 'ir' in the present tense — 'I give' is 'doy', 'you give' is 'das', etc.

Va al concierto. *He's going to the concert.*

Siempre van allí. *They always go there.*

tener — to have	
I have	tengo
you (inf., sing.) have	tienes
he/she/it/you (form., sing.) has/have	tiene
we have	tenemos
you (inf., pl.) have	tenéis
they/you (form., pl.) have	tienen

'Venir' (to come) follows a similar pattern to 'tener'. It also has an irregular 'I' form — 'vengo'.

Tengo cinco primos. *I have five cousins.*

Tiene mucho papel. *She has a lot of paper.*

'Tener' can also sometimes mean 'to be'

You can sometimes use '<u>tener</u>' + <u>noun</u> to mean '<u>to be</u>' + <u>adjective</u>.

You don't need an article for the nouns when you use them in this way with 'tener'.

Tienen hambre. *They are hungry.*

¿Tiene sed? *Is she thirsty?*

Tengo miedo. *I'm afraid.*

Tiene quince años. *He is fifteen.*

Tenemos calor. *We are hot.*

¿Tienen frío? *Are they cold?*

Grammar Questions

Correct the spelling mistake in each of these sentences.

1. Comenza a las tres.
2. Quieremos leche.
3. Yo do el libro a Lola.
4. Podes conducir.
5. Repeten las direcciones.
6. Penso que es importante.

Translate these sentences into **Spanish**, making sure the stem of each verb is spelt correctly.

7. I'm also coming to the party.
8. We're going there tomorrow.
9. I get dressed quickly.
10. I don't have a pen.
11. The students are hungry.
12. I recognise her from the film. [H]

Irregular verbs are a regular pain...

Just like the neighbour's cat, Pickles, who insists on leaving perfumed presents in my flowerbeds. I will stop you, Pickles, even if it's the last thing I do... Ahem. Sorry — I got a bit carried away there. As you were...

Quick Quiz

'Ser' and 'Estar' in the Present Tense

The verbs 'ser' and 'estar' both mean 'to be'. If that isn't confusing enough, they're used in different situations *and* they're both irregular. I'm starting to feel a bit dizzy...

Use 'ser' for permanent things

The verb 'ser' means 'to be'. It's used for permanent things. You need it to...

1) ...talk about nationalities.

Somos ingleses. *We are English.*

2) ...talk about someone's job.

Mi tío es profesor. *My uncle is a teacher.*

3) ...say someone's name or say who someone is in relation to you.

Nerea y Sabina son mis primas. *Nerea and Sabina are my cousins.*

4) ...describe the physical characteristics of a person or thing.

Es largo. *It is long.* Eres muy alto. *You (inf., sing.) are very tall.*

5) ...describe someone's personality.

Sois amables. *You (inf., pl.) are kind.* Son listos. *They are clever.*

ser — to be	
I am	soy
you are (inf., sing.)	eres
he/she/it/you (form., sing.) is/are	es
we are	somos
you are (inf., pl.)	sois
they/you (form., pl.) are	son

Juma was ser-tain he wasn't that tall...

Use 'estar' for temporary things and locations

'Estar' also means 'to be'. You use it to...

1) ...talk about things that might change in the future.

Estoy bastante enfermo. *I'm quite ill.*
(But you might not be ill next week.)

Estás muy triste hoy. *You (inf., sing.) are very sad today.*
(But you might not be sad tomorrow.)

estar — to be	
I am	estoy
you are (inf., sing.)	estás
he/she/it/you (form., sing.) is/are	está
we are	estamos
you are (inf., pl.)	estáis
they/you (form., pl.) are	están

2) ...talk about where someone or something is.

Madrid está en España. *Madrid is in Spain.* Estamos en casa. *We are at home.*

Grammar Questions

Decide whether you need 'ser' or 'estar' in each of these sentences.

1. Es / Está muy enojado hoy.
2. Siempre es / está trabajador.
3. Somos / Estamos de Hull.
4. Soy / Estoy en Bradford.
5. Es / Está mi hermano.
6. Mi padre es / está médico.

To be or to be — that's a question worth asking...

'Ser' and 'estar' are two of the most important verbs in Spanish — you'll need them all the time. It might take a while to get your head around when to use each one, but the more you practise, the easier it'll become.

Quick Quiz

The Preterite Tense

Fun fact: 'entire pester teeth' is an anagram of 'the preterite tense'. You heard it here first.

I went — *The preterite tense*

To form the preterite tense of regular verbs, find the stem (see p.127) and then add these endings...

-ar verb endings

I	-é	-amos	we
you (inf., sing.)	-aste	-asteis	you (inf., pl.)
he/she/it/ you (form., sing.)	-ó	-aron	they/ you (form., pl.)

-er and -ir verb endings

I	-í	-imos	we
you (inf., sing.)	-iste	-isteis	you (inf., pl.)
he/she/it/ you (form., sing.)	-ió	-ieron	they/ you (form., pl.)

Don't forget the accent — without it, you'd be saying 'I speak to Sonal'.

Habló con Sonal. *He spoke to Sonal.*

Some verbs are irregular in the preterite tense

1) Here are three important irregular verbs in the preterite tense. Watch out — 'ser' and 'ir' are the same.

ser — to be; ir — to go

I was / went	fui
you (inf., sing.) were / went	fuiste
he/she/it/you (form., sing.) was (were) / went	fue
we were / went	fuimos
you (inf., pl.) were / went	fuisteis
they/you (form., pl.) were / went	fueron

dar — to give

I gave	di
you (inf., sing.) gave	diste
he/she/it/you (form., sing.) gave	dio
we gave	dimos
you (inf., pl.) gave	disteis
they/you (form., pl.) gave	dieron

2) Some verbs change their stem in the preterite tense. If you know what the stem change is, you can predict what the verb is going to be in its other forms.

Infinitive	I	he/she/it/you (form., sing.)	Infinitive	I	he/she/it/you (form., sing.)
decir (*to say*)	dije	dijo	tener (*to have*)	tuve	tuvo
poder (*to be able to*)	pude	pudo	estar (*to be*)	estuve	estuvo
poner (*to put*)	puse	puso	hacer (*to do, make*)	hice	hizo
querer (*to want*)	quise	quiso	venir (*to come*)	vine	vino
traer (*to bring*)	traje	trajo			

The 'he/she/it/ you (form., sing.)' form is sometimes different to what you might expect.

Higher

3) Verbs ending in '-aer' and '-eer' add 'y' in the third person forms, e.g. 'cayó' (*she fell*), 'leyeron' (*they read*).

4) Other verbs only have stem changes in the 'he/she/it' and 'they' forms. Some change their 'e' to 'i' ('pedir' becomes 'pidió' / 'pidieron'). Some change their 'o' to 'u' ('dormir' becomes 'durmió' / 'durmieron').

5) Some verbs have spelling changes in the 'I' form of the preterite tense. Verbs ending in '-car' change from 'c' to 'qu' ('tocar' becomes 'toqué'). Verbs ending in '-zar' change from 'z' to 'c' ('cruzar' becomes 'crucé'). Verbs ending in '-gar' change from 'g' to 'gu' ('llegar' becomes 'llegué').

Grammar Questions

Put these verbs into the preterite tense. The subject is given in brackets.

1. venir (tú) **2.** cenar (ellos) **3.** dar (yo) **4.** ir (él) H **5.** pedir (usted) **6.** jugar (yo) H

Wanted: two irregular verbs masquerading as each other...

Don't panic —the context of a sentence should help you work out whether you're looking at 'ser' or 'ir'.

Quick Quiz

The Imperfect Tense

If you wanted to talk about what you 'were doing' before you turned the page, this is how you'd do it...

I was going / I used to go — *The imperfect tense*

1) To form the imperfect tense, find the stem (see p.127) and then add these endings. The 'I' form and the 'he/she/it/you (form., sing.)' form look the same, so you'll have to use the context to tell which is which.

-ar verb endings

		Higher	
I	-aba	we	-ábamos
you (inf., sing.)	-abas	you (inf., pl.)	-abais
he/she/it/you (form., sing.)	-aba	they/you (form., pl.)	-aban

Compraba manzanas.
I was buying / used to buy apples.

-er and -ir verb endings

		Higher	
I	-ía	we	-íamos
you (inf., sing.)	-ías	you (inf., pl.)	-íais
he/she/it/you (form., sing.)	-ía	they/you (form., pl.)	-ían

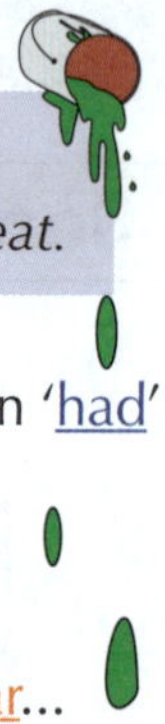

Comía carne.
I was eating / used to eat meat.

2) Some verbs have slightly different translations too — 'estar' can mean 'was/were' and 'tener' can mean 'had'.

There are three irregular verbs in the imperfect tense

1) 'Ser', 'ir' and 'ver' are the only three verbs which don't follow the pattern. 'Ser' and 'ir' are irregular...

ser — to be

		Higher	
I	era	we	éramos
you (inf., sing.)	eras	you (inf., pl.)	erais
he/she/it/you (form., sing.)	era	they/you (form., pl.)	eran

Era rubio.
He was / used to be blond.

ir — to go

		Higher	
I	iba	we	íbamos
you (inf., sing.)	ibas	you (inf., pl.)	ibais
he/she/it/you (form., sing.)	iba	they/you (form., pl.)	iban

Iba de compras.
I was going / used to go shopping.

2) ...but 'ver' is almost regular — just add the '-er' endings onto 've-', e.g. 'veía'.

Veía la tele. *I was watching / used to watch TV.*

Había — *There was / There were*

'Hay' and 'había' come from the verb 'haber'.

In the present tense, 'hay' means 'there is' or 'there are'. The imperfect form of 'hay' is 'había', which means 'there was' or 'there were' — it stays the same, regardless of whether the noun is singular or plural.

Había tráfico. *There was traffic.*

Había pájaros en el árbol. *There were birds in the tree.*

Grammar Questions

Put these verbs into the imperfect tense. The subject is given in brackets.

1. cantar (tú)
2. decir (él)
3. aprender (usted)
4. nadar (ella)
5. estar (yo)
6. tener (tú)

H
7. volver (ustedes)
8. seguir (vosotros)
9. ser (nosotros)
10. ir (ellos)
H

Learning the imperfect — a perfect way to spend your time...

Everyone has to learn the singular imperfect forms, but only Higher tier students need to learn the plural forms.

Using the Past Tenses

Quick Quiz

Choosing which past tense to use isn't always easy, but I'm here to help you crack it.

Learn when to use the preterite tense vs. the imperfect tense

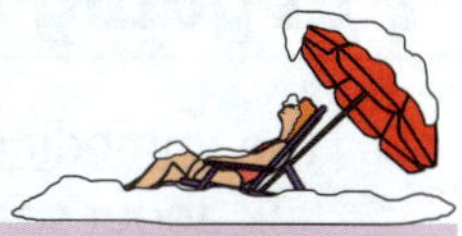

1) Use the preterite tense to talk about a single completed action in the past or an event that happened during a set period of time.

Fui al cine el jueves. *I went to the cinema on Thursday.*

Ayer hizo calor. *Yesterday it was hot.*

2) Use the imperfect tense to talk about what you used to do repeatedly or to describe something in the past.

Hacía calor. *It was hot.*

Iba al cine cada jueves. *I used to go to the cinema every Thursday.*

3) You can also use the imperfect tense to talk about something that was happening when something else happened. You need to use the preterite tense for the action that interrupts the imperfect.

Cuando paseaba al perro, vi a mi amigo. *When I was walking the dog, I saw my friend.*

I have done — *The present perfect tense*

1) You use the present perfect tense to say 'have done' or to talk about something that happened recently. To form it, you need the present tense of the verb 'haber' and the past participle.

haber — to have...

I	he	hemos	we
you (inf., sing.)	has	habéis	you (inf., pl.)
he/she/it/you (form., sing.)	ha	han	they/you (form., pl.)

Han jugado al tenis.
They have played tennis.

'Jugado' is a past participle.

2) To form a past participle, you remove the 'ar' from '-ar' verbs and add '-ado'.

ayudar *(to help)* → ayudado *(helped)*

3) For '-er' and '-ir' verbs, you remove the 'er' or 'ir' and add '-ido'.

comer *(to eat)* → comido *(eaten)*

The past participle always stays the same — you don't need to make it feminine or plural.

Higher

4) There are some irregular participles that don't follow these rules. You'll just have to learn them.

Infinitive	Past participle	Infinitive	Past participle	Infinitive	Past participle
cubrir	cubierto *(covered)*	poner	puesto *(put)*	hacer	hecho *(done, made)*
decir	dicho *(said, told)*	ver	visto *(seen)*	volver	vuelto *(returned)*
escribir	escrito *(written)*				

Grammar Questions

Translate these sentences into **Spanish**.

1. He has travelled to Spain.
2. She has run 500 metres.
3. They have finished the test.
4. Have you (tú) eaten already?
H
5. We have written a letter.
6. They have returned home.
H

Preterite or imperfect? It's a very tense business...

To say what 'has happened' very recently, use the present perfect tense. To say what 'happened' once or over a set time period, use the preterite. For descriptions or repeated actions in the past, use the imperfect tense.

Quick Quiz

The Future Tenses

You'll need to talk about things that are going to happen at some point in the future. There are two ways you can do it — and the first one's a piece of cake...

I'm going to... — *The immediate future tense*

This tense is also known as the 'periphrastic future'.

1) The immediate future tense can be used to talk about something that's about to happen, as well as something further on in the future.
2) To form the immediate future, take the present tense of 'ir' (*to go*) that goes with the person you're talking about.
3) Then, add 'a' and a verb in the infinitive.

ir — to go	
I am going	voy
you (inf., sing.) are going	vas
he/she/it/you (form., sing.) is/are going	va
we are going	vamos
you (inf., pl.) are going	vais
they/you (form., pl.) are going	van

voy
I am going
This is the present tense of 'ir'. + a + comer
to eat
This is another verb in the infinitive. = Voy a comer.
I am going to / will eat.
This is a sentence about the future.

I will... — *The proper future tense*

This tense is also known as the 'inflectional future'.

1) Use the proper future tense to say what will happen.
2) To form it, take the 'future stem' of the verb — for most verbs, this is the infinitive.
3) Add the ending that matches the person you're talking about (the endings are the same for all verbs).

hablar
infinitive + é
future ending = hablaré
I will talk.

Future endings	
I	-é
you (inf., sing.)	-ás
he/she/it/you (form., sing.)	-á

Higher

we	-emos
you (inf., pl.)	-éis
they/you (form., pl.)	-án

4) There are a few verbs that have a special future stem, so you just have to learn them off by heart. These are the most important ones.

Infinitive	'I' form
tener *(to have)*	tendré
hacer *(to do, make)*	haré
poder *(to be able to)*	podré
poner *(to put)*	pondré

Infinitive	'he/she/it' form
haber *(to have...)*	habrá

'Haber' is a bit different to other verbs — you only really need to use it in the 'he/she/it' form.

Higher

Infinitive	'I' form
saber *(to know)*	sabré
querer *(to want)*	querré
venir *(to come)*	vendré
decir *(to say)*	diré
salir *(to go out)*	saldré

Grammar Questions

Put these present tense verbs into the immediate and proper future tenses, keeping the subject the same.

1. haces **2.** tiene **3.** baila **4.** doy **5.** puedes **6.** juego

H: **7.** ponen **8.** venimos **9.** queremos **10.** vivís **11.** dice **12.** sabéis

Predicting the future might be tough, but talking about it isn't...

Use the immediate future tense to talk about something that's going to happen soon, e.g. scoffing a slice of cherry pie. Use the proper future tense to talk about things that 'will happen' further ahead in the future.

The Conditional

Quick Quiz

You could gloss over this page, but I would advise against it...

Future stem + imperfect -er / -ir endings — *The conditional*

1) The conditional can be used for saying 'would'. It uses the same stems as the proper future tense (see p.134) and adds these endings:

Pepe would eat the whole bowlful — if only Isuri would put it down...

Conditional endings

I	-ía
you (inf., sing.)	-ías
he/she/it/you (form., sing.)	-ía

Higher

we	-íamos
you (inf., pl.)	-íais
they/you (form., pl.)	-ían

comer
to eat
This is the infinitive. Not all verbs use the same future stem though (see p.134).

+

comía
I was eating.
This is the -er / -ir ending of the imperfect tense.

=

comería
I would eat.
This is a sentence in the conditional.

2) You can combine the conditional with other tenses to make more complicated sentences:

Bailaría, pero me duelen los pies. *I would dance, but my feet hurt.*

Le gustaría ir a la playa, pero no puede ir porque está lloviendo.
She would like to go to the beach, but she can't go because it's raining.

For more on conjunctions, check out p.113.

Irregular verbs in the conditional

The stems for irregular verbs are the same ones you use for the proper future tense (see p.134).
You just add the conditional endings instead:

Infinitive	'I' form
tener *(to have)*	tendría
hacer *(to do, make)*	haría
poder *(to be able to)*	podría
poner *(to put)*	pondría

Infinitive	'he/she/it' form
haber *(to have...)*	habría

Higher

Infinitive	'I' form
saber *(to know)*	sabría
querer *(to want)*	querría
venir *(to come)*	vendría
decir *(to say)*	diría
salir *(to go out)*	saldría

Saldría de la casa, pero estoy cansado.

I would leave the house, but I'm tired.

¿Podría ayudarme? *Could you (form., sing.) help me?*

Using 'poder' (to be able to) in the conditional lets you say 'could'.

Grammar Questions

Write these verbs in the conditional. The subject has been given to you in brackets.

1. ir (yo) **2.** cantar (él) **3.** poner (tú) **4.** hablar (usted) **5.** hacer (ella) **6.** pedir (yo)

H: **7.** decir (vosotros) **8.** venir (nosotros) **9.** querer (ustedes) **10.** saber (ellos) :H

I'll hand over the pizza on one condition...

You recite all those irregular stems while patting your head, rubbing your stomach and standing on one leg. I'll have a go too. Don't forget that regular and irregular verbs use the same endings in the conditional.

Quick Quiz

Modal Verbs

Modal verbs help you express desire, ability or obligation, so you might find this page rather useful...

Deber, poder, querer, tener que, saber

1) Modal verbs are usually followed by an infinitive.

Debo terminar la tarea ahora.
I must finish the task now.

Deben llevar un disfraz para la fiesta.
They have to wear a costume for the party.

Using 'deber' in the conditional helps you say 'should'.

2) As well as 'deber' (*to have to, must*), there are four other modal verbs you need to know:

a) Use 'poder' to say 'can' or 'could'.

No puedo ir al cine. *I can't go to the cinema.*

Scary films are better at home anyway...

b) Use 'querer' to say 'want to'.

Quiero viajar a más países. *I want to travel to more countries.*

c) You can also use 'tener que' when you want to say 'have to' or 'must'.

Tengo que volver a casa a las seis. *I have to go back home at six o'clock.*

'Tener' by itself isn't a modal verb. You need to add the 'que' to show the action that you have to do.

d) You can use 'saber' to say 'know how to'.

Sabe montar en bici. *She knows how to ride a bike.*

You could also translate this sentence as 'She can ride a bike.'

Quisiera, me gustaría — *I would like*

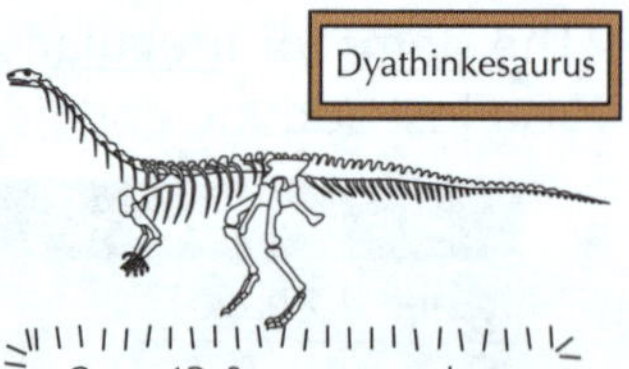

1) 'Quisiera' and 'me gustaría' are two common ways of saying 'I would like'. Just like other modal verbs, they are followed by an infinitive.

Quisiera / Me gustaría visitar el museo. *I would like to visit the museum.*

See p.12 for more on how to use verbs like 'gustar'.

2) You can use 'quisiera' and 'me gustaría' in polite requests.

Quisiera / Me gustaría reservar una mesa para tres personas. *I would like to reserve a table for three.*

3) Using other pronouns with 'gustar' in the conditional helps you say what other people 'would like'.

¿Te gustaría leer? *Would you (inf., sing.) like to read?*

Le gustaría comer. *She would like to eat.*

Grammar Questions

Translate these sentences into **English**.

1. Debes repasar para la prueba.
2. Juanjo no sabe hablar español.
3. ¿Pueden venir a la boda?
4. Tenemos que escuchar bien.
5. No quiero volver a casa.
6. Quisiera pagar la cuenta.

What do verbs say in the mountains? Modalay hee hoo!

Don't be put off by their fancy-schmancy name — modal verbs are really useful for talking about things you 'can' or 'have to' do. Using them confidently in your exams will get you top marks, so show off your skills.

Reflexive Verbs and Pronouns

Quick Quiz

Sometimes you'll have to talk about things you do to yourself — like 'washing yourself' or 'getting yourself up' in the morning. It sounds weird in English, but in Spanish they do it all the time.

Me, te, se... — *Reflexive pronouns*

1) Reflexive pronouns usually mean 'self'. They change form depending on who's doing the action:

myself	me
yourself (inf., sing.)	te
himself/herself/oneself/ yourself (form., sing.)	se

Higher

ourselves	nos
yourselves (inf., pl.)	os
themselves/ yourselves (form., pl.)	se

You can tell which verbs need 'self' by checking in the dictionary. 'To have a wash' is 'lavarse'.

2) When you use a reflexive verb on its own, the pronoun goes before it.

Me lavo. *I have a wash.*

3) If you have a verb followed by a reflexive infinitive, the reflexive pronoun goes before the first verb or at the end of the infinitive.

Me debo levantar. *I have to get up.*

Debes levantarte. *You (inf., sing.) have to get up.*

Higher

4) You can also use reflexive pronouns for reciprocal actions where two people do something to each other.

Nos hablamos. *We talk to each other.*

¿Os visteis? *Did you (inf., pl.) see each other?*

Lavarse, despertarse, levantarse... — *Reflexive verbs*

1) Reflexive verbs follow a straightforward pattern, e.g. 'lavarse' = to have a wash (literally 'to wash oneself'). You can use them in any tense as well — they take the same endings as their non-reflexive forms.

I have a wash	me lavo
you (inf., sing.) have a wash	te lavas
he/she/it/you (form., sing.) has/have a wash	se lava

Higher

we have a wash	nos lavamos
you (inf., pl.) have a wash	os laváis
they/you (form., pl.) have a wash	se lavan

¿Te sientes mal? *Do you (inf., sing.) feel ill?*

Me llevo bien con él. *I get on well with him.*

2) There are lots of these verbs, but here are the ones you really should know:

despertarse	*to wake up*	ponerse	*to get, become (+ adjective)*
levantarse	*to get up*	vestirse	*to get dressed*
sentirse	*to feel*	H acostarse	*to go to bed*
llamarse	*to be called*		

'despertarse', 'sentirse', 'vestirse' and 'acostarse' are all stem-changing verbs (see p.128).

Se puso nerviosa. *She became nervous.*

Me despierto tarde. *I wake up late.*

Grammar Questions

Write these reflexive verbs in the present tense. The subject has been given to you in brackets.

1. llamarse (yo) **3.** sentirse (él) **5.** acostarse (yo) **7.** vestirse (nosotros)
2. llevarse (tú) **4.** despertarse (usted) **6.** levantarse (ellos) **8.** ponerse (vosotros)

(Questions 5–8: H)

Just me, myself and I revising reflexive verbs...

The verbs on this page will be really handy in the exam. Now, where did I put that reflexive pronoun...

Quick Quiz

Verbs with '-ing' and 'Just Done'

The continuous tenses help you specify that something is ongoing at a particular moment.

Use the present continuous for what's happening right now

1) Most of the time you'd translate 'I am doing' with the present tense, e.g. 'hago'.
2) If you want to stress that something is happening at the moment, you use the present continuous.

Estoy cenando. *I'm having dinner.*

3) To form the present continuous, you need the correct part of 'estar' (*to be*) in the present tense...

estar — to be	
I am	estoy
you (inf., sing.) are	estás
he/she/it is you (form., sing.) are	está
we are	estamos
you (inf., pl.) are	estáis
they/you (form., pl.) are	están

4) ...and the '-ing' part — also called the present participle or gerund.
5) It's made up of the stem of the verb (p.127), plus the correct ending.

a) If it's an -ar verb, add '-ando'.

estoy (*present of 'estar'*) + habl- (*'hablar' stem*) + -ando (*-ar ending*) = estoy hablando (*I am speaking*)

b) If it's an -er or -ir verb, add '-iendo'.

estás (*present of 'estar'*) + com- (*'comer' stem*) + -iendo (*-er ending*) = estás comiendo (*you (inf., sing.) are eating*)

6) There are a few stem-changing present participles. For example, in verbs like 'pedir', the 'e' changes to 'i'.

pedir (*to ask for*) ⟶ pidiendo

decir (*to say*) ⟶ diciendo

The 'o' changes to 'u' in the stem of verbs like 'dormir'.

dormir (*to sleep*) ⟶ durmiendo

morir (*to die*) ⟶ muriendo

If the verb's stem ends in a vowel, you add '-yendo' instead of '-iendo'.

leer (*to read*) ⟶ leyendo

construir (*to build*) ⟶ construyendo

The imperfect continuous is for saying what was happening

1) If you want to stress that something was happening in the past, use the imperfect continuous.
2) The imperfect continuous is similar to the present continuous, except 'estar' has to be in the imperfect tense.

See p.132 for more on the imperfect tense.

estaba (*imperfect of 'estar'*) + habl- (*'hablar' stem*) + -ando (*-ar ending*) = estaba hablando (*I was speaking*)

Estaba buscando mis llaves. *I was looking for my keys.*

Se estaba cayendo, pero lo cogí. *It was falling, but I caught it.*

Estaba durmiendo cuando llegaron. *He was sleeping when they arrived.*

The preterite tense is used here to show that a sudden action — the people arriving — interrupted an ongoing action in the imperfect continuous — i.e. the person sleeping.

Pavel wasn't letting a falling *manzana* spoil his *mañana*.

There are a few other ways to say '-ing'

Higher

1) If you want to say you continue to do something or you'll still be doing something, you can use the present tense of the verb 'seguir' with a present participle.

sigo		habl-		-ando		sigo hablando
present of 'seguir'	+	*'hablar' stem*	+	*-ar ending*	=	*I am still speaking*

Siguen andando. *They continue to walk.*

Sigue lloviendo. *It's still raining.*

Ron and Sue should have checked the forecast...

2) To say you have been doing something for a certain amount of time, you can use the present tense of the verb 'llevar', followed by a time period and a present participle.

llevo		dos horas		escribiendo		Llevo dos horas escribiendo.
present of 'llevar'	+	*time period*	+	*present participle*	=	*I have been writing for two hours.*

Lleva treinta minutos ordenando su habitación. *He's been tidying his bedroom for thirty minutes.*

Llevamos casi cinco horas repasando. *We've been revising for almost five hours.*

3) You can also use the present tense with 'desde hace' to say how long you've been doing something.

Toco la guitarra desde hace cuatro años. *I've been playing the guitar for four years.*

'Acabar de' — *to say that something's just happened*

Higher

To say what's just happened, use the present tense of 'acabar', followed by 'de' and a verb in the infinitive.

'Acabar' is a regular '-ar' verb.

acabar de... — to have just...	
I have just...	acabo de...
you (inf., sing.) have just...	acabas de...
he/she/it/you (form., sing.) has/have just...	acaba de...
we have just...	acabamos de...
you (inf., pl.) have just...	acabáis de...
they/you (form., pl.) have just...	acaban de...

Acabo de llegar. *I have just arrived.*

Acaba de salir. *She has just left.*

Acabamos de verla. *We have just seen her.*

Grammar Questions

Put these verbs into the present continuous. The subject has been given to you in brackets.

1. traer (tú) **3.** decir (ellos) **5.** bailar (nosotros) **7.** servir (ustedes)

2. abrir (usted) **4.** correr (vosotros) **6.** leer (yo) **8.** seguir (ella)

Translate these sentences into **Spanish**.

9. He was asking for an orange. **11.** The cat was sleeping. H **13.** They have just seen the film. H

10. I was studying in my room. **12.** She was working well. H **14.** We have just had breakfast. H

The present continuous just goes on and on and on...

Careful, though — it isn't used as much in Spanish as it is in English, so don't be tempted to put it absolutely everywhere. Treat it like salt on chips — use sparingly for the best results. Then get it down the hatch ASAP.

Quick Quiz

Negative Forms

No, I won't write anything here about negatives. Nothing at all... except that they're pretty useful.

'No' in front of the verb means 'not'

1) To change a sentence to mean the opposite in Spanish, you have to put 'no' in front of the verb:

   Hablo español. *I speak Spanish.* → No hablo español. *I don't speak Spanish.*

2) You can do the same with all the tenses:

   No fui al parque. *I didn't go to the park.*

3) Sometimes you have to say 'no' twice. This is because 'no' in Spanish means both 'no' and 'not'.

   No, no quiero paella, gracias.
   No, I don't want paella, thanks.

4) You can also put 'nada' (*not anything, nothing*), 'nunca' (*never*) or 'nadie' (*nobody, no one*) before a verb to make it negative.

   Nunca canta. *She never sings.*

5) These words can be used with 'no' too. The 'no' goes before the verb and the other negative word goes after it.

   No vi a nadie. *I didn't see anybody.*

'nadie' can also mean 'anybody' or 'anyone' after a negative verb.

There are some tricky negatives to learn too

There are more negatives you need to understand — for top marks you should use them too.

(no) ... ningún / ninguna	*no, not ... any (pre-noun)*
(no) ... ninguno / ninguna	*no one, none, one (after a negative verb), anyone (after a negative verb)*
Higher: (no) ... ni ... (ni ...)	*nor, or (after a negative verb), neither ... nor ...*
Higher: (no) ... tampoco	*neither, either (after a negative verb)*
Higher: ya no	*no longer, no more*

See p.118 for more information on 'ningún'.

No hay ningún tomate. *There aren't any tomatoes.*

No queda ninguno. *There are none left.*

Higher

No van ni a Londres ni a Madrid ni a Barcelona.
They go to neither London, nor Madrid nor Barcelona.

In negative lists, you need a 'ni' before each item.

Tampoco hay uvas. *Neither are there grapes.*

No me gusta tampoco. *I don't like it either.*

Ya no voy a Sevilla. *I no longer go to Seville.*

Grammar Questions

Translate these sentences into **Spanish** using negative forms.

1. We didn't go to the library.
2. They don't have any apples.
3. There's nothing here.
4. Nobody is in the car.
5. (H) It's neither red nor green.
6. (H) We no longer go to the gym.

On a positive note, you've nearly finished another page...

Sometimes you'll need to say 'no' twice, especially if you're answering a question. In some cases you don't need 'no' at all — just put the negative word before the verb. I know, I know, but I don't make the rules...

Impersonal Verbs and the Passive

Quick Quiz

Quick — do your best impression of a sponge and soak up all the information on this page...

Impersonal verbs use a generic subject

You can make any Spanish verb impersonal by using its 'he/she/it' form and adding 'se' before it.

1) Impersonal verbs don't have a specific subject — they use a general one like 'it' or 'one'.
2) You can use 'se puede' to say 'you (general) / one can' and 'se necesita' to say 'you (general) / one needs to'.

Se puede comer. *You (general) can eat.*

¿Se necesita salir? *Does one need to leave?*

3) Use 'hace' and a noun to talk about the weather. See p.91 for more.

Hace calor. *It is hot.*

4) Here are some more important impersonal verbs you need to know:

Impersonal verb	Meaning	Example sentence
hay	there is / there are	Hay libros en esta caja. (*There are books in this box.*)
hay que	you (general) / one must	Hay que hacer la tarea. (*One must do the task.*)
parece	it seems	Parece un poco raro. (*It seems a little strange.*)
basta + infinitive	you (general) only have to (+ verb)	Basta hacerlo una vez. (*You only have to do it once.*)
falta (+ infinitive)	it's/is still to be (+ past participle)	Falta investigarlo. (*It's still to be investigated.*)
hace falta (+ infinitive)	it's necessary (+ verb)	Hace falta trabajar. (*It's necessary to work.*)
vale la pena + infinitive	it's worth -ing	Vale la pena esperar. (*It's worth waiting.*)

Higher (parece – vale la pena)

There are two forms of the passive

For the passive voice, past participles must agree with the subject. So 'escrita' is used because 'la carta' is feminine.

Higher

1) In an active sentence, the subject does something. In the passive voice, something is done to the subject.

Escribió la carta. *He wrote the letter.*

Fue escrita por él. *It was written by him.*

2) The passive is formed using 'ser' (*to be*), a past participle (see p.133) and 'por' (*by*).

fueron *they were* — This part changes depending on the tense and subject.
\+ limpiado *cleaned* — past participle of the verb 'limpiar'
\+ por *by*
= Las mesas fueron limpiadas por ellos. *The tables were cleaned by them.* — A sentence in the passive voice. The past participle has to agree with the subject.

3) You can also form the passive with 'se' and the third-person forms of any verb. Use the 'he/she/it' form for a single subject, and the 'they' form for a plural subject:

El arroz se cocina por diez minutos. *The rice is cooked for ten minutes.*

Las puertas se abren a las nueve. *The doors are opened at nine.*

Grammar Questions

Translate these sentences into **Spanish** using impersonal verbs.

1. You can relax now.
2. One must do exercise.
3. You need to go to class.
4. There are many festivals.
5. It's worth learning this content. (H)
6. It seems like a marvellous idea. (H)

One has to learn this — it's nothing personal...

These topics are plain sailing as long as you remember to use the 'he/she/it' or 'they' forms of the verb.

Quick Quiz

The Subjunctive

Oh yes, you're in for a treat — it's time to learn about the Spanish subjunctive...

Forming the present subjunctive

You only need to know the singular forms of these verbs in the present subjunctive.

Higher

1) Sometimes, the present subjunctive is needed instead of the normal present tense.
2) To form the present subjunctive of 'hacer', 'tener' and 'venir', take the stem from the 'I' form of the normal present tense and add the '-ar' verb endings.

hago → hag- + -a = haga

Verb	I	you (inf., sing.)	he/she/it/ you (form., sing.)
hacer (*to do, make*)	haga	hagas	haga
tener (*to have*)	tenga	tengas	tenga
venir (*to come*)	venga	vengas	venga
ir (*to go*)	vaya	vayas	vaya
ser (*to be*)	sea	seas	sea

3) You'll need to learn the subjunctive forms for 'ir' and 'ser' by heart — they are completely irregular.

Use the present subjunctive...

Higher

1) ...after 'cuando' (*when*) when talking about the future:

Cuando sea mayor, viviré en Italia. *When I am older, I will live in Italy.*

2) ...to request or command someone else does something:

Vyvan quiere que yo haga la cena. *Vyvan wants me to make dinner.*

It looks like Vyvan and Greg will be having a takeaway...

3) ...to express a wish or desire:

Espero que Noor tenga los billetes. *I hope that Noor has the tickets.*

You normally only use the subjunctive when there's a different person doing the second verb.

4) ...after expressing an emotion:

Es triste que no vayas de vacaciones. *It's sad that you (inf., sing.) don't go on holiday.*

5) ...after 'para que' (*so that*) to express purpose:

Mejoramos la app para que sea más fácil usarla. *We're improving the app so that it's easier to use it.*

6) ...after 'que' (*that*) to express possibility or necessity:

Es posible que venga a la fiesta.
It's possible that he'll come to the party.

Es importante que hagas los ejercicios.
It's important that you (inf., sing.) do the exercises.

Grammar Questions

Decide whether you need the present subjunctive or normal present tense in each of these sentences.

Higher

1. Piensan que Charvi ____ a su boda. (venir)
2. Lo explico para que ____ más claro. (ser)
3. Ya sé que ella ____ más hijos que yo. (tener)
4. Me preocupa que el libro no ____ bueno. (ser)
5. Llamo a mi novio cuando él ____ al café. (ir)
6. Es necesario que yo ____ mis deberes. (hacer)

Higher

It's sad that you're nearly finished with grammar *sob*...

If Spanish grammar were a video game (a truly frightening thought...), the subjunctive would be the final level. It can be a pretty tricky topic, so don't be afraid to revisit this page whenever you're feeling unsure.

The Imperative

Quick Quiz

Imperatives are words that give a command. They change depending on whether you're talking to one person or a group. So learn what's on this page and you'll be giving out orders in no time...

Singular informal commands

1) To form a singular informal command, take the 'tú' part of the present tense verb and take off the 's'.

escribes *you write* → ¡Escribe! *Write!*

escuchas *you listen* → ¡Escucha! *Listen!*

2) With commands, pronouns (e.g. me, them, it) are placed at the end of the word and you need to add an accent to show where the stress is.

¡Cómelo! *Eat it!*

¡Llámame! *Call me!*

3) There are a few common irregular imperatives you need to know.

Infinitive	Informal singular
ser (*to be*)	¡Sé!
ir (*to go*)	¡Ve!
tener (*to have*)	¡Ten!
venir (*to come*)	¡Ven!
hacer (*to do, make*)	¡Haz!
decir (*to say, tell*)	¡Di!
poner (*to put (on)*)	¡Pon!
salir (*to go out, leave*)	¡Sal!

¡Ven aquí, por favor! *Come here, please!*

¡Dime! *Tell me!*

¡Hazlo! *Do it!*

You don't need an accent when you use pronouns with the irregular imperatives.

Plural informal commands

Higher

1) To tell two or more people what to do in an informal way, take the infinitive and change the final 'r' to 'd'.

hablar (*to speak, talk*) → ¡Hablad! *Speak!*

conducir (*to drive*) → ¡Conducid! *Drive!*

mirar (*to look, watch*) → ¡Mirad! *Look!*

leer (*to read*) → ¡Leed! *Read!*

2) The verbs that are irregular in singular informal commands follow the same rules as regular verbs in the you (inf., pl.) form.

salir (*to go out*) → ¡Salid! *Go out!*

ir (*to go*) → ¡Id! *Go!*

poner (*to put (on)*) → ¡Poned la caja allí! *Put the box there!*

Laura was sure she could make space for more boxes...

Grammar Questions

Translate these sentences into **Spanish** using informal singular commands.

1. Sing this song!
2. Go to your room!
3. Write two sentences!
4. Take it!
5. Say something!
6. Drink the water!

Translate these sentences into **Spanish** using informal plural commands.

H
7. Learn these words!
8. Sign this document!
9. Wait here, please!
10. Buy that now!
11. Make your beds!
12. Cross the street!
H

Learn how to use the imperative... Go on...

Commands are far handier than you probably realise — you can order someone to tap dance, tell a really annoying person to go away, or request a llama to be delivered to your house... The possibilities are endless.

Verbs and Tenses — Grammar List

Regular Verbs

All regular verbs that end in '-ar', '-er' or '-ir' can be conjugated like these three examples.

-ar verbs, e.g. hablar (to speak, talk)

Subject	Present	Preterite	Imperfect	Proper Future	Conditional
yo	hablo	hablé	hablaba	hablaré	hablaría
tú	hablas	hablaste	hablabas	hablarás	hablarías
él / ella / usted	habla	habló	hablaba	hablará	hablaría
nosotros/as	hablamos	hablamos	hablábamos	hablaremos	hablaríamos
vosotros/as	habláis	hablasteis	H hablabais	H hablaréis	H hablaríais
ellos / ellas / ustedes	hablan	hablaron	hablaban	hablarán	hablarían

-er verbs, e.g. comer (to eat)

Subject	Present	Preterite	Imperfect	Proper Future	Conditional
yo	como	comí	comía	comeré	comería
tú	comes	comiste	comías	comerás	comerías
él / ella / usted	come	comió	comía	comerá	comería
nosotros/as	comemos	comimos	comíamos	comeremos	comeríamos
vosotros/as	coméis	comisteis	H comíais	H comeréis	H comeríais
ellos / ellas / ustedes	comen	comieron	comían	comerán	comerían

-ir verbs, e.g. vivir (to live)

Subject	Present	Preterite	Imperfect	Proper Future	Conditional
yo	vivo	viví	vivía	viviré	viviría
tú	vives	viviste	vivías	vivirás	vivirías
él / ella / usted	vive	vivió	vivía	vivirá	viviría
nosotros/as	vivimos	vivimos	vivíamos	viviremos	viviríamos
vosotros/as	vivís	vivisteis	H vivíais	H viviréis	H viviríais
ellos / ellas / ustedes	viven	vivieron	vivían	vivirán	vivirían

Important Irregular Verbs

You only need to know the subjunctive forms for ser, ir, tener, hacer and venir.

ser (to be)

Subject	Present	Preterite	Imperfect	Proper Future	Conditional	Subjunctive
yo	soy	fui	era	seré	sería	sea
tú	eres	fuiste	eras	serás	serías	H seas
él / ella / usted	es	fue	era	será	sería	sea
nosotros/as	somos	fuimos	éramos	seremos	seríamos	
vosotros/as	sois	fuisteis	H erais	H seréis	H seríais	**Imperative**
ellos / ellas / ustedes	son	fueron	eran	serán	serían	tú ¡Sé!

You need the present tense forms of 'ir' to make the immediate future tense (see p.134).

ir (to go)

Subject	Present	Preterite	Imperfect	Proper Future	Conditional	Subjunctive
yo	voy	fui	iba	iré	iría	vaya
tú	vas	fuiste	ibas	irás	irías	H vayas
él / ella / usted	va	fue	iba	irá	iría	vaya
nosotros/as	vamos	fuimos	íbamos	iremos	iríamos	
vosotros/as	vais	fuisteis	H ibais	H iréis	H iríais	**Imperative**
ellos / ellas / ustedes	van	fueron	iban	irán	irían	tú ¡Ve!

tener (to have)

Subject	Present	Preterite	Imperfect	Proper Future	Conditional	Subjunctive
yo	tengo	tuve	tenía	tendré	tendría	tenga
tú	tienes	tuviste	tenías	tendrás	tendrías	H tengas
él / ella / usted	tiene	tuvo	tenía	tendrá	tendría	tenga
nosotros/as	tenemos	tuvimos	teníamos	tendremos	tendríamos	
vosotros/as	tenéis	tuvisteis	H teníais	H tendréis	H tendríais	
ellos / ellas / ustedes	tienen	tuvieron	tenían	tendrán	tendrían	

Imperative
tú ¡Ten!

Only the irregular imperatives are included on these pages. You can find out how to form regular imperatives in the 'tú' and 'vosotros' forms on p.143.

hacer (to do, make)

Subject	Present	Preterite	Imperfect	Proper Future	Conditional	Subjunctive
yo	hago	hice	hacía	haré	haría	haga
tú	haces	hiciste	hacías	harás	harías	H hagas
él / ella / usted	hace	hizo	hacía	hará	haría	haga
nosotros/as	hacemos	hicimos	hacíamos	haremos	haríamos	
vosotros/as	hacéis	hicisteis	H hacíais	H haréis	H haríais	
ellos / ellas / ustedes	hacen	hicieron	hacían	harán	harían	

Imperative
tú ¡Haz!

venir (to come)

Subject	Present	Preterite	Imperfect	Proper Future (Higher)	Conditional (Higher)	Subjunctive
yo	vengo	vine	venía	vendré	vendría	venga
tú	vienes	viniste	venías	vendrás	vendrías	H vengas
él / ella / usted	viene	vino	venía	vendrá	vendría	venga
nosotros/as	venimos	vinimos	veníamos	vendremos	vendríamos	
vosotros/as	venís	vinisteis	H veníais	vendréis	vendríais	
ellos / ellas / ustedes	vienen	vinieron	venían	vendrán	vendrían	

Imperative
tú ¡Ven!

poner (to put (on))

Subject	Present	Preterite	Imperfect	Proper Future	Conditional	Subjunctive
yo	pongo	puse	ponía	pondré	pondría	ponga
tú	pones	pusiste	ponías	pondrás	pondrías	H pongas
él / ella / usted	pone	puso	ponía	pondrá	pondría	ponga
nosotros/as	ponemos	pusimos	poníamos	pondremos	pondríamos	
vosotros/as	ponéis	pusisteis	H poníais	H pondréis	H pondríais	
ellos / ellas / ustedes	ponen	pusieron	ponían	pondrán	pondrían	

Imperative
tú ¡Pon!

You also need to know the future and conditional forms of 'estar', but they are regular — you can use the '-ar verbs' table on the previous page to form them.

estar (to be)

Subject	Present	Preterite	Imperfect
yo	estoy	estuve	estaba
tú	estás	estuviste	estabas
él / ella / usted	está	estuvo	estaba
nosotros/as	estamos	estuvimos	estábamos
vosotros/as	estáis	estuvisteis	H estabais
ellos / ellas / ustedes	están	estuvieron	estaban

haber (to have done something)

You need these forms of 'haber' to form the present perfect tense.

Subject	Present
yo	he
tú	has
él / ella / usted	ha
nosotros/as	hemos
vosotros/as	habéis
ellos / ellas / ustedes	han

Verbs and Tenses — Grammar List

Other Common Verbs

The stems of these verbs change their spellings in certain tenses. See p.128 for more on stem-changing verbs.

decir (to say, tell)

Subject	Present	Preterite	Future (Higher)	Conditional (Higher)
yo	digo	dije	diré	diría
tú	dices	dijiste	dirás	dirías
él / ella / usted	dice	dijo	dirá	diría
nosotros/as	decimos	dijimos	diremos	diríamos
vosotros/as	decís	dijisteis	diréis	diríais
ellos / ellas / ustedes	dicen	dijeron	dirán	dirían

Imperative tú ¡Di!

You can find out how to conjugate the regular forms of these verbs by using the regular verb boxes on p.144.

dar (to give)

Subject	Present	Preterite
yo	doy	di
tú	das	diste
él / ella / usted	da	dio
nosotros/as	damos	dimos
vosotros/as	dais	disteis
ellos / ellas / ustedes	dan	dieron

salir (to go out)

Subject	Future (Higher)	Conditional (Higher)
yo	saldré	saldría
tú	saldrás	saldrías
él / ella / usted	saldrá	saldría
nosotros/as	saldremos	saldríamos
vosotros/as	saldréis	saldríais
ellos / ellas / ustedes	saldrán	saldrían

Imperative tú ¡Sal!

In the present tense, 'salir' is only irregular in its 'yo' form ('salgo').

ver (to see, watch)

Subject	Present	Imperfect
yo	veo	veía
tú	ves	veías
él / ella / usted	ve	veía
nosotros/as	vemos	veíamos (H)
vosotros/as	veis	veíais (H)
ellos / ellas / ustedes	ven	veían (H)

Hilde reckons she's nearly finished revising for her GCSE Spanish exams.

traer (to bring)

Subject	Present	Preterite
yo	traigo	traje
tú	traes	trajiste
él / ella / usted	trae	trajo
nosotros/as	traemos	trajimos
vosotros/as	traéis	trajisteis
ellos / ellas / ustedes	traen	trajeron

Reflexive Verbs and Pronouns

Reflexive verbs are useful for talking about things you do to yourself — they use reflexive pronouns.

Reflexive Pronoun		llamarse (to be called)
me	*myself*	me llamo
te	*yourself (inf., sing.)*	te llamas
se	*himself, herself, itself, oneself, yourself (form., sing.)*	se llama
nos (H)	*ourselves*	nos llamamos
os (H)	*yourselves (inf., pl.)*	os llamáis
se (H)	*themselves, yourselves (form., pl.)*	se llaman

For more on reflexive pronouns and where to put them in a sentence, see p.137.

Impersonal Verbs

These are the impersonal forms of 'haber':

Present	hay	*there is / are*
Imperfect	había	*there was / were / used to be*
Proper Future	habrá	*there will be / is going to be*
Conditional	habría	*there would be*

se puede	*you (general) / one can*
se necesita	*you (general) / one needs to*
hace + weather noun	*it is...*
hay que	*you (general) / one must*
parece (Higher)	*it seems*
basta + infinitive (Higher)	*you (general) only have to (+ verb)*
falta + infinitive (Higher)	*it's, is still to be (+ past participle)*
hace falta + infinitive (Higher)	*it's necessary (+ verb)*
vale la pena + infinitive (Higher)	*it's worth -ing*

Modal Verbs

See p.136 for more information about modal verbs.

querer (to want (to), love)

Subject	Present	Preterite	Imperfect	Proper Future	Conditional
yo	quiero	quise	quería	querré	querría
tú	quieres	quisiste	querías	querrás	querrías
él / ella / usted	quiere	quiso	quería	querrá	querría
nosotros/as	queremos	quisimos	queríamos	querremos	querríamos
vosotros/as	queréis	quisisteis	queríais	querréis	querríais
ellos / ellas / ustedes	quieren	quisieron	querían	querrán	querrían

poder (to be able to, can)

Subject	Present	Preterite	Imperfect	Proper Future	Conditional
yo	puedo	pude	podía	podré	podría
tú	puedes	pudiste	podías	podrás	podrías
él / ella / usted	puede	pudo	podía	podrá	podría
nosotros/as	podemos	pudimos	podíamos	podremos	podríamos
vosotros/as	podéis	pudisteis	podíais	podréis	podríais
ellos / ellas / ustedes	pueden	pudieron	podían	podrán	podrían

saber (to know (how to))

Subject	Present	Preterite	Imperfect	Proper Future	Conditional
yo	sé	supe	sabía	sabré	sabría
tú	sabes	supiste	sabías	sabrás	sabrías
él / ella / usted	sabe	supo	sabía	sabrá	sabría
nosotros/as	sabemos	supimos	sabíamos	sabremos	sabríamos
vosotros/as	sabéis	supisteis	sabíais	sabréis	sabríais
ellos / ellas / ustedes	saben	supieron	sabían	sabrán	sabrían

Past Participles

Use past participles with the verb 'haber' to form the perfect tense ('I have done').

Regular endings for past participles:

-ar verbs	-er / -ir verbs
-ado, e.g. habl**ado**	**-ido**, e.g. viv**ido**

These past participles are irregular:

Verb	Past participle	
decir	dicho	*said, told*
escribir	escrito	*written*
hacer	hecho	*done, made*
poner	puesto	*put*
ver	visto	*seen*
volver	vuelto	*returned*
cubrir	cubierto	*covered*

To say what's just happened use this phrase:

Higher

acabar de + infinitive — *to have just (+ past participle)*

Present Participles

Use present participles with the verb 'estar' to form the present and imperfect continuous ('I am/was doing').

Regular endings for present participles:

-ar verbs	-er / -ir verbs
-ando, e.g. habl**ando**	**-iendo**, e.g. viv**iendo**

These present participles change the spellings of their stems.

Verb	Present participle	
pedir	p**i**diendo	*asking for*
decir	d**i**ciendo	*saying, telling*
dormir	d**u**rmiendo	*sleeping*
morir	m**u**riendo	*dying*
leer	le**y**endo	*reading*
construir	constru**y**endo	*building*

Some set phrases in Spanish need a present participle:

Higher

seguir + present participle	*(to) continue to, still be + -ing*
llevar + time period + present participle	*(to) have been + -ing for X time*

Revision Summary Test for Section Fifteen

Here it is — the final revision summary. Test yourself if you dare. *Plays suspenseful music*

- Yep, these questions are **hard** — they'll really help you see **how well you know your stuff**.
- Tackle the **revision summary test** below, or scan the QR code to do it **online**.
  Use the CGP RevisionHub to **track your progress** and see **which areas need more work**.
- You can find **sample answers** here: www.cgpbooks.co.uk/BuenoExtras

Summary Test

The Present Tense

1) List all the present tense forms of these verbs: a) preparar b) beber c) recibir
2) Explain how the verb stem changes its spelling in the present tense for:
   a) jugar b) servir c) doler d) preferir e) repetir f) conocer g) salir h) empezar
3) Give a sentence in the present tense using these verbs: a) hacer b) ir c) ser d) estar e) tener

The Preterite, Imperfect and Present Perfect Tenses

4) List all the preterite tense endings for '-ar' verbs and '-er' and '-ir' verbs.
5) Give the 'I' form of the preterite tense for: a) ser b) dar c) traer d) poner e) querer f) decir
6) List all the singular imperfect tense endings for regular '-ar' verbs and '-er' and '-ir' verbs.
7) Translate these sentences into Spanish: a) She has danced. b) I have learnt. c) They have left.
8) Explain when you'd use the preterite, imperfect and present perfect tenses.
9) [H] Give the correct imperfect tense form for each of the verbs below. The subject is given in brackets.
   a) ser (vosotros) b) ir (nosotros) c) ver (ustedes) d) estar (ellos) e) tener (Luisa y yo)

The Future Tenses and the Conditional

10) Translate these sentences into Spanish using the immediate future tense:
    a) I am going to go to Spain. b) We are going to arrive tonight. c) He is not going to get lost.
11) Using the proper future tense, say that you will buy a present for your sister.
12) 'En un mundo ideal, comería patatas fritas todos los días.' Translate this sentence into English.
13) [H] Translate these sentences into Spanish, using the proper future tense or the conditional:
    a) I would come. b) They will tell you. c) She would know the answer. d) We will go.

Modal Verbs, Reflexives and -ing Verbs

14) List all the modal verbs and phrases in this section. There are 7 you need to know.
15) Translate these sentences into Spanish: a) She feels tired. b) Are you (inf., sing.) staying here?
16) What are the present participles of these verbs? a) pasar b) volver c) pedir d) dormir e) caer
17) [H] Describe two ways to say how long you 'have been doing' something. Give an example of each one.
18) [H] 'We have just found your (inf., pl.) keys.' How would say this in Spanish?

Negative Forms, Impersonal Verbs and the Passive

19) Write a sentence using each of these negatives: a) (no) nunca b) (no) nada c) (no) nadie
20) List all the impersonal verbs in this section. There are 5 you need to know (plus 5 for Higher tier).
21) [H] Say these sentences in Spanish: a) I no longer live there. b) I wear neither skirts nor dresses.
22) [H] Give a sentence using the passive voice with: a) 'ser' + past participle b) 'se' + a third-person form

The Subjunctive and the Imperative

23) What are the singular informal imperatives for these verbs? a) correr b) decir c) salir d) tomar
24) [Higher] In Spanish, use an imperative to tell two of your friends to open the door.
25) [Higher] Translate this sentence into Spanish: 'I hope that Dídac comes to my party.'
26) [Higher] List all the singular forms of the present subjunctive for: a) hacer b) tener c) ir d) ser

Spelling and Pronunciation

Spanish pronunciation can be tricky, so use this page to help if you're unsure how to pronounce a word. You can scan the QR code to hear the sounds and words in the tables spoken aloud.

Listening Track 20

Spanish pronunciation is quite different to English

The table below shows some of the main ways of spelling common sounds in Spanish.

Listen to the audio and practise pronouncing each sound out loud as you hear it.

Spelling	Example 1	Example 2
a	antiguo	abrir
o	copa	perro
e	esquina	viejo
i	ideal	instituto
u	comunidad	usar
ll	llevar	apellido
ch	noche	mucho
ca	campo	chica
co	comer	corazón
cu	discutir	excursión
cu + vowel	cuando	cuenta
ce	excelente	dulce
ci	estación	medicina
z	zapato	confianza
que	aunque	quedar
qui	quisiera	equipo
ga	lugar	gafas
go	luego	negocio
gu	gustar	segundo
ge	genial	argentino
gi	página	religión
gue	hamburguesa	juguete (Higher only)
gui	alguien	siguiente
j	jugar	bajo
ñ	sueño	compañero
v	varios	ver
-r-, -r	camarero	pasar
rr, r-, -r-	error	repetir
silent h	hermano	hora

In some Spanish-speaking countries, these (ce, ci, z) sound more like 's' than 'th' in English.

In Spanish, you don't pronounce the 'h' at the beginning of words.

"Knock knock."
"Who's there?"
"Sí."
"Sí who?"
"Sí what a bad pronunciation joke I've made!"

Some Spanish words have an accent to show you which vowel you need to stress when you say them.

á	pájaro	práctico
é	éxito	francés
í	increíble	típico
ó	montón	avión
ú	autobús	útil

It's useful to know how accents change the pronunciation of a word, but you'll only be tested on these if you're taking Higher tier.

The Listening and Speaking Exams

There are four separate exams for AQA GCSE Spanish and each one is worth 25% of your final mark. But never mind the maths — these pages are crammed full of advice to help you tackle the exams head on.

The listening exam has two sections

1) For the listening paper, you'll listen to various recordings of people speaking in Spanish.
2) The paper is 45 minutes long for Higher-tier students and 35 minutes long for Foundation-tier students. It's split into Section A and Section B:

Section A is the longer section — it's worth 40 marks at Higher tier and 32 marks at Foundation tier. It contains comprehension questions in English, and you'll write your answers in English.

Section B is a shorter dictation section — it's worth 10 marks at Higher tier and 8 marks at Foundation tier. You'll hear some short sentences and write them down in Spanish.

3) Read the paper thoroughly before the recording begins — the questions will give you a good idea of the topics you'll be asked about. This should help you predict what to listen out for.
4) Make notes while listening to the recordings, and listen to the end, even if you think you have the answer.
5) Don't worry if you can't understand every word — just listen carefully and try to pick out the key vocab.

The speaking exam has three parts

During your preparation time, you can make notes to use at any point during the exam.

1) Your speaking exam will be conducted and recorded by your teacher.
2) The exam is in three parts. Before you start, you'll get 15 minutes of preparation time. The time allowed for the exam is 10-12 minutes at Higher tier and 7-9 minutes at Foundation tier.

① Role-play

You'll get a card with a scenario on it. It'll have five tasks — four will be notes on what you should talk about. The '?' shows you have to ask a question.

② Reading aloud task

You'll get a card with several sentences in Spanish. You'll read them aloud, then your teacher will ask you four questions related to the topic of the sentences.

③ Photo card discussion

You'll receive a card with two photos on it. Your teacher will ask you to talk about them and then ask you questions related to the same theme.

Try to be imaginative with your answers

You need to find ways to show off the full extent of your Spanish knowledge. You should try to:

1) Use a range of tenses — e.g. for a question on daily routine, think of when something different happens.

Pero mañana voy a jugar al fútbol. *But tomorrow I'm going to play football.*

2) Talk about other people, as well as yourself — it's fine to make people up if it helps.

Me gusta el rugby, pero mi tía lo odia. *I like rugby, but my aunt hates it.*

3) Give loads of opinions and reasons for your opinions.

En mi opinión, debemos reciclar más. *In my opinion, we must do more recycling.*

You can use non-binary or gender-neutral pronouns in the exams — just make sure you're consistent and your adjectives agree.

Silence please! I'm taking my sneaking exam...

Don't panic if you make a mistake in the speaking exam — what's important is how you deal with it. You won't lose marks for correcting yourself, so show the examiner that you know where you went wrong.

The Reading and Writing Exams

The writing exam is a great way of showing off what you can do — try to use varied vocabulary, include a range of tenses, and pack in any clever expressions that you've learnt over the years. First up, though...

The reading exam has two sections

1) The Higher-tier reading paper is 1 hour long, and the Foundation-tier paper is 45 minutes. Both are worth 50 marks and have two sections.

2) In Section A, you'll be given a variety of Spanish texts and then asked questions about them. The questions and answers will be in English.

- Scan through each text first to get an idea of what it's about. Then read the questions that go with it carefully, making sure you understand what information you should be looking out for.
- Next, go back through the text, focusing on finding the information you need. If you're having trouble with a particular question, you might want to move on and come back to it later.

3) Section B will ask you to translate several short Spanish sentences (between 35-50 words in total) into English. The sentences will be on topics you've studied, so the vocabulary should be familiar. Here are some top tips for doing your translations:

- Translate a whole sentence at a time, rather than word by word — this will avoid any of the Spanish word order being carried into the English.
- Keep an eye out for different tenses — there will be a variety.
- Read through your translations to make sure they sound natural.

Not to brag, but I always sound natural...

There are various types of questions in the writing exam

1) The Higher-tier writing paper is 1 hour and 15 minutes long and the Foundation-tier paper is 1 hour and 10 minutes long. Some tasks are only for one tier, but others appear in both — these are explained below.

2) Each task is worth a different number of marks, so you should spend more time on the higher-mark tasks. For longer answers, make a quick plan before you start and remember to leave time to check your work.

Foundation

Photo Response Task (10 marks)
You'll be asked to write five short sentences in Spanish to describe a black and white photo.

Translation Task (10 marks)
You'll translate sentences from English into Spanish. The sentences could be on any topic you've studied. See above for some top tips for translation tasks.

Foundation

Grammar Task (5 marks)
You'll need to complete five short sentences by choosing the correct option, using your grammar knowledge.

90-word Writing Task (15 marks)
You'll be asked to write about 90 words in response to three bullet points. You'll have a choice between two questions. Make sure you write about each bullet point.

Foundation

50-word Writing Task (10 marks)
You'll be asked to produce a short piece of writing in response to five bullet points. You'll be expected to write about 50 words in total.

Higher

150-word Writing Task (25 marks)
You'll need to write about 150 words in Spanish, based on two bullet points. There will be two questions to choose from. This task is more creative — so don't forget to include some opinions with reasons.

And lastly, don't forget your pen...

When you're nervous and stressed, it's easy to misread a question or skip question parts. For writing questions with bullet points, make sure you talk about each bullet in turn — tick them off as you go along.

Answers

The answers to the translation questions are sample answers only, just to give you an idea of one way to translate them. There may be different ways to translate these sentences that are also correct.

For dictation and translation questions, this symbol (|) shows where to divide the marks. There is 1 mark awarded for the first part of the text, and 1 mark awarded for the second.

Section One — General Stuff

Page 5: Numbers and Times

1) a) 17 b) 88 c) the second street on the right
2) a) A+B b) B c) B

Page 7: Times and Dates

2) a) yesterday b) Bath c) on Friday

Page 9: Questions

2) a) ¿Cuál portátil | debería comprar?
   b) ¿Con quién | bailabas?
   c) ¿Cuántos | canales de televisión hay?
   d) ¿De qué | hablas?

Page 13: Opinions

1) a) watching films at home
   b) They seem boring to him.
   c) They are sometimes silly.
2) a) i) P ii) P+N
   b) i) N ii) P

Section Two — Identity and Relationships with Others

Page 21: My Family and Friends

2) a) three
   b) They enjoy the same activities.
   c) her dad, his wife and her stepbrother
   d) They're the same age and have the same birthday.

Page 23: Describing People

1) a) B b) A c) C d) D

Page 25: Relationships and Partnerships

1) a) A b) B
2) a) C b) C

Section Three — Healthy Living and Lifestyle

Page 29: Food

1) a) fat or sugar
   b) vegetables
   c) There aren't many dishes without meat at restaurants.

Page 31: Healthy and Unhealthy Living

2) a) It's as dangerous as taking drugs.
   b) not knowing where you are
      not knowing how much you've drunk
   c) They drank too much and had to go to hospital.

Page 33: Illnesses and Treatments

2) a) Water got into his tent on a camping trip.
   b) If he feels worse than when he returned home.
   c) He feels very cold.
   d) Any two from:
      Drink hot drinks.
      Try to relax.
      Wear more clothes if you're cold.
      When you go to bed, try to breathe slowly and deeply.

Section Four — Education

Page 39: School Life

1) a) 9:20 b) 10:30 c) 13:30
2) a) 800
   b) You can find everything you need there.
   c) enormous
   d) It's very dirty.

Page 41: School Pressures and Difficulties

2) a) C & D b) B & C

Section Five — Future Study and Work

Page 47: Career Choices and Ambitions

2) a) M b) H c) P

Section Six — Free-time Activities

Page 51: Cinema and TV

1) a) No le gusta nada | el cine.
   b) Recomiendo muchas películas | a mis amigos.
   c) Dijo que los personajes | hicieron cosas tontas.
   d) La escena al final de la película | era muy triste.
2) a) A b) B

Page 52: Music

1) a) It's very quick to download songs. / It costs less than buying music in a shop.
   b) Live music is always wonderful.
   c) Travelling around the world to give concerts.

Page 55: Going Out and Other Hobbies

1) a) The menu has a lot of variety. | I want to try a Chinese dish.
   b) The admission tickets are free | for small children.
   c) Reading newspapers is boring | and the articles can be very strange.

Section Seven — Customs, Festivals and Celebrations

Page 61: Customs and Festivals

2) a) la Tomatina, event
   b) spring, parades / processions

Section Eight — Celebrity Culture

Page 65: Favourite Celebrities

1) a) He loves cinema and how movies are made.
   b) The director is also a musician. /
      The director writes the songs for her films.
   c) She always wears unique clothing. /
      She has long hair. /
      She has blue hair. /
      She has brown eyes.
   d) She went back to her neighbourhood to help collect rubbish from the streets.

Page 67: Celebrity Life

2) a) B b) A c) A

Section Nine — Travel and Tourism

Page 71: Where to Go

1) a) B b) B c) A

Page 73: Accommodation and Travel

1) a) by train
   b) It's cheaper than travelling by plane. / It's more comfortable than travelling by bus.
   c) a flat
   d) Any two from:
      It has a kitchen.
      It has a nice balcony.
      It's close to the station.
2) a) Nuestro hotel | no tiene ascensor.
   b) Los turistas tienen | dos maletas y una mochila.
   c) Una habitación de lujo | cuesta mucho dinero.
   d) Habrá muchos retrasos | en el aeropuerto.
   e) Espero que la vista | sea maravillosa.

Page 75: Getting Around and What to Do

2) a) in the north of Spain
   b) a beautiful cathedral
      various museums
   c) going for a stroll through the streets.

Section Ten — Media and Technology

Page 79: Technology

1) a) P + N b) N c) N d) P

Page 81: The Internet

2) a) Spending time outside.
      Doing exercise.
   b) Being able to get information quickly
   c) Someone could steal your data.
   d) Some of them look real.

Page 83: Social Media

2) a) her parents
   b) To talk with her friends
   c) It annoys her having to wait a long time for a response.

Section Eleven — Where People Live

Page 87: At Home

2) a) B b) A c) B

Page 89: The Local Area

2) a) There isn't much to do in his region.
   b) They charge a lot for their products.
   c) There are some marvellous buildings. / The art museum in his town is very interesting.

Page 91: Directions and Weather

1) a) B b) C c) D d) A
2) a) La casa de mi amigo no está | muy lejos de la mía.
   b) Preguntaremos por | el camino correcto.
   c) El otoño pasado | apenas llovió.
   d) Las temperaturas frías | son las mejores.

Section Twelve — The Environment and Social Issues

Page 96: Environmental Impacts

1) a) Building more industrial zones | increases the use of energy.
   b) Air pollution can cause | serious illnesses.
   c) We have lost many species | due to the damage caused to forests.
   d) According to various recent studies, | the climate is changing.

Page 97: Protecting the Environment

1) a) i) Collect rubbish from the beach
      ii) It's important to protect the species of the sea.
   b) i) To walk or cycle to school
      ii) People should turn their lights off when they're not using them.

Page 99: Social Issues

2) a) poverty, initiatives
   b) discrimination, opportunities

Section Thirteen — Nouns, Articles and Linking Words

Page 103: Nouns

1) el zapato — los zapatos
2) la camisa — las camisas
3) la tradición — las tradiciones
4) el color — los colores
5) la vez — las veces
6) la mitad — las mitades
7) el monte — los montes
8) la dificultad — las dificultades
9) el ciudadano — los ciudadanos
10) la huelga — las huelgas
11) la impresión — las impresiones
12) el siglo — los siglos

Page 104: Forming Nouns

1) Me gusta comer la comida mexicana.
2) El francés es un idioma divertido.
3) Fumar está prohibido.
4) Los españoles son simpáticos.
5) No disfruto de ser famoso/a.
6) Alquilar un coche es caro.

Page 105: Articles

1) Comí un bocadillo de pollo.
2) El agua corre rápido.
3) Es profesora de inglés.
4) Quiere unas patatas fritas.
5) Juego al baloncesto los jueves.
6) Tardó unas horas.

Page 106: Subject Pronouns

1) ellos	3) ellos	5) él	7) ella
2) ustedes	4) vosostros	6) nosotras	8) él

Page 107: Object Pronouns

1) the window — la ventana **La** rompe.
2) the water — el agua (f) **La** bebo.
3) **Le** compró una falda.
4) **Les** enviaré un correo electrónico.
5) to you (inf., pl.) — os **Os** di el gato.
6) to us — nos **Nos** dijo el secreto.

Page 109: More Pronouns

1) What is your favourite colour?
2) the film that I saw yesterday
3) Have you eaten something?
4) That isn't true.
5) Yours is here.
6) I cooked for you.
7) They would go with you.
8) I will want that (thing).

Page 110: Prepositions

1) Hablamos sobre el tiempo.
2) El tren va hasta España.
3) Lo vi en la pared.
4) Son de Valencia.
5) El perro corrió hacia mí.
6) Vivo fuera de la ciudad.

Page 111: Prepositions with Verbs and Nouns

1) He/She organised a party without telling me.
2) They're doing the task again.
3) He/She has stopped smoking.
4) I play in order to win.
5) I will close the door before going out.
6) I'm trying to drink more water.

Page 112: 'Por', 'Para' and the Personal 'a'

1) The train for Paris is arriving now.
2) I'll do it for tomorrow.
3) The exit is around here.
4) I was walking through the countryside.
5) They were keeping it for their children.
6) They rarely used to go out because of the heat.
7) No, the personal 'a' isn't needed.
8) Yes, the personal 'a' is needed because there's a word for a human being ('gente') after the verb.
9) No, the personal 'a' isn't needed.
10) Yes, the personal 'a' is needed because there's a word for a human being ('abuelo') after the verb.
11) Yes, the personal 'a' is needed because there's a word for a pet ('las mascotas') after the verb.
12) No, the personal 'a' isn't needed.

Page 113: Conjunctions

1) La geografía es divertida, pero es dura.
2) Me gusta la historia porque es fácil.
3) Como estoy enfermo/a, me quedaré en casa.
4) Si hace calor, voy a la playa.
5) Hablo francés e italiano.
6) ¿Prefieres azul o verde?

Section Fourteen — Adjectives and Adverbs

Page 117: Adjectives

1) el perro feliz
2) una ensalada vegana
3) el coche azul
4) una botella reciclable
5) la hermana alemana
6) un problema evitable
7) El grupo está cansado.
8) ¿Ella está lista?

Page 119: More Adjectives

1) el primer día
2) pocos productos
3) cada familia
4) ningún plato
5) sus libros
6) esas películas
7) el bolígrafo mío
8) aquella manzana

Page 120: Comparative and Superlative Adjectives

1) Esta página es más fácil.
2) Soy tan alto como mi padre.
3) Faiza es mayor que Emilio.
4) Los libros son mejores que las películas.
5) Hoy es el peor día.
6) Ella es la menor.

Page 121: Adverbs

1) positivamente — positively
2) directamente — directly
3) socialmente — socially
4) diferentemente — differently
5) exactamente — exactly
6) perfectamente — perfectly
7) posiblemente — possibly
8) tradicionalmente — traditionally
9) evidentemente — evidently
10) estrictamente — strictly
11) nacionalmente — nationally
12) efectivamente — effectively

Page 122: Adverbs and Adverbial Phrases

1) Mis zapatos están aquí.
2) Quiero salir ahora.
3) A veces viajo.
4) Vivimos lejos.
5) Por fin puedo dormir.
6) La tienda está allí.

Page 123: Comparative and Superlative Adverbs

1) Wafa come más rápidamente que yo.
2) Yo pinto mejor que ella.
3) Luis baila tan bien como tú.
4) Alba es la que habla más tranquilamente.
5) Ellos son los que mejor conducen.
6) Inoke es el que peor corre.

Page 124: Quantifiers and Intensifiers

1) Hay demasiados gatos aquí.
2) Es bastante interesante.
3) Tengo muchos amigos.
4) Hablan tan rápidamente.
5) Es un libro muy bueno.
6) Hay una playa buenísima.

Section Fifteen — Verbs and Tenses

Page 127: Verbs in the Present Tense

1) bailo	3) discuten	5) aprende	7) escribes
2) bebemos	4) rompen	6) nadáis	8) visitan

Page 129: Irregular Verbs in the Present Tense

1) **Comienza** a las tres.
2) **Queremos** leche.
3) Yo **doy** el libro a Lola.
4) **Puedes** conducir.
5) **Repiten** las direcciones.
6) **Pienso** que es importante.
7) Vengo a la fiesta también.
8) Vamos allí mañana.
9) Me visto rápidamente.
10) No tengo bolígrafo.
11) Los estudiantes tienen hambre.
12) La reconozco de la película.

Page 130: 'Ser' and 'Estar' in the Present Tense

1) **Está** muy enojado hoy.
2) Siempre **es** trabajador.
3) **Somos** de Hull.
4) **Estoy** en Bradford.
5) **Es** mi hermano.
6) Mi padre **es** médico.

Page 131: The Preterite Tense

1) viniste 2) cenaron 3) di 4) cayó 5) pidió 6) jugué

Page 132: The Imperfect Tense

1) cantabas 2) decía 3) aprendía 4) nadaba 5) estaba 6) tenías 7) volvían 8) seguíais 9) éramos 10) iban

Page 133: Using the Past Tenses

1) Ha viajado a España.
2) Ha corrido quinientos metros.
3) Han terminado la prueba.
4) ¿Has comido ya?
5) Hemos escrito una carta.
6) Han vuelto a casa.

Page 134: The Future Tenses

1) vas a hacer, harás
2) va a tener, tendrá
3) va a bailar, bailará
4) voy a dar, daré
5) vas a poder, podrás
6) voy a jugar, jugaré
7) van a poner, pondrán
8) vamos a venir, vendremos
9) vamos a querer, querremos
10) vais a vivir, viviréis
11) va a decir, dirá
12) vais a saber, sabréis

Page 135: The Conditional

1) iría 2) cantaría 3) pondrías 4) hablaría 5) haría 6) pediría 7) diríais 8) vendríamos 9) querrían 10) sabrían

Page 136: Modal Verbs

1) You have to revise for the test.
2) Juanjo doesn't know how to speak Spanish.
3) Can they / you come to the wedding?
4) We have to listen well.
5) I don't want to return home.
6) I would like to pay the bill.

Page 137: Reflexive Verbs and Pronouns

1) me llamo 2) te llevas 3) se siente 4) se despierta 5) me acuesto 6) se levantan 7) nos vestimos 8) os ponéis

Page 139: Verbs with '-ing' and 'Just Done'

1) estás cayendo
2) está abriendo
3) están diciendo
4) estáis corriendo
5) estamos bailando
6) estoy leyendo
7) están sirviendo
8) está siguiendo
9) Estaba pidiendo una naranja.
10) Estaba estudiando en mi habitación.
11) La planta estaba muriendo.
12) Estaba trabajando bien.
13) Acaban de ver la película.
14) Acabamos de comer el desayuno.

Page 140: Negative Forms

1) No fuimos a la biblioteca.
2) No tienen ninguna manzana. / No tienen ningunas manzanas.
3) No hay nada aquí.
4) Nadie está en el coche. / No está nadie en el coche.
5) No es ni rojo ni verde.
6) Ya no vamos al gimnasio.

Page 141: Impersonal Verbs and the Passive

1) Se puede descansar ahora.
2) Hay que hacer ejercicio.
3) Se necesita ir a clase.
4) Hay muchas fiestas.
5) Vale la pena aprender este contenido.
6) Parece una idea maravillosa.

Page 142: The Subjunctive

1) You need the normal present tense 'viene'.
2) You need the present subjunctive 'sea' — it follows 'para que', which is used to express purpose.
3) You need the normal present tense 'tiene'.
4) You need the present subjunctive 'sea' — it follows a phrase that expresses an emotion.
5) You need the normal present tense 'va'.
6) You need the present subjunctive 'haga' — it follows a phrase that expresses necessity.

Page 143: The Imperative

1) ¡Canta esta canción!
2) ¡Ve a tu habitación!
3) ¡Escribe dos frases!
4) ¡Tómalo!
5) ¡Di algo!
6) ¡Bebe el agua!
7) ¡Aprended estas palabras!
8) ¡Firmad este documento!
9) ¡Esperad aquí, por favor!
10) ¡Comprad eso ahora!
11) ¡Haced vuestros camas!
12) ¡Cruzad la calle!

Index

SPAR42